THE ESSENTIAL

TOURING CYCLIST

SECOND
EDITION

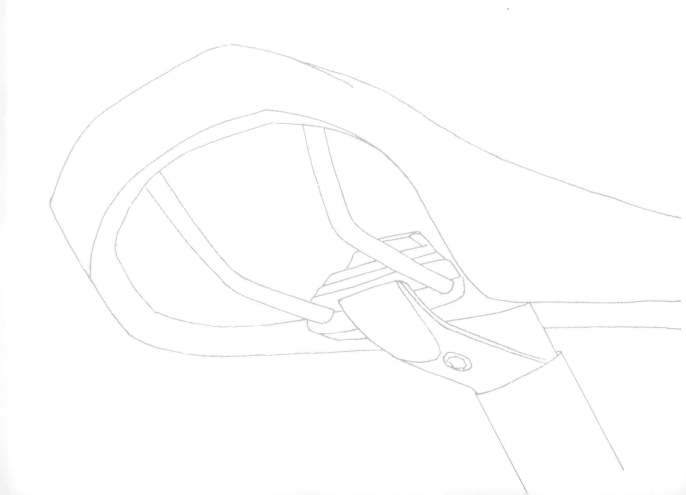

THE ESSENTIAL

TOURING

CYCLIST

SECOND EDITION

The Complete Guide for the Bicycle Traveler

RICHARD A. LOVETT

Photographs by Vera Jagendorf

RAGGED MOUNTAIN PRESS / McGRAW-HILL

CAMDEN, MAINE • NEW YORK • SAN FRANCISCO • WASHINGTON, D.C. • AUCKLAND
BOGOTÁ • CARACAS • LISBON • LONDON • MADRID • MEXICO CITY • MILAN
MONTREAL • NEW DELHI • SAN JUAN • SINGAPORE • SYDNEY • TOKYO • TORONTO

ALSO IN THE RAGGED MOUNTAIN PRESS ESSENTIAL SERIES
The Essential Backpacker: A Complete Guide for the Foot Traveler, Adrienne Hall
The Essential Cross-Country Skier: A Step-by-Step Guide, Paul Petersen
  and Richard A. Lovett
• *The Essential Outdoor Gear Manual: Equipment Care, Repair, and Selection*,
  2nd edition, Annie Getchell and Dave Getchell Jr.
The Essential Sea Kayaker: A Complete Guide for the Open-Water Paddler,
  2nd edition, David Seidman
The Essential Snowshoer: A Step-by-Step Guide, Marianne Zwosta
The Essential Whitewater Kayaker: A Complete Course, Jeff Bennett
The Essential Wilderness Navigator, 2nd edition, David Seidman and Paul Cleveland

Ragged Mountain Press
A Division of The McGraw-Hill Companies

10 9 8 7 6 5 4 3 2
Copyright © 1994, 2001 Ragged Mountain Press
All rights reserved. The publisher takes no responsibility for the use of any of the materials or methods described in this book, nor for the products thereof. The name "Ragged Mountain Press" and the Ragged Mountain Press logo are trademarks of The McGraw-Hill Companies. Printed in the United States of America.

Library of Congress Cataloging-in-Publication Data
Lovett, Richard A.
    The essential touring cyclist : a complete guide for the bicycle traveler / Richard A. Lovett ;
  photographs by Vera Jagendorf ; illustrations by Elizabeth Halsey.—2nd ed.
      p.   cm.
    Includes index.
    ISBN 0-07-136019-0 (alk. paper)
    1. Bicycle touring. I Title.
    GV1044.L68 2001
    796.6'4—dc21   00-034155

Questions regarding the content of this book should be addressed to
Ragged Mountain Press
P.O. Box 220
Camden, ME 04843
www.raggedmountainpress.com

Questions regarding the ordering of this book should be addressed to
The McGraw-Hill Companies
Customer Service Department
P.O. Box 547
Blacklick, OH 43004
Retail customers: 1-800-262-4729
Bookstores: 1-800-722-4726

This book is printed on 70 lb. Citation by R. R. Donnelley, Crawfordsville, IN
Design by Dede Cummings
Production by PerfecType and Dan Kirchoff
Edited by Tom McCarthy and Shana Harrington
Photographs by Vera Jagendorf unless otherwise credited
Illustrations by Elizabeth Halsey unless otherwise credited

Aleve, Ben-Gay, Bike E, Camelbak, Crescent, Cup O'Noodles, Gore-Tex, Grab On, Lycra, Mace, Mr. Tuffy, Pearl Izumi, Phillips, Pop-Tarts, Ping-Pong, Schrader, Spandex, Sting-Eze, Therm-A-Rest, TRIRI (Touring Ride in Rural Indiana), Tyvek, Velcro, Vise-Grip, and VistaLite are registered trademarks.

To Pat and Dick Lovett,
for nurturing the spirit of adventure.
And to the memory of John and Helen
Holland, for the encouragement
to share it.

CONTENTS

INTRODUCTION

Your bicycle slips gently along a winding ribbon of asphalt, smooth as glass. Pedaling seems effortless, as natural as breathing. Crossing a small creek, you watch the water leap over rocky ledges. A farmer waves at you from a field of new-mown hay; then for the next half mile you are overwhelmed by the sweet aroma of curing alfalfa. It is the last hour before sunset, when the motorized tourists have gone to ground and what little traffic remains is as benign as the warm glow of the sun, which bathes everything in gold and gives you a shadow 50 feet long.

Such is bicycle touring at its finest. Unless you wish it so, it is not a gasping effort, straining to climb hill after hill. There may be hills, but you don't have to race over them. The essence of touring is spontaneity and flexibility. If you tire, you stop. If you encounter the dream tailwind and you feel as though you could go on forever, you milk the day for all it's worth. But always you are immersed in the scenery, surrounded by sights, sounds, and smells denied those who travel in the fleeting, insulated world of an automobile.

There are as many styles of bicycle touring as there are types of vacation. Some are athletic challenges; others are relaxed excursions with time to bask in the sun, read a book, or share the camaraderie of a campfire. It's even possible to mix touring with fine wines and rustic B&Bs, with someone else carrying your baggage. Here are some possibilities.

- **Day Rides.** Single-day tours are the easiest and most frequent type of touring. Do them on your own to explore rural byways, finding treasures you'd never encounter by car. Or sign up for any of the thousands of group rides, be they hundred-milers or something considerably less challenging, conducted each summer wherever cyclists can be found.

- **Posh, Catered Touring.** For a fee you'll be put up in inns or motels and given meals, a guide, and a van to carry your baggage. This is touring at its most luxurious, combining cycling with southern mansions, California wineries, or New England fall colors.

- **Van-Supported Touring.** This is similar to catered touring, except you do the catering yourself, persuading a friend to drive the van or taking turns driving. You can stay in motels or rough it by camping.

- **Organized Touring.** These camping tours are conducted by bike clubs, state tourist departments, or budget-minded touring companies. They provide baggage transport and arrange camping on school lawns, country fairgrounds, or in parks. Group size ranges from a few dozen to thousands of other cyclists.

- **Credit-Card Touring.** For this form of lightweight touring, you need a credit card and little else. As on catered tours, you stay in inns or motels and eat in restaurants, and you carry what little baggage you need.

- **Light Touring.** In mild climates you can do short camping tours with little more than you'd carry on a credit-card tour.

- **Self-Contained (or *Loaded*) Touring.** With everything you need for a week (or longer), your load will weigh 40 to 60 pounds, depending on weather and how good you are at paring out unneeded luxuries and making what you do carry serve multiple purposes. With low gears this type of touring isn't as difficult as it sounds. It pays back the extra effort with a flexible schedule that gives you the ultimate in cycling freedom.

Know Your Author

Some people take up a sport as an act of deliberate volition; others drift into it by a series of steps so gradual they seem to have been born to it. I was the latter: when I was a preschooler on training wheels, my greatest ambition was to bicycle into the unexplored country 3 blocks away. From those beginnings it was simply a matter of extending my range and learning from experience—sometimes good, sometimes bad. By the time I was in my early 30s, I'd done a half dozen shorter bicycling trips before I struck out solo cross-country. It was a life-changing adventure, recorded in my book *Freewheelin': A Solo Journey across America*. Since then, I've continued touring, visiting a total of 40 states and 5 Canadian provinces, plus England, Mexico, and, most recently, Iceland.

Over the years I've introduced a number of friends to touring, watching them transform from beginners to seasoned veterans as they planned and carried out their first trips. *The Essential Touring Cyclist* offers you the same tutorial, combining the cycling lore I've learned from dozens of sources into a single volume that will serve as the foundation for your first trip.

My collaborator, photographer Vera Jagendorf, is the other type of cyclist, one who took up the sport by a sudden act of decision. Not previously an active cyclist, in 1986 she bought a touring bike and set off a month later on a mostly solo, 2,500-mile trek across the western U.S. Since then, she and I have done several shorter tours.

Who Are You?

Cycle touring isn't just for macho kids with perfect bodies. It's for anyone with a sense of adventure who is drawn to explore back-roads America or to poke along a seacoast unimpeded by the sense-deadening shell of an automobile. It's for people who want to discover a "real" America with as few barriers as possible—and it doesn't matter if you're 21, 41, or 61 if you're in sound physical condition and willing to take some time to prepare. You don't even have to be all that athletic. I've known people 80 pounds overweight who successfully completed mountainous 500-mile tours. Gearing and patience are more important than raw strength.

The Essential Touring Cyclist is aimed at beginners and intermediate cyclists, although it will be useful to experienced cyclists whose backgrounds do not include touring. It assumes you know how to ride a bicycle and are familiar with the basic operation of shift levers and brakes.

Families can tour if they keep distances and conditions within the abilities of the children (or within the ability of the parent to pull a trailer or do most of the work on a tandem). Many people with disabilities can also tour, although it may take special equipment.

Using This Book

This book's progression is logical but not completely linear. There is no reason you can't buy camping gear at the same time you're training—and no reason that part of your training for a long tour can't include a couple of short ones.

To make it simple, I've divided the book into two parts, Cycle Touring 101 and Cycle Touring 102, with a "midterm" and "final" for each. Think of it as two semester-long courses, because six to eight months is about what it takes to go from beginner to being ready to start your first weeklong tour.

Cycle Touring 101 deals mostly with preparation and training—things you'll do around home or on day rides, without going out overnight. Cycle Touring 102 takes you on the road for overnight tours, culminating with the prospect of an adventure lasting a week or longer.

A NOTE ON THE SECOND EDITION

Although bicycle touring isn't tied as strongly as some sports to changes in equipment design, I've taken the opportunity to update this second edition to reflect the latest equipment styles. I've also added more information on organized tours and new sections on the nation's best van-supported touring companies and on international touring. There's also more information on day riding, including how to train for the ever-popular century and half-century rides run by clubs throughout North America. Some of you will use these as training steps leading to an eventual self-contained trek. But many cyclists prefer these shorter outings. Whichever touring style you choose, this book will help you get where you want to go, as easily and comfortably as possible.

GETTING STARTED

I thought the matter over, and concluded I could do it. So I went down and bought . . . a bicycle. The Expert came home with me to instruct me. . . . We got up a handsome speed, and presently traversed a brick, and I went out over the top of the tiller and landed, head down, on the instructor's back, and saw the machine fluttering in the air between me and the sun. It was well it came down on us, for that broke the fall, and it was not injured.

   Five days later I . . . was carried down to the hospital, and found the Expert doing pretty fairly. In a few more days I was quite sound. I attribute this to my prudence in always dismounting on something soft. Some recommend a feather bed, but I think an Expert is better.

Mark Twain, "Taming the Bicycle"

This book assumes that you already have more experience than Mark Twain did in his initial encounter with his two-wheeled adversary. When starting a new endeavor, however, it's often reassuring to be reminded of how much you already know—not to mention how much bicycle technology has progressed from the high-wheelers of Twain's era.

If you bought this book, you've already made an initial commitment to the possibility of taking a cycling vacation. But if you're like most people at this stage, you have a welter of questions: What type of bike should I get? Do I really need those funny-looking cycling shorts? How much should I train? And how do I deal with dogs, cars, potholes, headwinds, or any of the other obstacles that experienced cyclists take in stride?

Cycle Touring 101 will reduce the intimidation factor inherent in these and similar questions. We'll begin by looking at equipment, keeping in mind that while the latest and greatest in specialized equipment may be appealing, it isn't necessary for an enjoyable touring experience. If you already have a well-maintained bicycle, odds are you can use it for your first touring experiences with only a few changes in gearing and accessories. And you can certainly use it for training.

In addition to equipment and training, we'll also look at basic cycling skills, such as riding in traffic, negotiating railroad crossings, and working together in a group to overcome headwinds. Finally, we'll look at fine-tuning your bicycle for added comfort.

The only prerequisites for this course are curiosity about cycling and a sense of adventure. For a midterm exercise, you can buy a bicycle and equip it for touring or you can retrofit the one you already own. For a final exam, you can take the bike out on the road for a 30- to 50-mile day trip.

RICHARD A. LOVETT

The ultimate in adventure travel. This well-equipped cyclist is touring the rugged landscape of Iceland's little-visited East Fjords.

CHOOSING AND EQUIPPING A BICYCLE

1

Bicycling can easily be dominated by gadgetry. Each year brings a new set of latest-and-greatest inventions. Some quickly become passing fads, but a few take the sport by storm and rapidly set new standards.

Cyclists with money to burn can get sucked into trying them all. Club rides sometimes look like showrooms on wheels, with everyone decked out in the latest miracle fabric, riding sleek new machines that look as though they've never seen rain or a chip in the paint.

As a touring cyclist, you can pronounce yourself above all that. Your equipment concerns are far more practical: Does it work? Is it comfortable? Reliable? Can you fix it or replace it if it breaks down in the middle of nowhere?

Avoid any gadget that hasn't been around at least a couple of years unless it's something you can't live without. The last thing you want is to stop in some small-town bike shop and have the mechanic study your misbehaving component only to say, "I've heard about these, but this is the first one I've ever seen."

If you haven't paid much attention to bicycle technology for a while, you've missed a virtual revolution and will be surprised by the number of new gadgets developed in the past few years.

Not that such revolutions are anything new. There was a time when high-wheelers were the height of fashion. Later, coaster-braked, balloon-tired 1-speeds and 3-speed "English racers" dominated the popular image of the bicycle. Then the 10-speed boom of the early 1970s brought drop handlebars, narrow saddles, and that strange French word *derailleur*.

The modern revolution is no less far-reaching. Very few 10-speeds have 10 speeds anymore—18, 21, 24, and 27 are more common. Similarly, the mountain bike boom and the explosion of "hybrid" designs following in its wake dominated the market virtually overnight and continue to do so today.

Other changes are more subtle. Click-stop "index" shifting went from avant-garde to standard in only a few years. Brake cables are hidden beneath the handlebar winding tape, and free-wheels have become easy-to-remove "cassettes."

This chapter won't turn you into a techno-freak gearhead. Rather, it will examine the basic styles of bicycles and components and assess their strengths and weaknesses for touring. If keeping abreast of the latest developments also appeals to you, subscribe to one of the bicycling magazines for a wealth of information each month.

TYPES OF BICYCLES

Touring doesn't require a special bicycle. Such machines are nice, but you can tour just fine on your old college 12-speed (with a few equipment upgrades) or a mountain bike. You can even do light-duty, self-contained touring on a racing bike. In fact, lightweight, sporty bikes are quite popular for day rides, van-supported tours, and weeklong organized tours. The first time you tour, concentrate on buying clothing and touring accessories—racks and panniers—rather than a new bicycle. If you find you like touring, decide then whether you want to further customize your existing bicycle or buy a new one.

There are five basic kinds of adult bicycles: racing, mountain, sport, dedicated touring, and hybrid. Some differences, such as the type of tires or handlebar styles, are immediately obvious; others are more subtle, showing up best if you compare the various bikes side by side.

Racing Bikes

Racing bikes are lightweight, with narrow, high-pressure tires that are typically no more than an inch wide. Everything about a racing bike is designed for going fast, on pavement, with no baggage. The thin tires, for example, reduce both rolling resistance and the weight of the wheels, making quick starts and sharp turns easier. The first time you ride a racing bike, the highly responsive

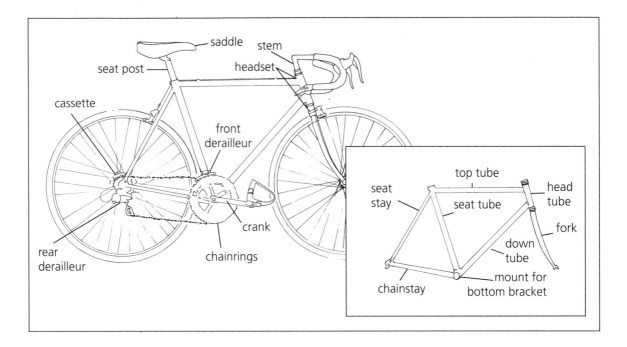

steering will probably feel unsteady, but it won't take long to get used to it.

To increase speed and responsiveness, racing frames are stiff, with the seat post and head tube closer to vertical than on other bicycle types. This keeps the frame from wasting energy by flexing when it hits bumps, but it also transmits the bump more directly to your body, which can be uncomfortable in the long haul.

Racing bikes aren't designed to carry gear and may become unstable when loaded down with panniers. But an entry-level racer can be good for light touring; I've used one for weeklong organized tours as well as credit-card touring with up to 20 pounds of baggage. I've even successfully navigated short stretches of gravel with such a load, although the thin tires increase the risk of flats.

Racing bikes are fast and fun to ride for short distances, but be wary about sitting on one for long hours, day after day. They're unlikely to be sturdy, or stable enough, for fully loaded touring.

Mountain Bikes

Mountain bikes—by far the most common bicycle sold in the past few years—are at the opposite end of the sturdiness spectrum. Built for rugged gravel roads or breakneck charges up and down steep trails, a good mountain bike will easily take the strain of a heavy pack.

But the traditional mountain bike is best designed for touring under Third World conditions. The fat tires, even if you replace the traditional knobby with a thinner road tire, often run at low enough pressure to slow you down appreciably, and the standard straight handlebar gives you only one hand position, something that can get tiring after a few hours.

A mountain bike can be improved for on-pavement touring by substituting lighter wheels and higher-pressure tires and by changing handlebar style or adding bar extenders (see pages 29–30). Some newer mountain bikes also have frames closer to traditional road-bike frames than do earlier models.

Mountain bikes are at their best for heavy touring when you need the strength and stability. They're the only way to go for rough gravel or trail riding, but they're at their worst on van-supported or organized tours, when they slow you down and give you little in return other than a softer ride and less pressure on your hands. If your only bicycle is a mountain bike, use it for your first touring experiments, but unless you plan to do a lot of off-pavement touring, you'll want to shift to a touring or hybrid bike.

Sport Bikes

Sport bikes are the descendents of the traditional 10-speed. Although not many seem to be selling today, there are still a lot of them on the road.

Sport bikes resemble racing bikes except that the angles of the head tube and fork are a bit farther from vertical to give a softer (but less efficient) ride. Expect heavier rims and slightly fatter tires than on a racing bike, but by no means the dramatically fat tires of a mountain bike. There is also slightly more curve (called *rake* in cycling terminology) to the fork, contributing to a more stable and shock-absorbing ride. Longer chainstays further increase stability by lengthening the wheel base. This also improves the function of triple cranks by allowing the chain to run straighter between the chainrings and the higher or lower gears on the rear cassette.

Sport bikes are a little better on gravel than are racing bikes, but they aren't designed to go off pavement for extended periods. They don't truly *excel* at any form of touring—they're slower than racing bikes for van-supported or organized tours and not quite as nicely designed for loaded touring as is a dedicated touring bike. But they make an excellent multipurpose compromise. I've done many tours on such a bicycle, including going cross-country. And the price is right: because these bikes aren't currently stylish, you might pick up a good used one inexpensively.

Dedicated Touring Bikes

A dedicated touring bike has the best design for long-haul touring on mostly paved roads. It may even be able to accommodate fairly beefy tires (about halfway between racing tires and mountain bike tires) for extended runs off pavement. Manufacturers' goals have always been stability, comfort, and the ability to carry heavy weight. There never have been many of these bikes on the market.

At first glance, a touring bike looks much like a sport bike, but it has some important differences. Its wheel base is longer for added stability and for even easier use of triple cranks, the frame angles are even farther from vertical, and the rake of the

Dedicated touring bicycle. Note the drop handlebars, midsized tires, preinstalled rear rack, triple crank, and relatively long wheelbase.

fork is more pronounced. A touring bike will also accommodate wider tires than will a typical racing or sport bike.

In addition, it should have a number of useful touring-oriented details, the most important being eyelets and braze-ons for front and rear racks. There may also be mounting attachments for three water-bottle cages instead of the traditional two, with the third cage attached to the front of the down tube, where the long wheel base leaves plenty of room.

Think of a touring bike as a truck on two wheels. On a test ride, it will feel sluggish and slower on the turns compared with a sport or racing bike but also very stable, happily maintaining its course on a straightaway with a minimum of steering effort. All of these characteristics are functions of the frame geometry.

A touring bike will have drop handlebars, a triple crank, and (hopefully) a wide-range gear cluster rather than the narrow-range "corncob" cluster found on racing bikes. The bike may even come with a rear rack already attached.

When loaded with panniers, it should remain stable or possibly become even more stable than ever, handling as though this is what it was created to do—which, after all, it was.

The rims will be strong, the tires probably 700 x 32c, although a good touring bike should be able to accommodate at least a 700 x 38c tire or even a 700 x 42c (the metric equivalents of 1.25-inch, 1.5-inch, and 1.65-inch widths, respectively). (See page 20 for an explanation of tire-width terminology). Brakes will likely be cantilevers, designed to stop

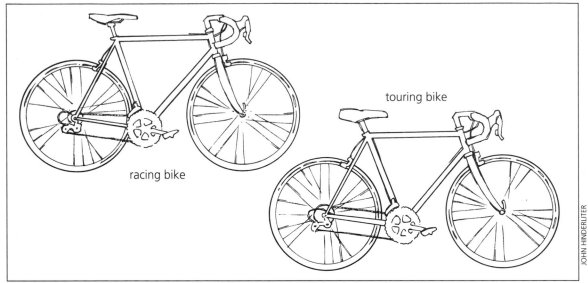

touring bike

racing bike

JOHN HINDERLITER

Touring and racing bikes have subtle but important differences. Note the touring bike's longer wheel base (compare distances between rear tire and seat tube) and comparatively swept-forward (raked) fork. Note also the less vertical angle of its seat and head tubes (exaggerated for illustration). All of these contribute to comfort and stability but reduce nimbleness and responsiveness. Touring bikes also tend to have larger rear gears for relaxed-pace hill climbing, but similar gearing can be put on racing bikes, too.

you plus 40–60 pounds of gear. These bikes will do anything sport bikes can do, although not quite as nimbly. On gravel, they'll outperform sport or racing bikes but won't do nearly as well as mountain bikes.

Hybrid Bikes

Hybrid bicycles mix the comfort, ruggedness, and security of mountain bikes with the quick steering response and reduced rolling resistance of wheels designed for road use. They typically have mountain bike gearing and straight handlebars, and some even have front and rear suspension systems designed to absorb road shock, just as mountain bike suspension systems absorb the shock of rough gravel or trails. However, hybrids are subtly different in their frame designs, which allow crisper handling than can be achieved on mountain bikes. Wheels vary; some hybrid bikes come with relatively narrow road tires, whereas others accommodate the same range of narrow to midwidth tires you can put on a dedicated touring bike. The available choices of hybrid bikes can get confusing, changing from year to year as manufacturers tinker with designs.

Narrow-tired hybrids work well on day rides, organized tours, and other forms of light touring, although the upright riding position encouraged by the straight handlebars increases wind resistance, slowing you down somewhat. Fatter-tired hybrids can be excellent for loaded touring. They may even have specific touring features, such as front and rear brazed-on eyelets and a third water-bottle cage, and many people will find the hybrid design more comfortable than a pure road bike.

If the bike can take a fatter tire, perhaps 700 x 42c, it will also allow you to traverse a wide range of gravel or dirt roads, even with a load, making it the best choice for wide-ranging conditions.

Don't limit your shopping only to hybrids claiming to be designed for touring. Bikes designed for commuting can make excellent touring bikes, since many of the desired features are similar.

Customizing Your Bicycle

When you buy a bicycle, it comes with stock components—gear clusters, wheels, tires, crank, saddle, handlebars, and so forth. Don't assume this is

Touring in the Big Chair

Recumbent bicycles are ones on which you sit in a seat that resembles a lawn chair, with your legs out in front of you. There are a multitude of designs; one that's popular on organized tours is the tiny-wheeled Bike E, made in Eugene, Oregon. Other recumbents use normal-size wheels, and there are even tandem recumbents, although they're rare.

Self-contained touring with a recumbent will probably require special equipment. The legs-forward, front-end design generally precludes a front rack, and the lawn-chair seat is likely to ensure that a standard rear rack won't fit. Any bike shop that sells recumbents, however, will probably be able to tell you how to obtain accessories for it. And many luggage trailers will be perfectly compatible with recumbents.

This cyclist is loaded for touring on a well-equipped recumbent bicycle. The plastic windscreen is called a fairing and greatly reduces wind resistance. The trailer appears to be custom-made. Mass-produced trailers are also available (see page 102).

a take-it-or-leave-it proposition. If you tell the shop what you want when you're buying the bicycle, you can negotiate the changes as part of the purchase price. You might get a discount if the shop can sell the unwanted components to someone else. A shop might even offer to swap components at close to the difference in retail prices, especially if the components you want are low-demand items that it would love to get rid of. But don't be surprised if you can't get a bargain; the components you're rejecting may be just the ones the shop already has in oversupply.

Expect to pay a labor charge for the substitutions, but it might not be large if you're willing to wait for the shop to assemble to your order a bike that just arrived from the manufacturer, rather than

It's in the Details

In marketing, the term *detailing* usually refers to paint stripes, decals, and other pieces of purely cosmetic trim. In biking, however, the details that matter are in the frame design, making the difference between bicycles that can carry camping equipment and those that can't.

If you want to do fully loaded touring, check the bike frame for the following details.

1. *Eyelets for attaching a rear rack.* Except for expensive racing bikes, most bicycles have these, but don't assume. Look for 2 threaded eyelets above or behind the slot (*drop-out*) on each side of the rear axle. You can mount a fender to one set, a rear rack to the other. Without them, there's no reason-

able way to mount either accessory, and the bike is *not* designed for touring.

2. *Seat-stay braze-ons for mounting a rear rack.* These are a second set of threaded eyelets, welded to the seat stays, near the top. Except on frames made of some exotic, crushable material like carbon fiber, you can mount a rear rack without them, with a clamp that holds it to the stays, but you won't be able to carry as much weight.

3. *Front ("fork") eyelets.* If you plan to use front fenders or a front rack—or want the option to do so—you'll want these. You can buy clamps that will hold a fender, but the eyelet is necessary to support the weight of a loaded rack. Any bike that does not have front eyelets will limit your baggage-carrying options and is definitely not suitable for self-contained touring. They look much like rear-rack cousins.

4. *Braze-ons for low-rider front panniers.* Like rear-rack braze-ons, these are welded eyelets on the outside of the fork, approximately at its midpoint. They're not essential, but they do simplify the task of mounting a low-rider-style front rack.

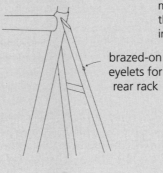

brazed-on eyelets for rear rack

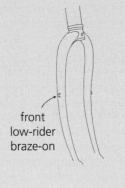

front low-rider braze-on

eyelets

drop out

Rear drop-out, with threaded screw eyelets for mounting rear rack and fenders. Look for similar eyelets in front if you want to attach a full front fender or a front rack.

Brazed-on threaded eyelets on seat stays and front racks indicate that a bicycle is designed to carry baggage. Although not mandatory, they facilitate the attachment of front and rear racks.

modifying one of the assembled bicycles on display. Manufacturers ship bicycles in a partially disassembled state, and some component changes involve labor that would have to be done anyway. The time to get what you want—possibly at a significant savings compared to what it would cost later—is when you buy the bike.

Although bicycles are increasingly designed as

packages, with all of the components selected to a well-thought-out plan, don't be too intimidated by the idea of overriding the manufacturer's equipment choices. Bike manufacturers attempt to rig their machines for the average user, and as a touring cyclist you aren't average. Among other things, the bicycle may not come with the ideal set of gears for real-world hills, especially for touring in mountains.

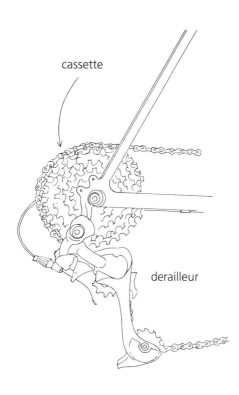
cassette

derailleur

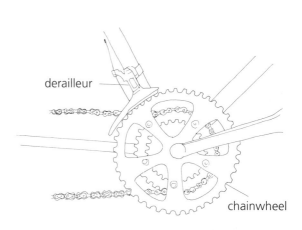
derailleur

chainwheel

Rear gears (left) and front gears (right).

GEARING

The importance of proper gearing is obvious—so much so that until recently bicycles were identified by the number of gears: 10-speeds, 5-speeds, 3-speeds, 1-speeds. (To calculate the number of speeds, multiply the number of chainrings in the front by the number of gears in the rear.)

Today, with the abundance of multispeed models, what matters isn't so much the number of gears as their range. It's also useful to have gears spaced uniformly across that range with a minimum of overlap and to have a shifting pattern that allows you to upshift or downshift by one gear without floundering around trying to figure out which one it is.

For touring, you're mostly interested in the low- and middle-gear ranges. Many bikes, even some that are sold for touring, don't have low enough gears. It's simple, however, to modify them. Just ask your shop to swap the gear cluster, the crankset, or both. You might also have to change derailleurs or bottom brackets (the bearing where the crank passes through the frame), but probably only if

you're making extreme changes such as changing from a double to a triple crank. Unfortunately, cranks are expensive, and these changes can quickly add up to hundreds of dollars.

In discussing gearing, it helps to be at least vaguely familiar with a mathematical construct called *gear inches*. You don't have to know precisely what this means, only that it's proportional to how far you go with each pedal revolution and is therefore a measure of how "high" or "low" a gear really is.

Any good bike shop will have a chart showing the number of gear inches for any combination of wheel size, front gear, and rear gear. But the formula is simple.

gear inches = (wheel diameter in inches)
x (teeth in chainring)
÷ (teeth in rear cog)

If the number is big, you're looking at a high gear—for example, a large chainring and a small rear cog. Low gears are produced by small chainrings and big rear cogs.

19

The lowest gear you want depends on how much baggage you're carrying and the hilliness of the terrain you're visiting. But don't ignore the low gears even if you plan to do all of your touring on a tabletop; a strong wind can kick you all the way down into your hill-climbing gears, especially if you're dragging bulky panniers directly into it. Unless you're a lot stronger than average, plan on a low gear of 30 inches or smaller, no matter what kind of touring you intend. When I do organized tours, other riders routinely covet my "granny" gear.

For loaded touring in hilly terrain, I like a gear range of at least 21–100 inches, but if you never plan on carrying much baggage, you can probably get away with a range of 27–100. The upper end isn't all that important because you'll rarely use it, but the lower end is: you want a low enough granny gear to allow you to comfortably pedal uphill at a pace barely faster than a walk.

If your bike shop can get a suitable cassette, I recommend an 18-inch gear as your lowest. You may never need it—and other cyclists may joke that you look as though you're geared to climb telephone poles—but such a gear allows you to maintain a pedaling cadence of 80 rpm at a pace of 4¼ mph. When carrying baggage, there are plenty of hills where that is precisely what you'll want. Smaller gears are theoretically possible, but they're overkill—you'd probably topple over at the slow speeds involved.

If all of this sounds horribly confusing, just tell your bike shop the gear range you want and ask for a rear cassette/crankset combination that provides it. Low gears of 18 or 21 inches aren't a common request, so expect disbelief and possibly an effort to talk you out of it. Stand firm. For self-contained touring, a low-low gear is a lifesaver. Unfortunately, if you have to change the crankset, it can be pricey, adding as much as $250 to the cost of your machine. Cassettes, on the other hand, can be changed for about $50, including installation.

WHEELS, TIRES, AND TUBES

Wheels come in a dizzying variety of widths, numbers of spokes, and spoking patterns—enough to make wheel building an esoteric art about which the average cyclist knows little.

Little, however, is all you really need to know. If you buy a good bicycle, it will have adequate wheels. Of most interest to you will be the wheel's diameter, the width of tires it can accommodate, and the type of tubes it's designed for.

In the U.S., wheels come in 3 diameters. The most common are 26 inches and a slightly larger metric size called *700C*; older bikes might have 27-inch wheels, but these are getting very rare. Currently, 700C is the standard for road bikes, 26 inches for mountain bikes. Fat tires are more readily available for 26-inch wheels, skinny ones for 700C.

The differences in wheel diameter are large enough that the tires aren't interchangeable. Nor is it likely you could replace your wheels with ones of a different diameter; your brakes are positioned for the size of wheel that came with the bike and probably can't be sufficiently readjusted. Other factors also limit your choice of tire size, including the clearance between the tire and the frame, and the width of the rim. You'll have some flexibility, but you won't be able to put everything on any given bicycle.

Tire widths range from less than 1 inch for the skinniest racing tires to upward of 2 inches for mountain bike knobbies. Small changes can make dramatic differences. A 700 x 32c (a 32 mm wide tire for a 700C wheel) gives you significantly more "float" on gravel than even a 700 x 28c, and a 1.4-inch (equivalent to 700 x 35c) is more stable yet. Wider tires also improve the smoothness of the ride, even on pavement.

(Don't worry about the oddity that the wheels are called *700C* while the tires are *700 x 38c*, etc. The reasons for this weird nomenclature are pretty much lost in history. The "700" itself doesn't mean anything; nothing about 700C rims measures exactly 700 millimeters. But as long as you say "700," everyone will know what you mean.)

Extremely fat tires and those with exaggerated "knobby" treads are for trail riding or rough gravel. On pavement, they slow you down. Even for a tour with a lot of gravel, you probably won't want anything fatter than 1.7 or 1.9 inches. On pavement, 700 x 32c is fine, with a 1.4-inch width acceptable if you want more freedom to take gravel shortcuts.

Tires should be kept inflated to the manufacturer's recommended pressure. Check them daily;

unlike automobile tires, bicycle tires can lose several pounds of pressure a day. You might have been told you can run them at slightly lower pressure for a smoother ride; the cost of doing so is wasted energy, increased tire wear, and potential damage to your wheels if you hit a bump. Cheap tires, I might add, are no bargain. They wear out faster and often can't be inflated to high pressure, causing the same problems as underinflation of better tires.

Most modern wheels have aluminum alloy rims. Old or inexpensive bicycles might have wheels with steel rims. Replace these with alloy, even though it's costly. Steel rims brake very poorly when wet.

All rims are designed for one of two types of tubes: those fitting Schrader or Presta valves. Schrader valve stems look like conventional automobile stems, fitting the same tire gauges and pumps, and they can be pumped up at a gas station. (You may have been warned against doing this for fear of bursting your tires, but that's not likely as long as you use common sense.)

Presta tubes have metal valve stems held in place by thin nuts. The valve itself opens by unscrewing a threaded pin. Presta valves are better for use with hand pumps because they're less likely to leak air when you connect or disconnect the pump.

Presta valve stems are narrower than Schrader stems, and the valve stem holes in the rim are sized accordingly. This means that in an emergency, a Presta tube will fit a Schrader rim, but not vice versa. If you find yourself desperate for a tube in a small town where the only ones available are Schrader, however, it takes only a few seconds with a circular file to (permanently) convert the rim to Schrader.

If you like to top off your tires at gas stations, you can still do so with Presta, using a $1 adapter that threads onto the valve stem. I've known people who have put such adapters on both wheels and left them there.

Quick-Release Hubs

These days, any good bike comes with quick-release wheels, which allow you to fix a flat quickly by removing the wheel without a wrench. They also help you pop a wheel off to load a bike into a car trunk or the back of a hatchback, where it otherwise wouldn't fit.

Make sure you know how to use quick-release

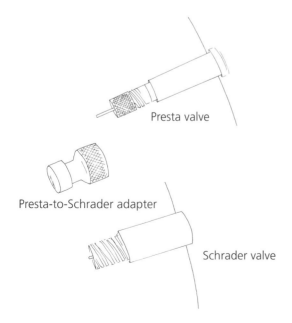

Presta valve

Presta-to-Schrader adapter

Schrader valve

Compromise Tires

If your touring plans involve a wide range of road conditions, picking the right tires can be difficult. It's easy to swap tires between tours, but sometimes a tour will have a mix of pavement and rougher surfaces. Tires that are right for one can be utterly wrong for the other.

Tire manufacturers have come to the rescue with various models of mountain bike tires designed to permit a wider-than-normal range of inflation pressures. These tires can be inflated to about 80 pounds for use on good roads, then deflated to about half that for rougher surfaces. They lack aggressive, knobby treads that would be inefficient on pavement but have enough tread depth to deter cuts from loose stones or other gravel-road obstacles. They're not optimal for either surface, but they're not bad, either, which makes them about as good as you can get for a mixed-surface tour. When shifting from pavement to gravel, make sure you bleed off enough air to drop the tires to the lower end of their range. Failure to do so will expose you to the risk of broken spokes.

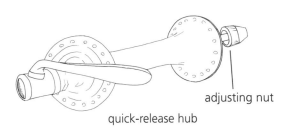

quick-release hub

adjusting nut

hubs. The release lever should be tight when folded closed, parallel to the wheel's plane—not sticking out where it might be bumped or might interfere with a pannier. Ideally the lever should be angled up and back, reducing the chance of something snagging it and accidentally releasing the wheel. This might be difficult if your front or rear rack is in the way, but do the best you can, checking periodically to make sure the lever is tight. This periodic check is a good idea anyway, especially if you've left the bike unattended where some street urchin with nothing better to do can maliciously flip your quick releases.

The best way to learn the proper tightness for quick-release levers is with a hands-on demonstration. Ask your bike shop to show you the difference between too loose and too tight. If the quick-release lever is misadjusted, fix it by flipping it open and tightening or loosening the nut on the other end of the spindle. A wrench is not needed.

Some bikes have wheel-retention devices to keep the wheel from coming loose if the quick-release pops open. These are designed primarily to reduce the manufacturer's liability if a quick-release opens at the wrong time—unlikely if it's properly tightened. Wheel-retention devices serve their function, but they do so by robbing the quick release of its convenience.

SADDLES

The part of the bicycle you sit on is called the *saddle*, not the *seat*.

Saddle design has long been controversial. One faction argues that the most comfortable saddles are firm but carefully contoured to support weight in precisely the right places; an opposing group sings the praises of padding. The advent of gel-filled saddles has produced a new generation of cushioned saddles while doing nothing to resolve the dispute.

The case for a soft saddle is obvious. When you first sit on it, it feels far more comfortable than a hard one. But the detractors of gel argue that shape is what matters, not cushion. A cushy saddle, they say, may actually make you more uncomfortable in the long run by allowing you to sink so deeply into it that your weight is improperly distributed, possibly onto portions of the anatomy not meant to bear it.

Many hard-saddle advocates recommend leather saddles, which are rock hard but gradually shape themselves to conform to your posterior. I'm dubious about using a leather saddle for touring, though. If it gets wet, you may have trouble drying it.

As far as the gel controversy goes, don't feel like a wimp if you decide you want some padding. Gel-filled saddles are nice; some even have springs.

More important than the padding dispute is knowing that there's a difference between men's and women's saddles. Women's saddles tend to be wider, with the "anatomical" supports for the bones of the pelvis placed farther apart than on men's. They may also have a depression on top to take the pressure off sensitive portions of the anatomy. Ask the shop which gender saddle comes on your bike, and realize that unisex means men's. Insist on a gender-appropriate saddle.

Some anatomical designs have strategically placed thin spots or Vs notched into the front of the saddle, again in separate men's and women's models. I've even seen saddles with slots that run their entire length, with no bridge between the right and left pelvis rests. In all of these, the purpose is to take the weight off places where you don't want it and redistribute it to places where it should be. Slotted saddles are becoming increasingly common but have yet to become the industry norm, although it's unclear whether that is because they don't work for all people or because the popular notion of what constitutes a "real" bicycle saddle is so firmly entrenched that the new designs face an uphill marketing battle.

Choosing a saddle is difficult, and the only way to be sure it fits is to take it on a long test ride. Saddles aren't outrageously expensive, though, so if you do get a bad fit, you can replace the saddle relatively easily.

TOE CLIPS

Toe clips position your feet properly on the pedals and increase your pedaling power by allowing you to pull upward on one pedal while you push down on the other. They have easily reachable straps that can be loosened or tightened as you ride. Loosen them in the city for frequent starts and stops. Tighten them in the country or for steep hills.

Toe clips often frighten beginners, who fear their feet will be trapped in them if they fall. In a serious crash this isn't likely; even a tightly snugged toe clip is easy to get out of—just pull the foot up and back. Try it a few times on a quiet back road, adjusting the strap to various tightnesses and seeing how much effort it takes to get your foot out. Most likely, you'll be cutting the circulation off to your toes long before escape becomes difficult.

Another beginner's fear is more realistic: if you've never used toe clips, you might topple over a couple of times when you forget to take your foot out of the strap. Practice dismounting a few times in a parking lot before venturing onto the road.

Getting your foot into the clip is also an art. Put one foot in before you start to move, letting the other clip drag until you're going fast enough to coast. Then position the remaining foot on the pedal with the spindle more or less directly under your arch. (The ideal location depends on your shoe size and the tightness of the clip.) Raise your foot slightly until the pedal, overbalanced in front by the weight of the clip, starts to roll forward. Catch its front edge with the sole of your shoe and gently flip it back-

ward. Bingo! Your toe should slide right into the clip. With practice, you can do this as one smooth motion without even having to stop pedaling.

As an alternative to toe clips, you may opt for "clipless" pedals (see page 37), which contain a step-in fastener to which a matching shoe affixes by a cleat on its sole. Because they're a little more intimidating to get into and out of, you probably don't want them until you're already comfortable with toe clips.

OTHER COMPONENTS

Chainrings, gear clusters, saddles, and tires aren't the only components on your bicycle, of course, but they're the ones you're most likely to tinker with. Others of interest are brakes, shift levers, handlebars, and cranks.

toe clip

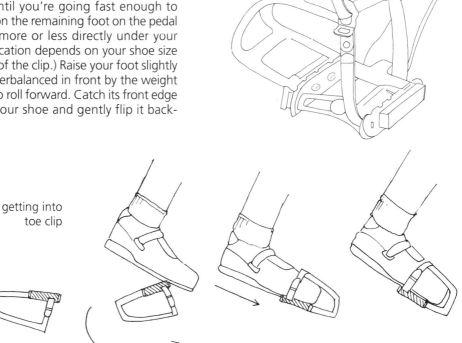

getting into
toe clip

Brakes. There are two common styles of brakes: side-pulls and cantilevers. Racing bikes generally come with side-pulls; mountain bikes and touring bikes usually have cantilevers. The difference lies in where the cable attaches to the brake arms. Side-pulls attach at the side, cantilevers in the center. Good brakes of either design have adequate stopping power.

Shift levers. The positioning of shift levers varies, but the most convenient places are where you can reach them with your hands still on the handlebars. With straight handlebars, this typically means that the levers are next to the handgrips, where you can reach them with your thumbs. On drop handlebars, modern bikes typically combine the shift lever with the brake lever in a system called *integrated brake–shift control*. But you may find a few "bar end" or "fingertip" shifters, located at the end of the handlebar, where they're most easily accessible from the drop position (look closely at the photo on page 15). If you *really* don't

like the location of your shift levers, you can change to a different style, but it will take new parts and a fair amount of work. First, try to get used to the levers you have.

Handlebars. The boundaries between bike types and their handlebars are crumbling, and people are mixing frame type and handlebars with an eye to comfort rather than style. In addition, prompted by the growing interest in mountain bike handlebars with more than one hand position, manufacturers have experimented with enough strange new shapes to satisfy anyone with an eye for novelty. If you don't like the handlebars that came with your bike, change them—even going so far as to swap between drop handlebars and upright ones.

Crank. Top-of-the-line cranks can cost hundreds of dollars. What you get for all that money are increased stiffness, so the crank doesn't waste energy by flexing on each pedal stroke, and reduced weight.

Since the crank is perhaps the single most

You Don't Have to Get a New Bike

If you already have a good bicycle, you don't need to buy a new one for touring. Or, if you're willing to settle for a bike that's anywhere from a couple of years out of date to a decade old, you can buy a good used one through the classified ads or for-sale signs posted in bike shops. Don't get an old model with 27-inch wheels, though, or you may have trouble finding high-quality tires and tubes. (To determine wheel size, read the label on the tire; it will say something like 700 x 32c, 26 x 1.5, or 27 x 1⅛. The first number is the wheel diameter; see page 20 for more explanation.)

Old bicycles, referred to both lovingly and sneeringly as "retro" bikes, have many advantages. For one thing, since they don't represent the cutting edge of fashion, they're a lot less likely to be stolen. Functionally, a

10-year-old bicycle isn't a whole lot different from a new one. Older bikes may also have greater tire clearance than modern ones, giving you a larger choice of tire sizes. So what if the brakes don't look aerodynamic, or the gears don't click when you shift?

Customizing a used bicycle for touring is no different from customizing a new one, except that you lose the advantage of being able to trade in the original components. The most expensive changes will involve the power train if the bicycle doesn't already have a triple crank. The cost will range from a few tens of dollars to several hundred, depending on which changes you have to make and how much you spend on components. But if the brakes and frame of the bicycle you're upgrading are good, when

you're done you may have a touring bike equivalent to a new one that would cost much more.

Here's a list of likely changes.

- Add a triple crank.
- Change to a longer spindle in the bottom bracket so the triple's granny gear doesn't rub the frame.
- Change the front derailleur to accommodate the triple.
- Replace the gear cluster with a wide-range touring cluster.
- Replace the rear derailleur if it won't accommodate all of the slack chain when you shift into the granny gear, or if it won't handle the large cog of the new rear cluster.
- Replace the chain, or at least add or subtract links to fit the new gearing.

expensive component on your bicycle, you aren't likely to change it except perhaps to swap a double for a triple or to improve your gearing as discussed on pages 18–20. High-quality bikes come with good cranks; cheap bikes come with cheap cranks. There's not much reason to put a $200 crank on a $350 bicycle.

ACCESSORIES

Accessories are items that mount onto the bicycle more or less permanently but aren't involved in the bike's functioning. They range from the essential to the trivial, from fun toys to gadgets that can be more of a nuisance than they're worth.

Four Essentials

Some accessories are so important for touring that you might as well install them when you buy the bicycle, viewing their cost as part of its purchase price.

Pump. Flat tires are part of cycling, so you'll need a pump. Even if you'll always be with a friend, each of you should have your own; you may occasionally get separated, and having two pumps between you also gives you a backup if one breaks.

Pumps aren't a place to skimp money. Inexpensive ones can break easily and might not be rated to reach the maximum pressure of your tires.

Pumps come in two styles (double- and single-action) and two lengths (full and "mini"). Double-action pumps inject air into the tire on both strokes of the handle. They're efficient but more prone to trouble than single-action pumps are—which means they're not ideal for remote-destination touring.

Pump length affects the volume of air delivered with each stroke. Long pumps (about the length of your top tube) are best, particularly for fat tires, which can take forever to inflate with a mini-pump. Some mini-pumps compensate by enlarging the diameter of the air chamber. That's fine for relatively low-pressure mountain bike tires, but it increases the effort needed to work the pump, making it impossible for people with weak arms to fully top off a high-pressure road tire. In a pinch, though, a mini-pump should still be enough to get you rolling again.

Full-length pumps have spring-loaded handles to fit firmly beneath the top tube or on the front side of the down tube. The top tube is best because that

saves the down tube for water bottles. Pumps come in a variety of sizes, typically with mounting brackets in case no length is right. If the pump can't be mounted securely enough to avoid being knocked loose every time it's jarred, tie it in place with a pair of short straps. Make sure the straps are padded or made of a material that won't scratch your paint. Velcro rubbing directly against your paint will gradually abrade it over the course of months.

Mini-pumps were invented for bike frames that don't have room to mount a full-length pump. Mini-pumps also come with brackets that mount to one of the frame's tubes, or the pump can be carried separately in your baggage. Another option for loaded touring is to carry a full-length pump on your rear rack, with your tent and sleeping bag (see pages 97–99 for suggestions on how to carry items on a rack).

Presta and Schrader valves require different pump nozzles, so make sure your pump is set for the right one. Most better-grade pumps will convert easily from one to the other. Learn how to make the conversion (usually something simple, such as unscrewing the pump head and reversing the orientation of one or more washers or gaskets) so you can use the pump if you switch tube types or need to help out a friend.

Your pump needs to be lubricated annually or it may not work when you need it. Lubricating is a two-minute job. Just unscrew the handle end and pull out the plunger. You'll find a gasket comprised of either a flexible cup washer or an O-ring that keeps air from escaping backward with each stroke. Lubricate that with petroleum jelly or a drop of oil. Make it part of your New Year's Day routine or some other annual event. If the gasket dries out com-

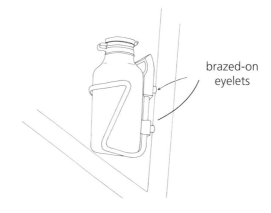

brazed-on eyelets

pletely, it will disintegrate to powder the next time you try to use it and will have to be replaced.

Water bottles. Get at least two water bottles and cages. Expensive ones aren't necessary, but the best bolt directly to the frame. Your bike should come equipped with attachments for at least 2 bottles: one on the down tube, one on the seat tube. If there is room, additional bottles can be mounted with clamps. To protect your paint, put a strip of rubber or other soft material behind any bare-metal clamp.

Rear rack. For any form of touring, you'll need to carry some baggage—at least rain gear and a change of clothes. If you're never going to carry more than that, you can get away with a light-weight rack, but otherwise this is another place you shouldn't skimp. Get a sturdy aluminum rack like those made by Blackburn, which bolt to the rear drop-out eyelets and seat-stay braze-ons.

Some racks have a flat surface on top, whereas others are an open framework. Both carry weight nicely, but the ones with a solid top serve double duty as a partial fender. They also reduce the chance of a loose strap getting into your spokes.

These racks aren't made to sit on, but they can carry a pretty healthy load through bumpy terrain. For heavy duty support on really rough surfaces, however, aluminum might not be strong enough. Chrome molybdenum or stainless steel racks are heavier, harder to find, and more expensive—but less likely to break. If they do suffer a mishap, they can be welded in virtually any small-town automotive garage or metal shop. Jandd, Bruce Gordon, and Ortlieb all make sturdy-looking designs.

rear rack,
unmounted

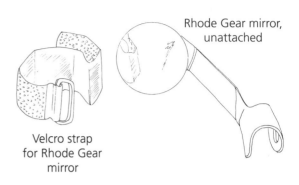

Rhode Gear mirror,
unattached

Velcro strap
for Rhode Gear
mirror

Mirror. If you want to know what's going on behind you, get a mirror and practice using it. It's no substitute for looking over your shoulder in city traffic, but it's great for advance warning of over-taking cars on rural roads.

I've experimented with a number of mirrors, and I prefer the type made by Rhode Gear, which fastens to the brake levers with a Velcro strap. Note that there are two types of these mirrors: one for drop handlebars, the other for straight handlebars. For either it's a good idea to carry a backup strap, because the straps have plastic buckles that break if cinched too tightly.

Another type of mirror mounts to the end of your handlebars. This type puts the mirror farther out from your body than the brake lever–mounting variety, making it easier to see directly behind you. But the bar end is more prone to vibration than the brake lever is, and the only time I tried one of these, I found that the extra vibration made it difficult to see. There are a variety of designs, though, so it may be a matter of how sturdily the mirror is attached. None of them, of course, works with bar-end shifters.

Using a handlebar-mounted mirror takes practice. If your hips, shoulders, or a wind-billowed jacket block the view, shift your body sideways on the saddle or steer ever so slightly to the left to give yourself a better view. It doesn't take much of a turn to open up the view considerably, so learn to do this without swerving into the path of a car or bicycle that may be starting to pass you. I can give myself a good half-second glimpse without veering any farther off course than I would to dodge a small rock. Also, take advantage of left-

Mountain Bike Shock Problems

Many mountain bikes have shock absorbers, or *suspension systems,* that can make it difficult to install racks. Some have only front shocks; others, called *full suspension*, have both.

The biggest problem is with a front-suspension system, nearly ubiquitous on newer bikes. Front-suspension systems have piston mechanisms encased in unusually fat fork blades. They don't have front-rack braze-ons (see page 18) because the outer casing isn't very strong. Made of a thin magnesium alloy, the casing's primary purpose is to keep dirt out of the shock absorber. In theory, you could clamp a front rack onto such a fork blade, but you might break the magnesium housing. Traditional front racks therefore aren't recommended for front-suspension bikes. At least one company, Old Man Mountain, now makes a (pricey) rack that attaches to the brake mounts and front-wheel spindle, however.

A less expensive solution, if you're not going somewhere extremely bumpy, is to change to a nonsuspension fork. You can probably find a used one very cheaply. When front suspension was introduced a few years ago, droves of mountain bikers replaced rigid forks with suspension systems, leaving the old forks at their bike shops. These forks will still fit new bikes, and the chances are that your bike shop has a whole shelf of them gathering dust. Just make sure you get one with front-rack eyelets. Swapping forks isn't a particularly difficult job, so it's feasible to switch back and forth between the rigid fork and the suspension fork that came with your bicycle, depending on the needs of a particular tour. Just don't expect the used fork's color to match the rest of your paint job.

Rear-suspension systems pose a different problem. These systems are located at the top of the seat tube, just below the saddle—right where you'd attach a conventional rack. Even if the rack were strong enough to withstand the stress, it couldn't be mounted there because the housing moves independently of the eyelets at the rear forks. Each time you hit a bump, you'd bend the rack, quickly breaking it.

Old Man Mountain has also found a way around this limitation by attaching the rack to the brake mounts and rear-wheel spindle, where it won't be repeatedly flexed by the suspension system. But for most types of touring, it's simpler just to get a bike without the rear suspension. Full suspension is needed only on extremely rough surfaces such as trails, where most people don't tour. If you do want to carry camping gear on a trail ride—or use a full-suspension trail bike for gravel-road touring—a trailer (see pages 102) might be a better option.

hand bends in the road to give you a good clear view behind.

A third type of mirror, discussed on page 36, mounts to your helmet.

USEFUL ADDITIONS

If you're on a budget, you might be able to live without the following accessories, but they can make life on the road a lot more pleasant. Unfortunately, not everything is compatible with everything else, at least not without modification, so I've included a brief description of potential problems and their likely solutions.

Cyclometer. A cyclometer is a bicycle computer that counts wheel revolutions or pedal strokes. Features vary from brand to brand, but most can function as odometer, stopwatch, cadence counter, and speedometer. Cyclometers aren't necessary, but they do serve as all-around fun toys. The odometer function is particularly useful for following route directions on organized tours or club rides, and on your own it's often nice to know just how much farther it is to the next town.

Compatibility problems: A cyclometer consists of a handlebar-mounting "head" and a magnetic sensor that attaches to the hub, spokes, or fork. Units with cadence counters have an additional sensor that mounts near the crank. The head's mounting bracket may conflict with a handlebar bag, although some tinkering can fix this. The wire connecting the sensor to the mounting bracket for the head is a weak link in most cyclometers. Reduce the risk of snagging by securing the extra length with plastic ties, but make sure there's enough play to allow the handlebars to be turned through their full range of motion. Mount the

AVOCET

This push-button cyclometer makes it easy for you to switch among its functions.

cyclometer head close to the stem to minimize the amount of slack needed to achieve this full range.

Altimeter. A few cyclometers contain startlingly accurate altimeters—just what you might (or might not) want to tell you precisely how far it is to the top of the mountain pass you've been climbing for the last hour. They'll also tell you how many feet you've climbed. Altimeter cyclometers are expensive, however, and they haven't had a good track record for reliability. Ask your shop how many returns have been received before investing in one, or consider buying a more reliable altimeter watch instead.

Inclinometer. Put this one solely in the fun-toy department. An inclinometer is a gadget like a carpenter's level, with a bubble that tells you the angle of the slope up or down which you're currently pedaling—a fun way to impress your friends. It clamps to your handlebars like a cyclometer and has the same compatibility problems—but magnified because now you've got both the inclinometer and the cyclometer to worry about.

Padded handlebar covers. People who spend day after day leaning on handlebars often find that their hands become numb or tingle from the constant pressure. One solution is padding. So what if the racers don't think it looks chic?

Grab Ons, the leading brand, mount by sliding over the handlebar tube. They aren't expensive, but installation is a real pain, partly because you have to remove brake levers and handlebar winding tape. Grab Ons slide onto the bare tube (with effort). For aesthetics—and to preserve the life of the Grab Ons— you can wind tape over the top after you're finished. If you can afford it, let the shop do the installation, even though the labor will probably cost more than the Grab Ons themselves.

A quick-and-dirty way to install Grab Ons is to slit them lengthwise and then fit them over the handlebar from the side. Use nylon strapping tape or strong plastic tape to hold the loose Grab On in place; then wind handlebar tape over the top to keep it from looking too sloppy. The result may have a tendency to twist, but I've ridden Grab Ons mounted in this manner for thousands of miles.

If you have tiny hands and find Grab Ons to be too bulky, look for cork-backed handlebar tape. It gives you an intermediate amount of comfort without bulking up the handlebars as much.

Mountain bikers, too, can get relief from jarring by using padded handgrips.

Compatibility problems: With mountain bike handgrips, there shouldn't be much problem, but for drop handlebars, anything that clamps to them—cyclometers, aero bars, and certain types of headlights—isn't designed to fit over the Grab Ons. The mount for your handlebar bag may also present a problem.

Solutions: Don't slide the Grab Ons all the way to the center of the handlebars; cut off the extra length, if necessary. You won't need to shorten them by much if all you're adding is a handlebar bag; an inch should be plenty. If you're mounting a cyclometer, decide which side of the stem you want it on and allow an additional 2-inch gap. A similar gap on the other side of the stem will leave room for a strap-on headlight.

For aero bars, you'll need to shorten the Grab Ons or cut a hole in it at the point where the bar attaches to the handlebars.

All of these changes are easiest when you first

install the Grab Ons, but you can make them retroactively by peeling back the winding tape and operating on the Grab Ons with a pocket knife. Use electrical tape or duct tape to reattach the loose end of the handlebar tape afterward, because you'll probably have ruined the glue.

Front rack. Depending on your bicycle and your coordination, you may not *have* to have a front rack, even with a full touring rig. But most bicycles are a lot easier to handle if you split the weight between the front and rear wheels. That requires a front rack.

There are two types of front racks. One looks like the mirror image of the rear rack and mounts above the wheel. The preferred model, however, is called a low rider. It is a strange trapezoidal contraption that holds panniers a few inches below the top of the

Low-rider-style front rack.

front wheel, which gives you a lower center of gravity for more stable steering. As long as you don't use enormous panniers, it still holds them high enough above the road that they won't drag.

Compatibility problems: Front racks are incompatible with headlights that clamp to the fork (such headlights are rare, however).

Solutions: See the previous discussion on cyclometers (page 27). Get the rack first; then figure out how to make a cyclometer work around it.

Thorn-resistant tire inserts. These thick pieces of plastic go inside the tire and provide an extra layer of puncture resistance between tire and tube. They work, but it helps to bevel the edges with a file or knife. The leading brand is Mr. Tuffy. If you're feeling cheap, split a pair with a friend, putting them only in the rear wheels, where most flats occur. To save on installation charges, do it yourself the first time you have a flat.

Compatibility problems: None.

Aero bars and bar extenders. Aero bars are metal tubes that clamp to your handlebars and loop far out in front of you. Pads on the handlebars allow you to rest your elbows and take your weight off your palms. They're designed more to reduce wind resistance than to provide comfort, and they reduce your steering control, so don't use them if you're carrying baggage.

Bar extenders (popularly known as *bar ends*) are a different matter altogether. They attach to the ends of mountain bike handlebars, giving you a variety of new hand positions. Unlike aero bars, they don't leave you lying forward on your elbows, so they don't rob you of steering control. There are a number of styles, all designed to make your bike a lot more comfortable for long distances on the road—in short, for touring.

Compatibility problems: Anything that mounts to your handlebars—such as bar end–mounting mirrors and handlebar bags—

29

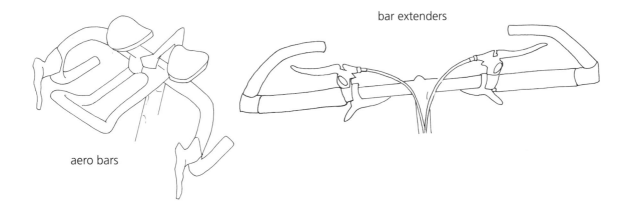

bar extenders

aero bars

may be in the way of some bar extenders or aero bars.

Solutions: Figure out what you want to mount on your handlebars; then look for a compatible bar extender.

Fenders. When you're riding in rain, the back wheel gives you a stripe up your backside, while the front wheel picks up water and dumps it in your shoes. For some people this is a badge of honor. For others it's a nuisance.

Loaded for touring, your panniers and the equipment on your rear rack will act as a partial fender, but there's no reason not to get true fenders unless you're offended by the aesthetics, live in a desert where it *never* rains, or fanatically count the extra ounces on your bicycle. For touring, none of these reasons makes much sense; you might as well get fenders.

Fenders come in two styles: those that mount permanently with a series of struts, and clip-ons made mostly for mountain bikers. I prefer the permanent kind because they're always with me when I need them. Some are short and stubby; others curve much of the way around the wheel. The long ones usually work better.

Compatibility problems: Your fork or seat stays may be too narrow to accommodate a fender; also fenders are potentially incompatible with front or rear racks. If you have a bike with a short wheel base (or if you have really big feet), the fender and your toe may meet at the front of the pedal stroke on a sharp turn.

Solutions: Some people view toe overlap as a safety hazard; others are willing to learn to live with it. Installing a fender isn't likely to be a serious problem on a touring bike, as long as you get one designed for your tire width. It will be more difficult to get fenders for a narrow-wheeled racing bike, though, since there's not much market for them.

Handlebar Relief for Gadget Fans

Short on room for all the goodies you want to mount on your handlebars? Don't dismay; Minoura makes the Space Grip, a short T-shaped bar that clamps to your handlebars to give you room to mount two items in the space normally occupied by one. Sidetrack makes an even larger gadget bar that will hold even more than two items. Combine a couple of these, and you can have cockpit controls that would make an airplane pilot feel at home.

A word of warning, however. For safety, you should mount these bars so that they point *forward* (a potential incompatibility with most handlebar bags), rather than upward. Otherwise, the bar and anything attached to it are potential hazards in a crash, positioned right where they might catch you in the stomach or groin if you take a tumble over the handlebars.

Taking the Kids

Going with children makes touring more difficult. If they're young, you can pull them in a two-wheeled trailer, as you would around town. It's possible to lug a pair of tots plus camping gear over the Continental Divide. But unless you're a real animal, you'll probably want to stick to day rides and organized tours. Van-supported touring also works, because the children can ride in the van if they don't get too bored. When pulling children in a trailer, it's best if the other parent rides along behind, watching the children. Trailer-age kids have a penchant for throwing things overboard, and it's good to catch them in the act rather than miles afterward.

It's also possible to carry children on bike seats, but trailers are more comfortable for the children and make for a more stable load, with a lower center of gravity. Cargo compartments are a real plus, as are child trailers that can be converted to luggage trailers after the children grow up.

For children who are too big for a trailer but too small to go it alone, it's possible to put the child on the back of a tandem, with the pedals jacked up so the child can help. It'll be a few years before the child can pull her weight, but many parents opt to use this approach to take children on organized tours. Even if the parent is doing most of the work, it's rewarding for the child to feel that she's helping.

Another option is a single-wheeled contraption called a *trailer cycle* that attaches to the back of your bike. It has its own saddle and handlebars, and pedals so the child can—at least in theory—assist in the work. Unlike a tandem, the child's pedals drive only the trailer cycle's wheel, which is independent from your own drive chain. This allows the child to rest or work as desired, and a separate gearing system means the child isn't forced to accept your cadence. That's good, but these aren't designed for high-speed travel; the child will run out of gears long before you do.

In general, child carriers and trailers of all sorts are incompatible with rear panniers. But Burley makes a trailer cycle that attaches via its own special rear rack that allows you to carry panniers. It's innovative but comparatively expensive.

Children over age 8 or 9 may be able to ride part of an organized tour with you. By the time they're 12 or 13, they may even be able to go all the way on their own, particularly on the shorter, flatter tours. Of course, they should be well schooled in bike safety, and you should avoid the Little League–parent syndrome that leads proud parents to push too hard. Motivated children can have a good time bike touring, but if it's not fun, they may wind up hating your sport.

HOW MUCH MUST I SPEND?

You can buy a bicycle cheaply. Discount-store models still sell for as little as $100, but they are utterly unsuitable for the rigors of touring.

The best way to tell the difference between a good bicycle and an inexpensive one is by comparing them. Go to a discount store and check out what they're selling, paying particular attention to the frame. Notice how the drop-outs of the front and rear wheels look cheap and fragile compared with what you find on more expensive bicycles. Compare the welding on the frame. Inexpensive bicycles often look cheaply constructed, although it takes an expert eye to really spot the differences.

To get a feel for what makes the difference between fine workmanship and average, look at bicycles you can't afford. You don't need a $2,000 bicycle, but you do need one whose frame won't break if you hit a big bump with a heavy load. Good components also reduce the frequency of repairs or minor adjustments.

Don't buy a used bicycle that looks as if it's seen a lot of hard use. Unless you're an expert bike mechanic, these aren't bargains. Particularly, don't buy one with a rusty frame or one that's been repainted, possibly masking a host of flaws. If the frame is bent or cracked even slightly, reject it. Damaged frames are dangerous.

If in doubt, take a knowledgeable friend with you before making the final purchase or, even better, have a mechanic look at the bicycle before you commit to buying it.

All told, it costs at least several hundred dollars to purchase and customize a touring bike. The chart below shows how to do it on three budgets: economy, midprice, and luxury. The economy column assumes you're upgrading a used bicycle, either one that you already have or one that you purchased. The midprice range assumes you are buying a new bicycle and are willing to spend a little money to do it right. The luxury column assumes that budget really isn't a factor.

The same goes for accessories. The economy budget allows for only the four essentials: rear rack, water bottles, pump, and mirror. It assumes, though, that you'll purchase good ones since they need to be durable. The midprice budget adds fenders, thorn-resistant tire inserts, a cyclometer, and padded handlebar covers. The luxury column includes a top-of-the-line pump, a gel saddle, and a fancy cyclometer. The chart also includes entries for clothing and bags, which are discussed in subsequent chapters.

General prices to fit your budget.

Item	Prices		
	Economy	Midprice	Luxury
Bicycle	$0 – $400	$450 – $800	$900 – $1,500+
Accessories	$90 – $110	$300 – $400	$400 – $500
Touring bags*	$110 – $130	$200 – $250	$350 – $450
Cycling clothes**	$150 – $175	$325 – $420	$650 – $1,100
Total	$350 – $815	$1,275 – $1,870	$2,300 – $3,550+

* Not necessary for all types of touring.
** Economy level includes only helmet, gloves, cycling shorts, and cycling shoes; midprice improves the quality of these and adds tights and a cycling jacket; luxury includes a full suit of clothing plus eye shields, waterproof-breathable-fabric rain gear, aerodynamic helmet, and more.

A Bicycle Built for Two?

Touring doesn't have to be done on conventional single bikes. In fact, it's disproportionately popular among tandem riders. Tandems are slower going uphill but faster in headwinds and much faster on downgrades. They're popular on day tours and club rides, but many tandem riders are also self-contained-touring enthusiasts.

Your biggest problem doing a self-contained tour by tandem is where to put two people's gear on a bicycle that has about the same amount of luggage space as a single bike. You can buy a second handlebar bag for the rear rider (*stoker*) and narrow bags that hang beneath the seat tubes, but these give you only a modicum of additional capacity. Most tandem riders just stack the extra luggage on the rear rack. "We add something new every year," one tandem couple once told me as they relaxed around camp in lawn chairs. "No problem."

Don't take that "no problem" attitude too cavalierly when you're starting out, however. As with all tandem parts, you may need extra strength in your racks to carry the double load. It may be easier to abandon the racks and pull a trailer (see page 102). Or you could decide to use racks *and* a trailer. Might as well put that stoker to work, right? Whatever you do, tell your shop it's for a tandem when you buy equipment. Shops that support tandems should be able to give you good advice.

RICHARD A. LOVETT

EQUIPPING YOURSELF 2

Bicycle clothing has become chic, which means it's also expensive. If you set out to be the most stylish rider in your group, you can easily spend as much on attire as for a top-notch touring bike.

Thankfully, you don't have to buy the best of everything, and if you're an otherwise outdoorsy person, several potentially expensive items—such as jackets and rain gear—can be scrounged from whatever camping equipment you already have. On my first forays into touring, I had virtually no cycling clothes, and I've known people to go cross-country with no specialty clothing except a helmet and shoes.

Going to extremes, though, is no more practical than the clotheshorse, money-is-no-obstacle attitude. A student-budget approach will leave you pedaling around in blue jeans and tennis shoes, carrying a vulcanized rubber rain suit for bad weather. If you're 20 years old that might be acceptable, at least under mild conditions, but it's not much fun, and you're likely to seek out another sport without ever giving cycling a fair chance.

Set up a personal priority list for clothing—not according to the whims of fashion, but according to its functionality and the frequency that you'll need it.

HELMETS

Bicycling without a helmet is like driving without a seat belt. You might get away with it, even for your entire life. But it might be a short life. Head injuries are far and away the leading cause of cycling deaths and disabilities, a large percentage of which could be prevented by wearing a helmet. You may

have heard stories of cyclists who received neck injuries *caused* by their helmets. (The theory is that the hard shell of the helmet transmitted the stress of the blow into the neck.) Helmet designs make this possibility unlikely, at least in people who wouldn't have received similar injuries anyway. But even if a few of these anecdotes are true, they—like tales of auto passengers miraculously "thrown free" unhurt because they weren't belted in—are more than offset by the number of helmetless riders who are unnecessarily injured.

I've only truly *needed* a helmet once. But when I did, I was glad I'd worn one for years. I was riding near home on a lightly traveled back road—the type of place where it's tempting to go without a helmet. I'd just stood up on the pedals to power up a small rise when, suddenly, the derailleur skipped and then threw the chain (my fault—I'd been trying to ignore the fact it was out of adjustment). I teetered precariously, then fell sideways, bouncing the side of my helmet off the pavement so hard I worried about whiplash. A moment later I realized that the simple fact that I *could* worry was a blessing. I wound up with a bruised hip but was able to remount my bicycle and pedal home. Without a helmet, I'd certainly have been heading for the hospital instead—perhaps worse. I won't ride ten feet without a helmet.

In addition to protecting your head, wearing a helmet sends an important message to motorists, telling them you're a serious cyclist and expect to be treated as one. Motorists will give you greater respect simply because you respect yourself.

Typical helmets consist of a foam interior covered by a hard plastic shell. The shell is designed to hold the foam in place, distribute impact, and allow your head to skid smoothly over a rough surface without twisting your neck. The foam is designed to crush under impact, giving you lifesaving cushion.

Pick a helmet that meets the two accepted safety standards, ANSI and Snell. You'll find this information stamped somewhere on the box and probably on a label in the helmet itself. Don't try to substitute a construction worker's hard hat or a mountaineering helmet; these don't have the crushable foam that protects you on a bicycle.

As long as the helmet meets the safety standards, choose it based on fit, price (which ranges from $40 to over $100), and your tastes for appearance. What you'll get from the more expensive models is styling, aerodynamic shaping (valuable for racers but not much use for touring), and lighter weight (nice). You might also get better ventilation. (If your helmet has really big ventilation louvers, beware of sunburning a bald spot or the part in your hair through them.) Many helmets have a molded plastic stabilizer that snugs against the back of your head. This is a useful accessory that helps hold the helmet at the proper angle on your head. Reflective tape is also useful for night riding.

Fit is more important than price and styling. Try several models, and don't be surprised if the fit varies even among styles made by the same manufacturer. Before pinching pennies on a poor-fitting helmet, remember that fit affects safety—especially if a poor fit discourages you from wearing the helmet in the first place.

Helmets come in a variety of colors, but basic white is the best if you care about being seen. A white helmet will show up from a long distance; a dark one, even if it's fire-engine red, will blend into the scenery. White is currently out of style and may be hard to find. Yellow is your second-best choice.

If you crash and hit your head, replace your helmet even if there's no visible damage, unless an expert assures you it's safe. Often the manufacturer will exchange it for a new one at a nominal price.

BELL SPORTS INC.

White is the safest color for a helmet; this lightweight model with plenty of vents will help keep your head cool.

Helmet Adjustments

Helmet fit can be adjusted three ways. One is by using the plastic headband, inside the helmet, which alters fit over a wide range of hat sizes. Adjust this in the shop when trying on helmets, so you're sure the helmet fits. The second adjustment is by using the chin strap, which should be tight enough to keep the helmet firmly positioned on your head, but not so tight that it gives you a headache or cuts into your jaw.

The third adjustment is the one beginning cyclists tend to overlook. If you examine the chin strap, you'll discover that on each side it splits near your ears, attaching to the helmet at two positions. This, in combination with the plastic stabilizer at the back, keeps the helmet from rocking on your head and being easily knocked loose in a crash, where it would become a hazard dangling around your neck.

The angle of the V formed by the junction of these straps is crucial to keeping the helmet in position. It is controlled by adjusting the buckle where the two straps come together. On most helmets, that buckle should be positioned approximately at your earlobe, but test it to make sure you can't easily rock the helmet forward and back. It will gradually get out of adjustment, so check it periodically.

Helmet-mounting mirrors. I prefer a rearview mirror that mounts on the handlebars. But there are also mirrors that clip to your helmet or eyeglasses or mount to the helmet with Velcro fasteners. If you get a helmet-mounting type, make sure the mirror fits your helmet. Helmet styles change, and the mirrors stocked by your bike shop could be dated. Some people swear by these mirrors, but I find them hard to use while still paying attention to what's going on in front of me.

GLOVES

For long-distance touring, cycling gloves are one of the most useful inexpensive purchases you can make. The leather palms provide much-desired cushion as you lean on the handlebars, while the fingerless design and thin fabric on the backs of your hands allow sufficient cooling. The leather palm also serves to prevent painful abrasions in a fall and allows you to (carefully) skim your palm against a moving tire if you've just ridden through a patch of glass and are afraid of a flat.

Gloves come with various amounts of padding, ranging from simple leather to gel filled.

EYE SHIELDS

Eye shields are sometimes mistakenly called *goggles*. They are a luxury but a nice one, keeping everything from dust and rain to insects out of your eyes. Good ones are considerably more expensive than sunglasses, but they also do a better job of blocking the wind from drying out your eyes—particularly important for middle-age and older riders. Some have interchangeable lenses so you can choose between tinted and clear, depending on the weather. Inexpensive shields aren't much better than sunglasses, however.

Don't expect shields to fit over eyeglasses. Eyeglass wearers will have to either switch to contact lenses or have their shields custom-fitted with prescription inserts, at a cost roughly comparable to prescription sunglasses. On the other hand, eyeglass wearers don't need shields as much as other people do, since glasses themselves provide a good deal of protection. If you purchase custom lenses, find an optician who carries a brand of shields that supports lens inserts, rather than attempting to retrofit shields purchased elsewhere.

SHOES

To increase your speed or the distance you can cover in a day, cycling shoes are, dollar for dollar, one of the best investments you can make. Unlike running shoes, which have cushioned soles, cycling shoes are firm in order to transfer the energy of your pedal stroke directly into turning the crank. No energy is wasted squishing and unsquishing shoe material. Cycling shoes also have more durable soles and reinforced uppers so toe clips won't wear holes in them, and they often are easier to slip into and out of a toe clip.

When I bought my first pair of cycling shoes, after years of riding without them, I was amazed by the difference. The day I got them, I tried out both my new shoes and the old ones on a favorite 10-mile course. The results, though not scientific, were dramatic: I was 25 percent faster with the cycling shoes.

There are three basic shoe types: touring, mountain biking, and clipless.

Touring shoes are designed for use with toe clips. They look a lot like running shoes, except for the firmer sole and reinforced upper. They should have reasonably smooth soles that slide easily out of toe clips. You may have to shop around; traditional touring shoes once dominated the market, but they're becoming scarce. Mountain biking shoes are similar but have aggressive tread patterns, almost like hiking boots. They're designed for hopping on and off the bicycle on muddy hillsides and generally aren't well suited for use with toe clips unless you keep the clips extremely loose. Otherwise, the lugged soles hang up on the pedals and won't come free. They're a poor substitute for touring shoes unless you're doing rough country mountain bike touring.

Clipless shoes are designed to snap into specially designed *click-in, step-in,* or *clipless* pedals.

(Newcomers may find the term *clipless* confusing because the shoe "clips" into the pedal. They're called *clipless* because they don't need toe clips.) Clipless pedals won't work without matching shoes, but the shoes can be used without the pedals. Well-made clipless shoes make excellent touring shoes—and may be your shop's only alternative to mountain biking shoes.

Until recently, clipless shoes weren't practical for touring because they attached to the pedal with a thick cleat under the ball of the foot. This made them uncomfortable for even short walks. New models, however, have recessed cleats on which you can walk perfectly normally. Most even have a snap-on dirt cover to keep grit out of the cleat mechanism.

Riding with clipless pedals takes a little practice because the shoe has to be placed just right before it will snap into the pedal. Starting up from a halt, it's generally best to have one shoe engaged before you begin. Then pedal one-legged for a few seconds to build up speed, and coast while you snap the other shoe into position. Getting out is simpler, but you have to remember to do it correctly. Click-in cycling shoes have their ancestry in downhill ski bindings, and their release is similar, by rotating the heel of your foot outward or inward. They'll also release

RICHARD A. LOVETT

from a sudden blow, as in a crash. With adjustable tension, you can choose how easily they pop free.

Part of the process of learning to use clipless shoes may involve a few slow-motion crashes when you forget about the cleat and try to lift your foot off the pedal normally at a stop. You may also experience the ignoble fate of reaching for the ground with one foot only to topple slowly in the opposite direction, with the other foot still firmly attached to the pedal. Some people never make such mistakes. For others, they are simply part of the learning curve. If you are fortunate enough to own an indoor trainer (see page 70), you may be able to minimize the number of mishaps by familiarizing yourself with your clipless pedals while your bike is on the stand, where you can't fall.

Clipless shoes must be adjusted to align your foot properly with the pedal. The owner's manual will instruct you on how to do this. On old models, precise adjustment was critical because even a small error could give you a sore knee, but most recent models allow your foot to "float" freely over a range of motion, rather than holding it rigid. Ask how much freedom of motion you have with each brand. The larger the range of motion is, the easier it will be to get the shoe properly adjusted.

Socks. Any athletic socks can be used for cycling. I prefer the lightweight anklet variety that isn't much higher than the tops of my shoes.

CYCLING SHORTS

It's possible to cycle in blue jeans or cutoffs—I did for years. But many people find cycling shorts much more comfortable. Put them high on your priority list.

The distinguishing feature of cycling shorts is a sewn-in seat patch, called a *chamois* because years ago that's was what it was made of (now it's imitation). Good cycling shorts are designed with the seams placed where you won't have to sit on them.

These shorts are either the stretchy, tight-fitting variety that have become so popular they're part of the public image of cycling, or baggier touring shorts, complete with pockets.

The choice is mostly one of taste. Compared to blue jeans or cutoffs, both offer much greater freedom of motion, and compared to running shorts, both have longer legs, preventing the inside of the thigh from chafing against the saddle.

The loose-fitting variety probably will have an elastic waist with a drawstring and an inner lining like in men's boxer-style swimming trunks. If you're on a budget, you could substitute any other form of loose-fitting, long-legged shorts, particularly if you have a soft saddle and don't need the cushion of the chamois.

Form-fitting cycling shorts are made of Lycra, Spandex, or a similar fabric designed to be fast drying and to provide low friction against the saddle. The chamois material not only pads but also wicks

To Clip or Not

Click-in pedals and shoes allow you to pedal more efficiently than do even the best touring shoes because they bolt you firmly to the bicycle, making it easier to pull up with one leg as you push down with the other. But they're not for everyone. Here are a few factors that may help you decide.

- How much are you willing to spend? Your bicycle already has pedals. Step-in pedals can be expensive.
- How much cycling experience

do you have? If you're a beginner, you may want to wait awhile before graduating to clipless pedals. Not only are they more difficult to get into, but they're a lot more frightening to get out of.
- How much are you a creature of habit? This will affect how easily you can make the change.
- Are you a downhill skier? If you are, you may already feel reasonably familiar with the clipless binding system.

- Where do you intend to bicycle? Clipless pedals are at their best on rural roads. In stop-and-go urban traffic, toe clips may be better because they allow you to make faster starts. When you're riding on gravel or dirt, clipless systems can also be a disadvantage because you want to be able to get your feet free at a moment's notice.

moisture from your body, increasing comfort and further reducing chafing.

Surprisingly durable unless you snag them on something, these shorts should last for years. They are designed to be tight, both to cut down on wind resistance and, more importantly, to prevent chafing. Try on a few pairs in the shop, and ask the sales staff to tell you which ones fit.

Prices vary. Expensive shorts will be better tailored, with a more comfortable chamois material. When choosing a pair, feel the chamois material to decide whether it might become abrasive with repeated washings. It can be hard to guess, but you often get the quality you pay for.

If you have a fixed budget for shorts, it's better to buy two or three less expensive pairs rather than a single expensive one. On a multiday trip, you'll have one to wear, one clean and dry, and another drying in the sun, instead of a single pair that gets dirtier and dirtier, day after day.

Some cycling shorts come in separate men's and women's models, cut differently in the hips and waist and with differences in the shape of the chamois. Cycling shorts that claim to be unisex are probably men's, although many women will find the fit acceptable.

If you temporarily need a pocket on Lycra-style shorts, you can stuff things like your wallet or spare change under the elastic of the leg without too much worry of it falling out. Don't put anything in there that will get sweat damaged, though, and don't ride with anything hard and sharp, such as car keys, that you wouldn't care to land on in a crash.

This style of cycling shorts is designed to be worn without underwear to reduce the risk of chafing. But for many people, the very idea of wearing such shorts makes them feel naked, so going without underwear is unthinkable. If that's you, wear underwear and see if you chafe. If so, the pain will probably overcome your modesty quickly enough.

Tights

Cycling tights are another piece of functional attire you probably won't want to be without. Light and easy to carry, they provide freedom of motion you can't get with street pants and are more durable than cotton warm-ups. Tights also dry out better when wet and keep you surprisingly warm on chilly mornings. Wear them over your cycling shorts so

you can take them off easily as the day warms up.

You don't need to buy expensive, name-brand tights; running tights work equally well and may be lower priced, especially if you get them at a discount sporting goods store.

Another option is a pair of leg warmers to cover the gap between your cycling shorts and socks. Usually made of a slightly heavier fabric than tights, they can give you a bit more warmth, for a lower price. When in use, the top end tucks under the elastic of your shorts; if the weather warms up, just shove the leg warmers down to your ankles until you're sure you won't need them again.

SHIRTS AND JERSEYS

Browse the pages of any cycling magazine, and you'll see that everybody's dressed in form-fitting cycling jerseys gaily decorated with the logos of racing-team sponsors. Since racing fashion drives much of the rest of cycling fashion, don't be surprised to find that you, too, can buy jerseys that make you look like a traveling billboard.

But this is money you don't need to spend. T-shirts work fine; on hot days, their loose-fitting cotton or cotton blend fabric makes them more comfortable than most jerseys. On cooler days, though, the quick-drying jersey fabric is likely to have the edge over cotton. It'll also keep you warmer when it's wet. For racers, the biggest advantage of jerseys is that they reduce wind resistance. When you're touring, your shirt's wind resistance isn't all that important; pick shirts for comfort and visibility.

For visibility, look for bright, solid colors whenever you buy souvenir T-shirts; such mementos, even if they aren't from bike trips, make perfect cycling shirts. For slightly cooler weather, long-sleeved T-shirts are also valuable, giving you a pleasant bit of warmth on your arms. Because the best colors tend to fade quickly in the sun, you'll be needing a constant supply of new shirts, both short sleeved and long.

If you want a jersey, of course there's no reason not to get one. Sometimes it's fun to feel like a racer. Also, many jerseys have elasticized pockets at the small of the back, where you can stuff a banana or your wallet—a true convenience. Some even come in cool, comfortable cotton.

If you get a racing jersey, avoid those plastered

These well-equipped cyclists are wearing Lycra shorts, touring shoes, and lightweight polypropylene jerseys. Light-colored stripes on cycling shorts and tights add to twilight visibility; solid-colored jerseys in bright colors are best for both day and night, as are light-colored helmets.

with logos. Even with bright colors, from a distance the effect is still a bit like military camouflage. And be warned—any of these jerseys will show every extra ounce of fat. But then, that can make their purchase a great incentive for a diet!

JACKETS AND WIND SHELLS

On any ride longer than a few hours, include a lightweight jacket in your pack as a combination wind shell and light-duty rain repellent.

If you're on a budget, an inexpensive nylon jacket is more than adequate. Tyvek jackets are also nice. Made from a type of plasticized paper and frequently sold or given away in place of T-shirts on bicycle tours, these jackets are windproof, reasonably rain resistant, and surprisingly durable,

considering what they're made from. Since they're designed specifically for cycling, they often come in good, bright colors.

If you want to invest some money in a cycling wind shell, there are also some nice jackets made from a new generation of fabrics that are reasonably breathable, fast drying, and somewhat water-repellent. Look for ones using bright colors, so the traffic can see you on a dim, drizzly day. Pearl Izumi, for example, makes a jacket from a vivid yellow fabric that practically glows in the dark.

A less expensive, lightweight specialty item for cool-weather riding is a set of arm warmers similar to the leg warmers described earlier. They won't do anything to cut the wind on your torso, but they effectively convert a short-sleeved shirt to long sleeves.

RAIN GEAR

It's easy to make fabrics rainproof, and it's easy to make them breathable, but it's difficult to strike a happy medium, especially if you're going to be working hard and sweating.

A fisherman's rubberized rain suit, for example, is impressively waterproofed, but you'll take a sauna in it on a bicycle. A nylon jacket is an improvement but not a big one, unless it has zippered air vents on the sides or back panel. Nevertheless, even an inexpensive rain shell is adequate for mild conditions. You might indeed take a sauna, but saunas are warm, and that's what really matters. Expect to feel chilled, though, when you stop exercising and all that trapped sweat starts to cool.

Gore-Tex and other waterproof, breathable fabrics offer a more expensive alternative based on a different principle. The fabric's weave is fine enough that liquid water can't pass through, but water vapor will, driven by the temperature differential between the inside of the jacket and the outside.

The trouble with these fabrics is that people have heard them described as "miracle" fabrics and expect too much. Yes, they can be far more comfortable than traditional rain gear, but they're not panaceas for all conditions. They work best if you're idle—for example, a hunter waiting for ducks on a rainy day. If you're working hard, you'll overload them by generating sweat faster than it can pass through, bringing on at least a partial return of the sauna. A new generation of fabrics, called *micropore fabrics*, strike a different trade-off, sacrificing some degree of waterproofing in favor of increased breathability.

Good cycling jackets, regardless of the fabric, have side or back vents. If expensive cycling jackets are out of your price range, look for a cyclist's poncho. I once had one long enough that I could sit on its tail, while thumb loops let me pull the front out to block wind-driven rain. It worked well in warm rain, keeping me reasonably dry while giving a lot of ventilation. In cold rain, however, a poncho will let in too much wind and water around the edges.

In addition to a raincoat or poncho, invest in rain pants, choosing from the same range of fabric options that you have for your raincoat. On a limited budget, get a better-grade fabric for your raincoat than your rain pants. You'll probably find that your legs don't mind overheating as much as

For riding in rain, this cyclist has a Gore-Tex jacket, nylon rain pants secured at the ankles with Velcro bands, and a waterproof, billed cap under his helmet. The bicycle has full front and back fenders.

your upper body does, and that even if they get wet, they'll warm up faster afterward.

Good rain pants have zippers near the ankle so you can take them on and off over your shoes, then zip them shut so they aren't too baggy. If there's any loose fabric around your ankles, carry something to tie the cuffs out of the way on both legs. Inexpensive elastic straps with Velcro fasteners are best. Rubber bands are cheaper but are liable to break inconveniently.

Keeping your feet warm and dry is a problem. Most people just opt to get wet, but one solution is neoprene booties that pull on over your cycling shoes. If those are too warm, some manufacturers make booties from lighter weight nylon or Gore-Tex. Booties may also help keep your feet warm on cold, dry mornings. They're designed, however, for people with clipless pedals (there's a hole cut into the bottom for your cleat). Neoprene won't fit under toe clips; Gore-Tex or nylon does but will eventually fray from rubbing against toe clips and pedals.

For your head, consider a helmet cover or a jacket with a hood that fits over or under your helmet. If you wear eyeglasses, try wearing a cotton cycling cap underneath your helmet, with its bill pulled down practically on top of your glasses. A friend of mine says this is the best thing going to keep glasses from getting rain spattered. The best head cover I've ever found is a floppy rain hat with an elastic band that keeps it from blowing away in a gust of wind. Made by Burley (headquartered in rainy Eugene, Oregon), it has a bill like a baseball cap to keep rain out of your face, and it slopes onto the shoulders so water doesn't run down your neck.

COLD-WEATHER CLOTHING

Most people hang up their bicycles for the winter when the days grow short and temperatures dip. But even if you don't try to stretch the season far into the fall or early spring, you should be equipped for cold weather, especially for mountain touring in the western U.S., where morning temperatures in the 30s or 40s can occur even in August, and long descents can expose your sweaty body to the chill of a self-generated 40-mph wind. The same clothes can also be used in camp, mornings and evenings.

Steal a trick from backpackers and dress in layers you can peel off or add, one at a time. For the upper body, carry at least 3 layers. The inner one should be a wicking layer, made of wool, polypropylene, or any of a number of new synthetics that pull the moisture away from the skin and keep you warm if they get wet. This is a good use for that fancy racing jersey, if you've got one, since it's probably made of an appropriate fabric.

Many people, myself included, sometimes use a T-shirt instead, assuming that eventually this is what we'll strip down to when it warms up. It works, but if the weather stays cool, you'll find sweat-soaked cotton cold and uncomfortable. To avoid the risk of getting dangerously chilled, be prepared to swap the T-shirt for a more suitable fabric.

The middle layer is your bulk or warmth layer (use multiple layers, if you prefer). You won't use it when you're pedaling hard unless it's *really* cold, but you will need it for cold downgrades or to keep rest breaks from turning into "freeze breaks." Again, get a material that will keep you warm if it gets wet. Wool is traditional, but imitation-fleece synthetics are superb, seeming to shed moisture rather than absorb it. They're also a lot lighter in weight. Their only serious disadvantage is that, unlike wool, which has an amazing ability to neutralize body odor, many synthetics wick away the sweat but retain the aroma—making you wish for a self-service laundry daily.

Full zippers are better than pullovers, allowing you to add or subtract a layer without removing your helmet. But if you're cutting costs, this isn't important—a well-worn wool sweater will work perfectly. You can get one inexpensively at a secondhand store or moving sale.

The third layer is a wind shell. Use the same one you carry for light-duty use in milder conditions, but make sure it's large enough to fit comfortably over everything you want underneath. If you're really trying to save money or baggage, your rain jacket will work, but if it's not breathable you'll overheat too easily.

If you can afford expensive specialty clothes, buy a warm cycling jacket that combines the middle and outer layers by covering the front, shoulders, and arms—but not the back—in wind-proof nylon. This gives you wind protection where you need it while allowing the back of the jacket to breathe. Such a jacket might also have zippered pockets at the small of the back and additional pockets at the sides. Since you'll be using it as an outer layer, look for one with bright colors, especially on the back. Another specialty item is a heavyweight jersey with rear pockets, made of a wicking fabric that stands alone in cool weather or works well as an inner layer when it's really cold.

That takes care of the upper body. But it's also important to keep the legs warm, if for no other reason than to reduce the risk of straining cold, stiff muscles.

I've found two methods that don't overly restrict my freedom of motion. Most often, I combine my lightweight cycling tights with rain pants, an approach that has worked adequately for 20-mph coasts at temperatures as low as 40°F.

The other approach, which I used on my cross-country trip, when I knew I'd be spending a lot of time at high elevations, is to buy a warmer set of

This cyclist is geared for the cold, dry conditions of early autumn or frosty mountain mornings. She's wearing a polypropylene head warmer beneath her helmet, thick long-fingered gloves, heavy tights with a layer of windproof, nylon toward the front, and a windproof, breathable jacket roomy enough to cover a bulky sweater. The Gore-Tex jacket can serve double duty as a rain-coat, if needed.

tights with fabric that is more breathable. Such tights are expensive, though, especially considering that you might not use them often. Some even come with a chamois, but you can save money by buying ones without and wearing cycling shorts underneath (useful anyway, if you think the weather's going to warm up).

A budget alternative is long underwear. As with all clothing that might get wet, use fabrics that dry quickly and wick the moisture from your skin. That means no cotton long johns or cotton warm-up pants. Blue jeans are even worse. Not only will they *not* keep you warm when wet, but they restrict your freedom of motion, have uncomfortable seams, and are heavy to lug around.

Your biggest problem with long underwear is that it will draw stares. Of more practical concern, it isn't made to sit on and will wear out quickly from friction against the saddle, and it might also chafe. Reduce the first two problems by wearing cycling shorts over the top, if they'll fit. Chafing, though, is a problem for which there's no solution except the cumbersome thought of wearing another pair of shorts or Lycra tights as yet another layer underneath. If you find yourself resorting to this more than occasionally, it's time to buy those warm tights.

For your hands, wear a pair of wool or cotton gloves over or under your cycling gloves or buy cold-weather cycling gloves with full-length fingers. For your ears, try a bandanna or ear warmers, if they'll fit beneath your helmet.

MAKING FRIENDS WITH YOUR BIKE AND STAYING FRIENDLY

3

A bicycle is like a suit of fine clothes. It needs to be tailored for ideal fit. Unless you're experienced, don't try to do all of the adjusting yourself—just as you wouldn't try to tailor your own clothes.

Some choices, such as frame size, must be made before you buy. Others are a matter of fine-tuning and can be done after you've chosen the bike. Many bike shops will do this for you using a bike-fitting approach called the Fit Kit. Not a kit in any conventional sense, this approach puts your bike on a stand so you can sit on it while a mechanic tinkers with the adjustments.

Even if you've paid an expert to adjust your bike, don't feel wedded to the result. There's a lot of disagreement over adjustment rules, and people's bodies differ. What matters is what's best for you. Use the advice given by your shop and the suggestions that follow as a starting point, but don't be afraid to tinker. It can take a lot of experimentation to customize your bike to its "perfect" fit, and even then a change in shoes, saddle, or riding posture can start a whole new round of adjustments.

BEFORE YOU BUY

Frame Size

Bicycle sizes are distinguished by such measurements as the distance between the top of the seat tube and the center of the bottom bracket.

To test frame size on a road bike, straddle the top tube with your feet flat on the ground, wearing shoes with approximately the same heel thickness as those you'll ride with. You should clear the tube with about an inch to spare. Mountain bike frames are often smaller—and are a lot less standardized—so the 1-inch rule won't apply; ask dealers for the sizing rules for the brands they carry.

Such rules aren't absolute, so the straddle test won't necessarily find the perfect fit, even for a road bike. However, you shouldn't buy a bike so large you can't comfortably straddle it, since you

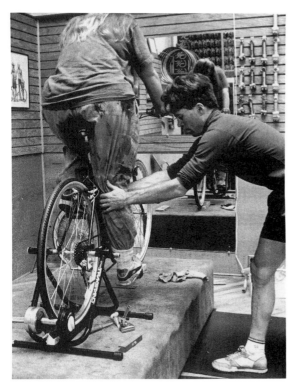

The best way to custom fit your bicycle is to put it on a stand and have a trained mechanic examine how it affects your riding posture.

4

may have to dismount in an emergency. Conversely, one that's far too short won't fit your back and might force you to put the seat and handlebars up as high as they will go, robbing you of adjustment flexibility.

Once you've found approximately the right frame size, test ride your chosen frame and the next smaller one. Try out the next larger size, too, if you can straddle it. Do this because height isn't the only variable that changes with frame size. Make sure the bicycle isn't too long or too short, either stretching you too far forward as you reach for the handlebars or bunching you up uncomfortably (although moderate variations in length in a bike that otherwise fits can be adjusted by changing the stem, as discussed in the following section). For the same reason, if you're looking at more than one brand of bicycle, don't assume that the frame size that's right for one will be right for the others.

A good bike shop is invaluable in making these decisions, especially for your first few test rides. A knowledgeable salesperson can watch you ride and help determine what's right. Later, after you've test ridden a few models, you'll develop your own ideas about what feels comfortable.

STEMS AND CRANKS

Once you've chosen a frame size, certain other component sizes come with it, such as crank length, stem height (which controls the range of heights you can set the handlebars), and stem reach (the distance the stem holds the handlebars out in front of you). These are chosen by the manufacturer, based on its image of the average cyclist. That may or may not be you.

Cranks are fairly easy to swap, although the components are expensive. Consider doing this if you are particularly long- or short-legged for your height. Most people do fine with the crank length that comes with the bike.

Stems can also be changed. For stems, however, the component is relatively inexpensive but the

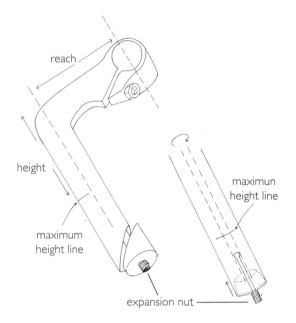

Anatomy of a bicycle stem. When the stem is installed, tightening its bolt pulls the expansion nut into the stem's hollow interior, pressing it against the inside of the head tube.

installation is more complex, especially if you're using Grab Ons. The best time to swap stems is when you're buying the bike; if you do it later you not only won't get to trade in the original, you'll also pay a more substantial labor charge.

You're more likely to want to change stems on road bikes than on mountain bikes. Road bikes are often designed to look like racing bikes, and racers, concerned about aerodynamics, set their handlebars lower than many comfort-minded touring cyclists do. Racers don't need long stems, and the bike might come equipped with one that's so short you'll have to use it at maximum height, wishing you could raise it farther. If that's the case, swap it for a longer one. Similarly, if you have a particularly long or short back, you might want to change the stem reach for greater comfort.

Stemming Bad Cycling Posture

Many cyclists have bad upper body posture, exhibited by leaning onto the handlebars with locked elbows. This transmits bumps directly from the front wheel into your hands, wrists, and elbows; it's tiring and can even make your fingers go numb after a few hours of riding.

Proper posture involves leaning forward enough at the waist to bend your elbows. The ideal amount of bend depends on the type of bicycle you're riding and the degree to which you want a head-up or head-down riding position. Touring cyclists and mountain bikers generally want to see the scenery, favoring less elbow bend than racers, who are after better aerodynamics. But even a little bit of bend lets your arms serve as shock absorbers, greatly reducing the effects of road jar.

Several factors, including your arm strength and your body's flexibility, affect cycling posture. But one factor you can change immediately is the stem. Too long a stem forces you to reach forward, stiff armed, rather than holding the handlebars with a more relaxed grip. Changing stems is a quick fix to a potentially nagging problem.

Left: Poor cycling posture. Note the straight elbows and severely flexed wrists. Right: Good cycling posture: elbows are bent for shock absorbance and wrists are in a more comfortable, straighter position. Gripping the brake hoods, as this cyclist is doing, isn't necessary, but it's a comfortable way to vary your hand position. Good posture is easier to achieve on a properly adjusted bike.

Unfortunately, choosing the perfect stem isn't as easy as you might wish: if you get a taller one, it could also have a longer reach—something you might not want. One way to increase your range of options is by putting a mountain bike stem on a road bike. Whenever you change stems, make sure you know what you're getting before you buy. The wrong stem can substantially alter the handling characteristics of your bicycle. Undoing a goof will cost you not only another stem but also a second labor charge.

ADJUSTMENTS

You can make the following adjustments after you've taken delivery of the bicycle.

Toe Clips

Begin by learning where to put your feet on the pedals. Most beginners try to place the pedal under the arch of their feet, which is inefficient and uncomfortable. But if you've never used toe clips or clip-in pedals before, this is almost certainly what you've been doing. The ball of your foot should be directly over the spindle so the power of your stroke transfers to the crank smoothly and naturally. Getting the foot into the proper position may require a minor adjustment.

With clip-in pedals, the adjustment is to your shoes. Follow the manufacturer's instructions to shift the cleat to the right place for your foot. With toe clips, all you need to do is make sure they're the

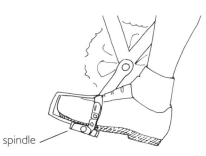

spindle

Toe clips should be sized so they're just barely long enough to hold your foot in proper position. This will keep your feet from sliding forward, inefficiently putting the pedal beneath your arch. With clipless step-in pedals, follow the shoe manufacturer's instructions to adjust the cleat on the bottom of the sole to achieve a similar foot position.

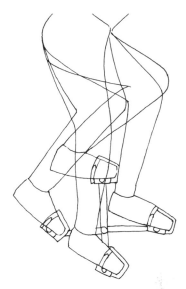

Knee bend during pedal stroke.

right length to guide your feet into proper pedal position. For comfort and to extend the life of your shoes, there should be a small gap between the clip and the toe of the shoe. If necessary, exchange the clips that came with the bike for ones that fit correctly. If you can't get the right size, you can make one that is slightly too large fit by taping a piece of foam inside its front end.

Saddle Height

From the feet, adjustment moves to the saddle. When you buy the bicycle, the shop should help find approximately the right saddle position for you, but this is an adjustment where millimeters count and it's going to take some fine-tuning to get it right.

There is no consensus on ideal seat position. The only thing that most experts seem to agree on is that a great many cyclists ride with their saddles too low. And within limits, too low is worse than too high.

If you think about the motion of your leg during each pedal stroke, you'll quickly understand why saddle height is so important. At the bottom of each stroke, your knee is almost straight, but at the top it's bent fairly sharply. The higher the seat, the less bend there is in the leg, and the less knee stress there is on the downstroke. Set your seat high but not so high it hyperextends the knee at the bottom of the pedal stroke or robs you of power because your feet lose contact with the pedals.

Saddle height is too high. Note the tilt of the pelvis, greatly exaggerated here for illustrative purposes. Any "tick-tock" motion is too much.

To find this point, sit on the bicycle with some-one holding it upright to help you balance. Sitting normally on the saddle, put your feet in the toe clips or clip-in pedals and pedal backward until your foot reaches the bottom. Racers, who draw power from calves and ankles as well as thighs, will tend to have their toes pointing downward at this point. Touring cyclists are more likely to have their feet closer to level, but what matters is putting the foot in the same position you'll be using on the road. If that changes as you gain experience, you can always readjust your seat height.

With your foot in this position, your knee should be slightly bent. If your knee is locked, you're too high. Adjust the seat accordingly.

Another approach is to take the bike out on the road or put it on an exercise stand. Pedal, while another cyclist watches you from behind. If your pelvis rocks back and forth, your seat is too high, forcing you to reach for the pedal at the bottom of each stroke. Lower it to the point slightly below the one at which you start to rock.

A third, time-tested approach is to pedal back-ward with your heels on the pedals, adjusting the seat until you find the maximum height at which your feet maintain easy contact with the pedals all the way around.

These three approaches probably won't give you the same result. Try them all, and since too low is worse than too high, pick a height near the upper end of the resulting range. If you feel twinges of knee pain on your first excursions after a change in saddle height, adjust the seat by a couple of millimeters (probably upward), and see whether they go away.

You might think that once you get your seat properly adjusted, you'll never need to change it. But that just isn't the case. Buying a new pair of shoes with a different sole thickness will require a change in seat height, as will the purchase of a new saddle. And some days, the height you've always used just seems inexplicably wrong.

Remember that saddle-height recommenda-tions aren't immutable laws. One of my cycling friends has ridden for years with her saddle so high her pelvis always rocks. It has never seemed to bother her.

Making the adjustment. Adjusting seat height is a 30-second job, faster if your bike, like some mountain bikes, has a quick-release lever on the seat post. Loosen the seat post (either with the quick release lever or an Allen nut at the top of the seat tube), pull the seat up or down as needed, and tighten it again. Work in small increments; for fine-tuning, ¼ inch is a *big* change. To keep from losing track of your starting point, mark it with tape or by lightly scratching the seat post.

Whatever you do, don't exceed the maximum safe-height line inscribed on the seat post. Look for this line the first time you adjust your saddle height so you're sure you know what it is. If you need to go higher than that, get a longer seat post.

When adjusting saddle height, wear your cycling shoes—otherwise, you'll have to readjust the saddle when you're dressed for riding.

Forward-and-Back Position of the Saddle

In addition to adjusting your saddle height, you can adjust its tilt and forward-and-back positions. Begin with the latter.

Adjusting the forward-and-back position might have some impact on knee comfort, but more than anything else, it affects the power delivery of your pedal stroke. The classic rule of thumb is that when the pedal is in its extreme forward position, a plumb line dropped from the point of the bone that protrudes just below your kneecap should go through the ball of your foot, bisecting the spindle of the pedal. Bike shops experienced with making this kind of adjustment actually have plumb lines

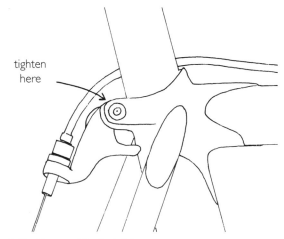

tighten here

Adjusting saddle height.

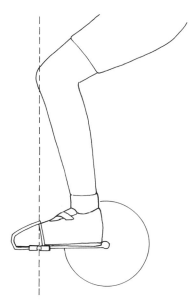

Correct knee position.

they use for this purpose. If you decide to do it yourself, have a friend eyeball your knee and foot position as you sit stationary on the bicycle.

Making the adjustment. The saddle is clamped to the seat post by a pair of metal rails that are part of the saddle's frame. Loosen the bolt securing the clamp, and slide the saddle to the desired position. Don't remove the nut completely, or you might have trouble reinstalling it.

If the saddle won't go far enough forward or back, you might need to change the seat post. Clamp position varies from brand to brand.

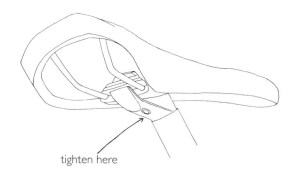

tighten here

Adjusting saddle tilt and forward-and-back position.

Saddle Tilt

Too much forward saddle tilt throws weight uncomfortably onto your hands, while too much backward tilt can cause groin discomfort. It's a trade-off you'll have to make for yourself. Men should start with the saddle level or tilted slightly upward in front. Women may want to tilt it slightly downward, although a well-designed woman's saddle will reduce the need for doing so.

Making the adjustment. This is usually controlled by the same bolt that controls forward-and-back position. Because it comes under a lot of torque as you shift your weight in the saddle, this joint often uses a notched mechanism to keep it from slipping; you'll have to adjust your saddle by full notches rather than partial steps.

To adjust tilt, you shouldn't need to loosen the nut as much as you did to slide it on the rails. Adjusting the seat forward and back might accidentally disturb your tilt adjustment but not vice versa—convenient, since tilt is the adjustment you're more likely to tinker with.

Handlebar Height

This is largely a matter of personal choice. For racing the issue is one of aerodynamics; for touring it's one of lower-back comfort and getting the weight off your hands. An old rule of thumb is to start with the top of your handlebars an inch lower than the top of the saddle. I like to keep the handlebars higher, nearly even with the top of the saddle, sacrificing a little in wind resistance in exchange for comfort and an easier view down the road without craning my neck.

As with saddle height, don't exceed the maximum height line inscribed on the stem. Raising the handlebars higher than this risks breaking the stem, which could leave you cruising along with no way to steer.

Making the adjustment. The stem is held in place by a long expansion bolt inserted from the top (see drawing page 45). Tightening the bolt enlarges the diameter of the stem slightly, pressing it firmly against the inside of the head tube.

To change your handlebar height, loosen the stem bolt with an Allen wrench but don't remove the bolt completely. If it loosens ¼ inch or so but the stem won't move, rap on top of the bolt with something hard to knock the expansion nut loose. Then slide the stem to the desired position.

Retighten the bolt firmly enough that the handlebars won't twist when you hit a bump but not so tightly that the bar ends might impale you rather than twist in a crash. To test for proper tightness, stand in front of the bike holding the front wheel between your knees. The stem should rotate—grudgingly—to a hard twist. If you don't know how tight is tight enough, ask a bike mechanic to demonstrate.

Handlebar Tilt

The tilt of your handlebars affects how comfortable it is to reach the lower position on drop handlebars and how much weight rests on your hands. Tilt isn't as important on upright handlebars, although it will affect the orientation of your extension levers.

Even for drop handlebars, there are enough styles on the market that there's no simple rule of thumb for this adjustment. Most people, however, will probably want the handlebar ends pointing somewhere between level and aimed at the rear hub. Tilting them dramatically upward or turning the handlebars upside down, as a few people do, is dangerous because it puts the bar ends right where your stomach might hit them in a crash.

Making the adjustment. Loosen the bolt clamping the handlebars to the stem, and rotate the bars as desired. When finished, make sure this bolt is tight. If it slips, you'll be lucky not to crash. Don't tighten it absurdly; I watched a mechanic do that once, shearing it and sending the broken end shooting across the room like a bullet. Do that on the road, and you'll be stranded.

Brake Lever Position

Brake levers can be moved, too, but doing so will ruin your handlebar tape and Grab Ons if you're using them. Don't make this adjustment until you've tried the brakes for at least a couple of weeks in the position in which they were installed. The odds are you'll get used to this position.

With straight handlebars, you really don't have much choice about brake positions, although you can rotate the levers. With drop handlebars, there are a lot of places to put the brakes. But think before you get too wild about it. Make sure you can reach them easily from the down position, since that's the most stable for hard braking. In addition, you want to be able to rest your hands on the brake hoods as you ride (see photo page 46). For beginners, this feels truly weird, but with practice, it's a comfortable variation with the nice side effect of changing the pressure points on your hands. You can even reach the brake levers from there for lazy, gentle braking.

Making the adjustment. Squeeze tightly on the brakes, and peer into the gap that opens up at the top of the brake lever. On most brakes, you'll see a large screw. Loosen it, slide or rotate the levers as desired, and then retighten the screw. In the process, you'll almost certainly have to remove handlebar tape, Grab Ons, or both. They're in the way, and the brake cables run underneath and need to be moved along with the levers.

BASIC RIDING SKILLS

By now, you have a bicycle, you've rigged it for the kind of touring you plan to do, and you've had a shop help you fit it to your body. Now it's time to start having fun on the roads and bike paths near your home.

This book assumes you already know basic riding principles: balancing on two wheels, starting, stopping, shifting gears. While riding a bicycle is definitely something you never forget, you can spend a lifetime honing your skills.

This chapter covers basic skills—ones you'll need regardless of where you ride. Later chapters

cover more advanced skills and topics such as desert or mountain riding, useful if you live in the relevant parts of the country or visit them on a bicycling vacation. A few regional topics, such as cattle guards and rumble strips, are included here because they have much in common with ubiquitous problems like railroad tracks and bumps.

PEDALING CADENCE

Experienced cyclists call it *spinning*. Beginners are more likely to call it impossible. But to increase your efficiency and comfort, especially on a long ride, the single most effective way is by increasing your pedaling rhythm, or *cadence*.

If you've ever seen bike racers, you might have noted that their feet spin at a fantastic pace—well over 100 revolutions a minute. That's because racers know something that most beginning cyclists don't: spinning at a rapid cadence is easier—both on knees and on stamina—than grinding along in high gears.

To test your cadence, go out on a calm day to a flat, smooth road or bike path long enough to ride several minutes without slowing down. If you have a cyclometer with a cadence sensor, put it in cadence mode (sometimes called *rpm*). Otherwise use a watch or the clock mode of your cyclometer.

Your goal for the moment is not to see how fast you can spin but to determine your normal cadence. After you've warmed up, settle into an easy cruising speed in a comfortable gear. Count the number of full pedal revolutions you make in a minute. Do it several times, trying not to let the test influence your rhythm. If your cadence is 85 rpm or higher, congratulations—you can skip the rest of this section. If it's 75 or below, there's room for improvement. Between 75 and 85 you're doing OK but may still want to improve.

Increasing your cadence takes practice. Partly it's merely the cumulative experience of thousands of miles of lifetime cycling, but you can speed up the learning curve. Riding at your normal cadence, try downshifting one gear, spinning faster to maintain speed. Your cadence should increase by 10–15 percent—for example, from 65–75 rpm.

Try to maintain this faster cadence for a minute or two. It'll feel strange and hard to maintain for long, but that's OK. This is your goal; practice will make it feel natural. If you want to increase your cadence by more than 10 rpms or so, take an incremental approach, targeting a series of more easily achievable small changes. Check your cadence periodically to see how you're doing, especially on hills or in headwinds, when you'll be tempted to grind it out in overly high gears. Because these are the times of greatest stress, they're the most important times for rapid spinning.

You may wonder if you can spin *too* fast. The answer is yes, but it's not a problem for most cyclists. Shift to a low gear and pedal as fast as you can. You'll probably find yourself bouncing up and down on the saddle. *That's* spinning too fast. It's uncomfortable, and you're not likely to do it unless you're sprinting and run out of gears.

What is the ideal cadence? That'll depend on your body and your bike, but the answer will be somewhere between 75 and 100 rpm. I have two bicycles: one for touring, the other a sport/racer. On the touring bike, my natural cadence is 84. On the racer, it's 10–15 rpm higher. The difference comes in the way the two seats position my body above the pedals. I would expect most touring bikes and mountain bikes, which are designed for long-haul comfort rather than nimbleness on the sprint, to encourage lower cadences.

RIDING IN TRAFFIC

Riding in traffic can be reduced to two watch-words: confidence and predictability. Being visible (as discussed on page 39) is also important.

Confidence and predictability are linked. Knowing what you're doing and acting like it earn motorists' respect by telling them you understand

Spinning Classes

Looking for a quick, structured way to pick up your cadence? Try a spinning class at a health club. These are the stationary-bicycle equivalent of aerobics classes; workouts typically mix high-rpm sprints with slower-rpm recovery intervals. You can do something similar on your own on any exercise bicycle with a cadence sensor. Spinning classes typically use an interval-training, sprint-and-recovery approach, but that isn't necessary. For long-haul riding, what you really want is to pick up your average cadence, not just your sprinting cadence.

One caveat: exercise bicycles are designed differently than road bikes are. Those broad cushy seats are inefficient, and your normal exercise-bicycle cadence may be slower than your road-bike cadence. Don't worry; the goal is simply to teach your legs to spin faster, and that should carry over to your road bike.

and will follow the rules of the road. Timid cyclists who wobble all over the place trying to keep away from traffic are as disturbing to drivers as maniacs who run stoplights or bring everyone else to a halt by riding the wrong way on one-way streets. The maniacs make drivers gnash their teeth, confirming beliefs that bicycles don't belong on the road. Timid cyclists bring up thoughts of children darting unpredictably in any direction.

The basic rule for cycling in traffic is simple: you are a vehicle, with all the privileges and responsibilities of an automobile. In general, you follow the same rules as a car.

Except in a traffic jam, however, you are a much more slowly moving vehicle—and one particularly vulnerable to accidents. Most of the skill of riding in traffic comes from learning to live with those two important differences. Here are a few specific pointers.

Ride on the right-hand side of the road. It's amazing how many cyclists don't understand this. Pedestrians walk facing traffic; cyclists ride with the traffic. If you're not convinced, think about this: pedestrians can always leap into the ditch to keep from being hit; cyclists can't. You need to *share* the lane, which is easier if you're moving in the same direction.

Look behind you. Keeping track of what's going on behind you is as important as knowing what's happening in front. Get a mirror and use it. Seeing cars behind you slow down or pull to the left lets you know whether they see you (and respect you); with experience you'll soon be able to tell pretty accurately how closely someone is going to pass.

Often you need to supplement your mirror by looking over your shoulder. To keep from veering in the direction you turn your head, shift your weight a bit to the opposite direction on the saddle. Practice until you can take a thorough look over either shoulder while steering a straight line.

When looking backward, be careful to avoid swerving. The author has kept the bicycle moving in a straight line by shifting his hips to offset the lean of his upper body. He's angling left because he's already started a lane change.

Ride as far to the right as safety permits. You have a right—unfortunately, one not always recognized by law—to avoid rocks, chuckholes, and broken pavement at the edge of the road. Furthermore, steering a straight course far enough out into the lane to automatically miss the bulk of these obstructions is usually safer—and more predictable to the traffic—than veering around the obstacles one at a time.

Some cyclists ride as close to the edge as they can, steering unerringly straight lines 2 inches or less from the lip of the pavement. I'm not one of them. Not only does that make it hard to watch the scenery, it's also dangerous. One gust of wind, one lapse of concentration, and you're off the road, heading for a crash. It also gives drivers an open invitation to pass without crossing the centerline.

Mark Twain once wrote about a lady whose health was failing and who had no bad habits like drinking or smoking to give up. There she was, quipped Twain, a foundering ship with no ballast to throw overboard to lighten the load. When it comes to lane position, don't be like Mark Twain's lady. It pays to retain some "ballast" to throw overboard in times of trouble—ballast in the form of space between you and the edge of the road. Not only does this give you room to wobble, but it also gives you somewhere safe to go if you're crowded by a passing car.

For normal cruising on a level road, I like a cushion of about 12–18 inches—more on fast downgrades, less on upgrades. If you find yourself in very heavy but slow-moving traffic—for example, downtown in a big city—you may even want to "take the lane" by riding in the middle of it, making yourself more visible and preventing cars from crowding you off the road. This is particularly useful if traffic is moving so slowly that you can easily keep up with it.

It's also appropriate to take the lane in situations where there isn't room for you and a car to safely share it. But here it may not be wise to ride in the center—that comes across as overly aggressive and can anger drivers (or traffic police). All that you really need to do is position yourself far enough out to force overtaking cars to cross the centerline to get around (see photo page 130). Watch carefully, and be prepared to throw away some "ballast" if necessary.

Proper lane use can also mean waiting your

The author is maintaining a modest cushion between himself and the edge of the pavement. Not only does this leave room to veer away from cars that crowd too closely, but it also avoids rough surfaces near the edge of the road.

turn. Trying to zip between lanes at a traffic light or other traffic slowdown is rude, often illegal, and unwise because drivers aren't expecting it.

Turns and stops. Always signal, both to drivers and to other cyclists. The signals are standard; you were probably taught them in grade school. For a left turn extend your left arm in that direction, straight from the shoulder. For right turns the traditional signal is to use your left arm, bent 90 degrees upward at the elbow. This rule was developed for cars, however, where all hand signals must necessarily be given with the left arm. For cyclists it's becoming acceptable to signal a right turn with the right arm, in the mirror image of the left-turn signal.

To signal a stop, extend the left arm downward, slightly out from your side. It's best to hold the palm open rather than pointing with one finger, so it doesn't look like you're merely pointing to something on the ground. Some cyclists make the gesture more emphatic by waving backward with the palm.

When turning, lean into the turn and raise the pedal on the inward side (left for a left turn, right for a right turn) if there's any risk it might drag. With practice, this becomes habitual, not only on city streets, but also on steep, winding downgrades.

Get into the habit of using both brakes to stop. Many beginners are afraid of the front brake because they've been told it can flip them over. This is true, but you need to know how to use it for emergencies or for stopping on steep downgrades. Practice using both brakes, carefully at first then more firmly as you gain confidence. Most of your stopping power comes from the front, with the rear brake contributing to control and stability. Except at very slow speeds, it really isn't all that easy to flip. A more realistic worry is skidding the front wheel on slippery surfaces. If the road is wet or covered with sand or gravel, use the front brake gingerly; it's better to skid the rear wheel than the front.

With either brake, if the wheel thumps or grabs once a revolution, you have a bad wobble in your rim. This can cause the wheel to lock and skid, so get it fixed immediately.

Intersections. Even experienced cyclists can approach intersections improperly. This is one time when the stay-to-the-right rule doesn't necessarily apply, especially on multilane roads.

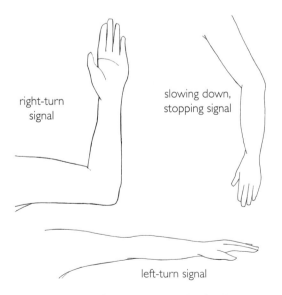

right-turn signal

slowing down, stopping signal

left-turn signal

Front views of turning signals (cyclist coming toward you).

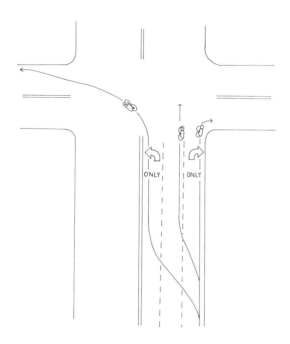

How to execute a right turn and left turn, and how to go straight in a multilane intersection.

Right turns are simple. Use the right side of the right-hand lane.

To go straight, stay to the right but watch for right-turning traffic cutting in front of you. If there is a designated right-turn lane, you can avoid it (not to mention obey the law) by moving over to the next lane. At red lights this shift frees the turn lane for people wanting to turn right on red and announces your intention to go straight. If heavy or fast-moving traffic makes it dangerous to leave the right lane, you can either move to the sidewalk, dismount, and become a pedestrian, or go straight from the right-turn lane, making *sure* the traffic understands what you're doing.

For left turns, move to the left half of the left lane (but don't hang across the centerline in front of the oncoming traffic!). Executing the turn, move directly to the right side of the road, even if it has multiple lanes. This might not be technically legal in some states, but anything else blocks traffic and can trap you in the wrong lane.

Changing lanes to turn left is scary the first few times you do it. Time your approach to the intersection to coincide with a gap in the traffic. Then signal a left turn, look over your shoulder to check for traffic (don't rely solely on your mirror; you have blind spots just like an automobile driver does), and move to the center of the left lane, "taking" it so that no one tries to squeeze past. If there is traffic close behind you, try to make eye contact with the leading driver before making your move. Many will give you the right of way, but make sure of their intentions.

Sometimes traffic is just too heavy or fast to make a conventional left turn with safety. If this is the case at a driveway or side street where there's no stoplight, pull to the side, wait for a gap in the traffic, then cross as though you were a pedestrian. Even at stoplights you'll sometimes have to do the same, crossing one way with the green light, then waiting for it to change to cross the other way. It's frustrating, but at least you'll live to tell the tale.

Even more frustrating are magnetic sensors at low-traffic intersections. If you are the only traffic, you can wait forever for the light to change. Often, one or two bicycles simply don't have enough metal to trip these sensors.

There are no good solutions to this problem. A few cyclists have become expert at understanding the polygonal cuts in the road marking the sensor's location. Laying the bicycle on its side in just the right manner can apparently trigger some of them. Other cyclists become pedestrians, pushing the walk button, although that won't give you a left-turn arrow if that's what you need. Most cyclists simply run the light, figuring that anything else is beyond the call of duty.

If there is enough traffic, I sometimes wait until someone comes up behind me, triggering the signal for both of us. If you do this, make sure the car pulls onto the sensor, beckoning the driver forward if necessary. Otherwise you'll both wait.

Some cities are beginning to install special bike sensors, tuned to detect two-wheeled travelers. They're marked with cartoon bicycle symbols and arrows showing you where to stand. Those in my town work quite well.

Parked cars. On busy streets, parked cars are a nuisance, forcing you to swing farther out into the traffic lane than you'd prefer. Since most of the drivers behind you will be oblivious to your plight, signal your intent in advance, trying to make eye contact so they'll let you in. A full-fledged left-turn signal gets their attention but may be misunderstood, so try signaling this minor change of lane position by holding your hand down to the side and pointing left. Most drivers will get the idea.

Another common hazard comes from parked cars that suddenly sprout open doors into your path. Always be alert to this possibility, especially if you see someone in the car. If traffic conditions permit, try to stay far enough away that a door can be opened to its full extent without hitting you.

If there are a lot of parked cars, stay in the traffic lane; don't swerve into and out of it for every car. If they're spaced erratically with occasional large gaps, courtesy—and self-preservation—dictates that you pull into the parking lane periodically to let the cars get by. Plan ahead; it's easy to get trapped. And be careful when you reenter the traffic lane; changing lanes is always dangerous.

Highways. Any road with a high speed limit requires extra caution. If it has a paved shoulder, use it. Even a 2-foot shoulder can do a lot to separate you from the traffic. If there is no shoulder, check your rearview mirror frequently, being prepared to pull off the pavement and stop (a mountain bike makes this a lot easier, allowing you to pull safely onto a gravel shoulder while still moving). Also be alert to pickup trucks with odd loads, such as planks, hanging farther out to the side than the drivers realize.

Highways aren't good places to aggressively "take the lane," but it can still be useful to have a cushion of spare room. When a car passes, you can ease closer to the edge, adding a foot or so to the room the driver intended to give you. That can make a big difference.

Keep an eye on the oncoming traffic as well. If cars reach you at the same time from both directions, you might be in for a tight squeeze, especially if the road is narrow. Watch the car behind you, and listen to the sound of its engine to hear whether it's slowing down to wait. If it isn't, this is a good time to pull off the pavement before you have to make an emergency bailout.

Watch oncoming cars because they occasionally pass each other, scaring you badly if you've been dozing. If there's any risk at all that the passing car won't be back in its lane by the time it reaches you, pull off the pavement and stop, immediately.

Trucks can also be frightening; watch them carefully while also keeping your eyes on the road. Farm trucks are rarely a threat. They're usually local, not in much hurry. Semis or logging trucks are a different matter. They'll seldom deliberately crowd you, but they're not all that likely to slow down and wait for a safe opportunity to pass. The deep throaty growl of a diesel engine behind you, followed by a blast on the air horn, should be interpreted as "I'm coming through. If there's no oncoming traffic, I'll give you room. If not, you'd better get out of my way." Get angry if you want, but it's a message you'd better heed.

At highway speeds, any passing truck produces wind gusts that buffet you unpredictably. If a truck passes within half a lane's width of you, you might also feel a suction trying to pull you toward it. Or the truck may suddenly block a crosswind, causing you to swerve. Prepare for all of these possibilities before the truck arrives. Grip the handlebars firmly, crouching low to reduce your susceptibility to wind. With drop handlebars, your hands should be spaced wide apart for best steering control and easy reach of the brakes. If you have drop handlebars, it's best to be in the down position. This is good riding posture any time you are facing the prospect of gusting crosswinds.

Defensive cycling. A bicycle might have the same right-of-way as a car, but defending it isn't worth a trip to the hospital. The confidence necessary to ride comfortably in traffic should be accompanied by a healthy dose of skepticism about the sanity of any given motorist.

The single most common threat comes from people making right turns in front of you, treating you like a lamppost—something that won't move after they've passed. Always be prepared for cars to make right turns immediately after they pass you, with or without signaling. When this happens (and it will), yell for attention, brake hard, and if necessary execute an emergency right turn in unison with the car. More rarely, left turners will also cut in front of you, forcing a similar maneuver. Be alert to traffic going in both directions.

Another danger is that a child playing in front of a parked car will run out in front of you or throw a ball into the street at just the wrong moment. Trucks and vans are tall enough to block your view even of an adult. Make a habit of looking underneath such cars when you're still at a distance, checking for feet or other signs that someone's in front. When you see feet or a ball rolling across a lawn toward the street, slow down and be prepared to take evasive action before it becomes an emergency.

Don't pull up too close behind a stopped car at traffic lights, stop signs, or in parking lots. People have been known to back up without looking, and it doesn't take much of a bump to ruin your front wheel.

Unguarded intersections (that is, those with no stop sign or stoplight in either direction) are also dangerous. Theoretically, the right-of-way belongs to whoever gets there first (the vehicle on the right in the event of a tie), but only a fool races somebody to such an intersection.

Another good place to practice defensive cycling is when you see a driver poised to pull out of a driveway or side street. Don't assume you've been seen; slow down or stop until you make eye contact with the driver—and are sure he won't pull out even *after* he's seen you.

Riding in traffic is never as much fun as riding on a quiet country lane, but if you're cautious and alert (but not paranoid) it can still be enjoyable and low risk.

TRAFFIC LAWS

Bicycle laws vary from state to state as well as change from year to year as states grant increasingly explicit recognition to the special needs of cyclists. Here is a summary of what to expect.

1. You are a vehicle. Bicycles have the same rights and duties as autos except for those that by their nature cannot apply. This means you don't need brake lights, but you do have to stop for stop signs and stoplights—and you can't go the wrong way on one-way streets.

2. Stop signs. I once asked a police officer, himself a cyclist, what he believed constituted a legal stop. His answer was liberal: slowing to a jogging pace and not stealing the right-of-way from someone else. But if you get a ticket, good luck defending that interpretation in court! Technically, a full, legal stop is a complete cessation of motion. If a police car is around, it's best to put one foot on the ground to prove that you have indeed stopped.

3. Lane use. Older laws require bicycles to stay "as far as possible" to the right of the road. Since it's *possible* to ride through chuckholes, broken glass, and gravel, that verbal formula is much resented by cyclists, and bike clubs have lobbied long and hard to substitute the more liberal phrase "as far as practicable." Whether the term *practicable* includes taking the lane when necessary for safety, however, isn't always clear. The most bike-friendly states have rules that explicitly permit this in appropriate circumstances.

4. Corners and one-way streets. Expect the law to allow you to move to the left for left turns or to avoid right-turn lanes when going straight. On one-way streets it will probably allow you to ride on the left, but don't make a habit of it. The traffic doesn't expect you to be there, and your cycling mirror is on the wrong side of your bike for seeing what's going on behind you and to your right.

5. Two abreast. Some states require you to ride single file. Others allow you to ride two abreast. Only ride two abreast, though, if it doesn't block traffic; it's common courtesy, if not the law. (Three abreast is illegal in most states, if not all.)

6. Bike lanes and bike paths. This is a hotly controversial subject where bike law often hasn't caught up with reality. Must you use a bike path if one is provided? What if it's full of grit or stops for every driveway? Learn the rules of your own town by asking other cyclists. Elsewhere the best rules of thumb are practicality, courtesy, and safety. If the road is a nightmare of heavy traffic, any bike path is better than none. If the road is ridable and the path unappealing, you're faced with a trade-off that you may not be able to explain satisfactorily to a ticket-happy police officer.

7. Sidewalks. Bikes and pedestrians don't mix. If you must ride on a sidewalk, the law will probably require you not to go too fast or to do stupid things like suddenly popping into the street in front of a car. You may be required to give an audible warning before passing pedestrians from behind. Beware, though, that this makes many pedestrians panic. It is also my experience that more than 50 percent of them react to announcements such as "Bicycle on your left" by stepping directly into your path. Give your warnings well in advance. Or you may want to try using a bell instead of giving verbal warnings. These thumb-operated ringers—once quite popular—avoid the left/right confusion that afflicts so many startled pedestrians, although you still shouldn't expect them to realize instantly what's going on.

8. Helmets. A growing number of states require helmets for children on bicycles. Helmet laws for adult cyclists may well be the wave of the future.

9. Miscellaneous provisions. Typically, you must have a seat on your bicycle (good idea!), and you can't cling to the back or side of a motor vehicle or carry more passengers than your bicycle is designed for. Also, you must keep at least one hand free for the handlebars. The law may also dictate how far in advance you should give turn signals, although the rules may not be practical if they're written for cars, not cyclists.

10. Learning the law. To find out your state's laws, ask at your local driver-testing station. If they don't know, they can almost certainly tell you who does. It's also a good idea to know the cycling laws of any states you're planning to visit on a tour. (Try asking the state police, the department of motor vehicles, or a bike shop.) In practice, though, most cyclists merely follow the rules of common sense, one of which is taking the most conservative approach whenever a police officer is in sight.

WIND

Headwinds are a cyclist's worst enemy. They're bad enough on a sleek, aerodynamic racing machine, but on a loaded touring bike or a mountain bike, they can practically stop you in your tracks.

One solution is to avoid wind. It sounds simple-minded, but there's a lot you can do. On training rides or social outings around home, you'll quickly become adept at interpreting wind patterns. I once lived where the standard summer weather pattern saw a brisk west wind spring up at midday then die out a couple of hours before sunset. Riding east, I'd take advantage of that by departing when the wind was strong and returning as it was fading. Riding west I'd leave early, while the wind was light, so it could blow me home at its strongest. Usually. It's a good idea to allow some leeway in case the wind doesn't cooperate.

Another trick is to let the wind determine your route. Go upwind first, saving the easy downwind leg for last. Better yet, do the upwind section on a road that's relatively sheltered, emerging into the open for a free ride home.

If you do get caught in a headwind, be patient.

Gear down, keep up your cadence, and don't push too hard.

Drafting

Another approach to headwinds is to team up with one or more other cyclists in a drafting, or *pace*, chain. When drafting, you ride in the slipstream of the cyclist in front of you, letting your friend break the wind while you rest. Taking turns so the leader never fatigues, you go faster than either of you would alone. It even works when there's no wind.

Proper drafting formation depends on the wind direction. In a straight-on headwind or one that's nearly so, the most efficient way to ride is closely spaced, single file. *How* closely spaced is a trade-off between energy savings and the risk of colliding. Drafting efficiency falls off rapidly with distance; if you're more than a bicycle length apart, you've lost much of it. Closer is scary, though, because you can't see much except the rear tire of the cyclist ahead of you, and there's not much time to react.

The trade-off between safety and efficiency is one you have to make for yourself. My own compromise is to stay well back—at least half a bicycle length—from people I haven't cycled with several times or whose skills I don't trust. I also like to move slightly off to one side. That exposes me to a bit more wind, but allows me to see what's ahead and gives me a safe direction to veer if necessary. In a larger group you can achieve the same benefits by forming a staggered line, giving each cyclist a little bit of extra time to react.

Drafting in an angling headwind is the same, except now each cyclist offsets to the same side, downwind. The ideal position depends on the precise wind direction. As a rule of thumb, imagine a line through the center of your two bicycles. That line should point directly into the perceived wind (the combination of the wind itself and your own forward velocity). Get into approximately the right position, and move forward or back a few inches to see what's most comfortable. If this leaves you with part of your front wheel beside the rear wheel of the rider in front of you, think about dropping farther back or moving well off to the side. At least make sure the other rider knows where you are. You're "lapping wheels," and if he swerves, you'll hit the pavement, hard.

"Why Is Everything Always Upwind?"

Most cyclists believe that when it comes to wind, they're jinxed. A random poll of cyclists would probably find that 75 percent of the time, they think they're going upwind.

Scientifically, that's unlikely. What's really happening is that cyclists often don't recognize gentle tailwinds when they've got them. Many times, in fact, I've had experienced cyclists complain to me about headwinds when actually we were running with a light following breeze. What fools them is the perception of wind in their faces, generated by their own forward motion.

For a tailwind to truly *feel* like it's coming from behind you, it has to be going faster than you are, which takes a near gale or an upgrade steep enough to slow you significantly.

There's no real harm, of course, to this failure to recognize light to moderate tailwinds. But psychologically, it can be depressing. Next time you wonder why the world's always stacked against you, ask yourself the following questions.

- What direction was the wind blowing the last time I stopped? (If you don't know the answer, why not stop and find out?)
- What speed am I going? (If you're making good progress at relatively low effort, that perceived headwind must be an illusion.)
- Which way are roadside grasses, leaves, or flags blowing?
- Am I just getting tired at the end of a long day?

The results might surprise you.

Crosswinds are similar. Since the perceived wind still has a headwind component from your own velocity, the most efficient place to ride won't be directly beside the upwind rider, but with your front wheel somewhat behind hers.

In a straight-on headwind, there's no theoretical limit to the length of a pace chain, although chains of more than a half-dozen riders tend to stretch and contract accordion style, much to the irritation—and occasional panic—of the people in back. It's often simpler and a lot more sociable to form a double pace chain, with two lines of cyclists, side by side. But do this only if you have a wide road shoulder; otherwise the riders nearest the traffic don't have time to get out of the way of approaching cars. If there's no shoulder, ride single file, and keep the group small enough that it's not too much of an obstacle to traffic.

In a crosswind or angling headwind, long pace chains don't work because the necessary stagger will force the trailing riders too far to the side. The leader can help by riding as far to the upwind side as safety permits, but it's best to break into pairs or trios.

Drafting Etiquette

Riding in a pace chain is a good cure for a nasty headwind, but it's inherently dangerous. If you're going to do it—and at some time or another even the most cautious cyclists usually do—it requires careful attention to technique and group etiquette. It's not something to do when your primary interest is in the scenery.

Don't even consider drafting if you have trouble holding a constant pace or tend to wobble around a lot. At best you'll drive your drafting partners batty; at worst you'll find yourself in the middle of a crash. Also beware of drafting at high speed downhill. At 30 mph, you don't need a windbreak anyway.

Pace chains don't work well uphill either; in this case everyone has an individual way of climbing hills, and it's hard to keep a group together.

In a drafting chain, the leader is responsible for road hazard warnings, pointing downward on the side where an obstacle will soon appear and calling out "rock" a second or two beforehand. Cyclists in the middle of the chain often echo the warning to those behind them, but overdoing this can be irritating.

Keep the warnings simple: "rock," "gravel," "glass," "stick," "road kill," "hole," "bump." If the obstacle doesn't fit any obvious category, call it a bump or a hole—the last thing you want is for other riders to be saying "Excuse me?" when you've tried to warn them about an unidentifiable car part or a bag of litter. If there are several obstacles, wave your hand broadly on the proper side

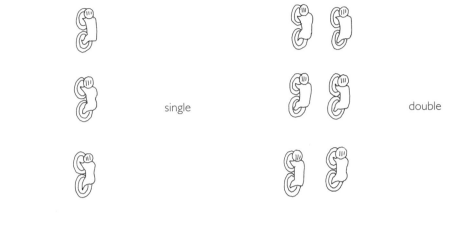

single

double

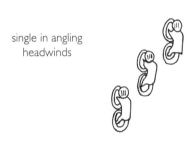

single in angling
headwinds

Drafting or pacing chains allow riders to work together against a headwind. They will also speed you up on calm days but require care to avoid colliding with fellow riders.

and call out "rocks" or whatever. Plan ahead, so you never have to swerve violently, and try to steer at least 2 feet away from the obstacle so the riders behind you don't come too close. People who can't remember to do these things consistently shouldn't be trusted in pace chains.

If the obstacle is a railroad track, stop sign, corner, or anything else that requires a major speed or course change, warn well in advance, letting the pace chain spread out as people find their own ways through. Regroup afterward.

Whether you're the leader or in the middle, don't slow down abruptly, and particularly not without warning. A hand signal and a shout of "Slowing!" or "Braking!" should *precede* the action if at all possible. If you're drafting closely (with a gap of, say, less than 2 feet), don't miss even a pedal stroke without announcing it.

Riders in the back of the chain are responsible for giving warnings about traffic. Since it's not safe to take your eyes off the rider in front of you long enough to look over your shoulder, a mirror is mandatory. Traditional warnings are "car back," "truck back," "RV back," or simply "another one," if you're being passed by a string of traffic. In appropriate circumstances—as when the group is about to make a left turn—you can also call out "clear back" if there's no traffic behind. Always indicate what direction is clear, since other riders may be wondering about what's going on ahead or to the side.

If this all sounds tricky and dangerous, it is. It requires constant attentiveness. But it has its rewards—not only the tangible ones of getting there faster and easier but also the psychological ones of facing a headwind and *doing something* about it. And drafting with a single partner or a small group of friends is a wonderful exercise in teamwork and camaraderie.

The first time you draft, the reduction in effort will feel almost magical. The best way to learn is by practicing with a close friend in a headwind strong enough to hold you back to a speed of less than 10 mph. That will give you plenty of time to react, and even if you do bump each other you're not likely to have a serious crash.

DOGS

Dogs may be man's best friend, but they aren't a cyclist's. There's nothing like a snarling mongrel threatening to take a chomp out of your Achilles tendon to make you wonder why you didn't take up a nice tame sport like bungee jumping.

Cycling lore is full of suggestions for defending yourself against canines. Some cyclists carry Mace; some bend pump handles over the beasts' skulls. I find dogs to be a much-overrated hazard. They're usually harmless, running with you simply for the joy of the chase. Mace might discourage such dogs, but it could also turn them into cyclist haters, creating bigger problems for the next cyclists to pass by. If you feel you really *must* squirt a dog with something, use water.

The really dangerous dogs are the ones that don't growl or bark. They're on you before you know what's happening and—as in the case of the only dog that's ever bitten me—gone before you could possibly have armed yourself with the pump or a can of Mace.

So what do you do when a dog charges toward you out of a farmyard? Try not to get worried or excited, even if it's a 100-pound shepherd that looks like it could have both you and your bike for breakfast. Dogs sense fear, and it brings out something atavistic in them, greatly increasing the threat.

With most dogs, especially those that wag their tails and obviously mean no harm, it's best just to ignore them. You usually can't outrun them, and suddenly speeding up may excite them further. Consider doing the opposite, coasting if the terrain and wind direction permit. That way your heel is no longer going up and down, up and down, where even the friendliest pooch may be tempted to grab it.

When all else fails, the best defense is often to dismount, use the bike as a shield, and yell at the dog or scream for help. If you're lucky, the very act of dismounting will take the fury out of the attack. Sometimes it's not people a dog dislikes—it's people on bicycles.

One other caution: beware of dog walkers on bike trails. The dog is unlikely to chase you, but it may step suddenly into your path. Never pass between a pet and its owner without being certain there's no leash between them. In some light, leashes can be virtually invisible.

RAILROAD TRACKS, CATTLE GUARDS, AND RUMBLE STRIPS

Cross railroad tracks at a right angle or close to it. Too shallow an angle—what that is depends on your skill, your tires, and the weather—and the track will grab your wheel, and you'll crash before you know what happened.

To cross a sharply angling track, plan on using most of the lane. On a quiet farm lane or a highway with a full-width shoulder, this is no problem. If the traffic is too intense, as on a busy narrow-shoulder highway, dismount and walk. In a town or city or on a low-speed rural road, look for a suitable gap in the traffic and give the arm signal for slowing down. If you're with other cyclists, give one another plenty of maneuvering room. Slow to a fast walking speed—less if the crossing is bumpy. Depending on which way the tracks angle, move to the right or out into the lane until you can cross comfortably while staying in your lane.

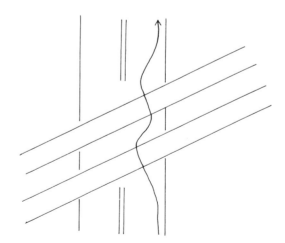

When crossing multiple angling tracks, steer a W-shaped course to cross each pair of tracks squarely and to avoid interfering with oncoming traffic. Don't pull out into the path of cars coming up from behind you, but once you start your crossing, don't hurry, even if traffic builds behind you.

If there are multiple tracks, you might not be able to cross them all at once. Use the space between them to curve back in a W-shaped course until you've gained enough room. If there's no traffic, you can also use both lanes of the road to cross the tracks in a single hitch.

If a car comes up behind you while you're zigzagging across a multiple track, let it wait. Your right to the road includes the right to cross railroad tracks safely, and it won't help anybody if you crash in front of the car because you hurried.

Even if the railroad track crosses at right angles to the road, be careful—some crossings are extremely rough. Reduce the stress on your bicycle by rising slightly out of the saddle, knees and elbows bent to absorb some of the shock. Also, watch for metal flanges that can slice big gashes in your tires. And remember that wet railroad tracks are extremely slippery, even if you're going very slowly. It's a good idea to unclip your feet from the pedals so you can catch yourself if the bike starts to slip. Sometimes it's best just to dismount and walk.

Cattle guards. Cyclists in the western U.S. are all too familiar with these wheel-jolting contrivances. Easterners, on the other hand, often stop in open-jawed amazement the first time they see one.

Cattle guards, or grates, are parallel metal bars spaced several inches apart, crossing the entire road from shoulder to shoulder. The grating is usually several feet wide, with a 2-foot-deep trench

Cattle guards are generally smoother than they look. The flat-topped rails of this one would provide an easy ride at speeds as high as 30 mph. However, beware of joints such as the one in the middle of this guard, and watch for big bumps where the road surface may have sunk or been broken up at the grate's edge. Ideally, this cyclist should be braced for bumps, as in the drawing below left, but that's not possible when you're pedaling uphill, as here.

beneath it. Hoofed animals such as cattle won't cross it for fear of getting their feet trapped. Wheeled animals such as cyclists are usually just as intimidated on their first encounters.

Unlike crossing railroad tracks, the trick to crossing cattle guards is keeping up your speed, especially on newer guards that use flat-topped I-beams instead of round rods. Cross too slowly and you'll be bounced to death as your wheels go thump-thump-thump from one bar to the next. Take a good look at the guard, however, before venturing across. Some, especially on gravel roads, have big bumps as you enter them or exit. If a grate is really rough, dismount and walk, but be careful not to twist an ankle.

Some cattle guards use bars that aren't as long as the road is wide, with joints in the middle of the lane. Watch for these; they often have gaps that are the perfect width to eat your wheels. Also, as with railroad tracks, rising out of the saddle, knees

crossing a bump

bent to absorb shock, reduces wear and tear on your bike. This also goes for speed bumps, chuckholes, rumble strips, and any other potentially damaging bump.

Rumble strips. Rumble strips are the bane of midwestern cyclists, although they can be found wherever road surfaces are made of concrete rather than asphalt. A series of closely spaced seams cut crosswise into the concrete, rumble strips mark hazards such as stop signs or warn drivers that they are straying onto the shoulder. At 55 mph, they make car tires buzz loudly enough to catch the attention of dozing motorists. On a bicycle, they seem to vibrate every bolt loose from its housing.

An occasional set of rumble strips is merely a nuisance. If the road engineers were thinking of bicyclists, they may even have left a gap for you on the shoulder. Rumble strips designed to keep traffic from straying onto the shoulder, however, also force you out into the traffic lane. That can make the traffic hostile, since the drivers can't figure out why you aren't using that nice, wide shoulder. Find a different road.

Bicycle-jolting rumble strips may eventually become a thing of the past. Highway engineers in the Midwest have developed a new way to cut grooves into the concrete that makes them far less jarring—bicycle friendly enough that you can just ride across them, mile after mile.

Drain gratings and manhole covers. Most modern drain gratings are crosshatched or turned sideways to keep your wheels from dropping in. But don't let this lull you into complacency. Not all storm sewers are so bicycle friendly, and all of them, along with manhole covers and any other metal object, can be slippery when wet. Avoid them if traffic conditions permit.

DAY TOURS AND TRAINING RIDES

5

You now have most of the equipment and skills to take on the most popular form of touring: day rides into the rural countryside near your home or to a favorite vacation destination. You may want to do these alone or with a few close friends, but many people are drawn to the challenge and high-energy camaraderie of organized club rides, popularly called *century rides*.

In cycling parlance, the word *century* doesn't mean 100 years; it means *100 miles*. For a few dollars, these rides provide maps, snacks, scenic low-traffic routes, and the camaraderie of riders of a wide range of skills and speed. Every summer weekend is likely to bring at least one; some events feature distance medleys that also include a metric century (62 miles), a half century (50 miles), or a metric half century (31 miles).

RICHARD A. LOVETT

Other than a handlebar bag or rack pack to hold your rain gear and the route map (see page 96), and perhaps a bike rack on your car to get you to the start (see page 139), the only thing you may be lacking is enough training mileage for the ride to be an exhilarating challenge rather than a battle between willpower and an undertrained body. This chapter will discuss how to prepare for an enjoyable outing, whether it's a full century or something considerably shorter.

With minor adjustments, the same training methods apply to any other form of touring. Even heading out into the mountains for a week doesn't take much more preparation than a long day ride—and a tough century may require considerably more intensive training than a week of low-key, van-supported touring. But you'll get better results on longer trips with a slightly altered training schedule that focuses on toughening your body for consecutive days in the saddle. This chapter therefore presents a continuum of training techniques from early spring start-up to focused training designed to peak your body for a multi-day tour.

TRAINING BASICS

There is no ideal, one-size-fits-all training method. What works when you're 25 might not work when you're 45, and experienced riders, who are well practiced in pacing themselves to avoid exceeding the limits of their conditioning, may be able to get away with less training than beginners can.

Training is a process of experimentation. Don't wed yourself to anyone's training schedule—including the one presented here. One of the most important components of training is learning to listen to your own body's ways of conveying such information, such as *I'm feeling great; it's time to move on to the next step*, or *You've been pushing too hard for a week; if you don't take a break soon, I'll force you to.*

Set each year's goals according to how much previous cycling experience you've had. It's just common sense that if you're so new to the sport that you can't imagine pedaling 10 miles, let alone 50–100, you shouldn't aim for an 80-mile-a-day tour by the end of your first season. Go ahead and plan a tour, but keep the distance shorter.

SPRING TRAINING

If you're fortunate enough to live where you can ride year-round, getting in shape after a winter layoff isn't an issue. But if you live in colder, snowier climes, the first weeks of spring can make you feel as though you're beginning all over again from scratch. And if you've taken a long layoff for some other reason or are just beginning the sport, start with a spring-training regimen regardless of the season.

The basic rule of spring training is to ease back into cycling. Gentle, rapid spinning is the name of the game. Avoid the temptation to race other cyclists and, if possible, avoid big hills, especially for the first month or so. If you can't dodge the hills, go at them gently until you've toughened up not only your muscles but your tendons and ligaments as well. If something starts to hurt, back off immediately; it's too early in the season to be macho.

Some cyclists advise staying in this spinning mode until you've accumulated at least 1,000 miles, but unless you bike a lot, that could take months. A better rule is to keep your training gentle until you've put in at least 20–30 percent of last year's mileage. (If this is your first year of serious cycling, stay in spinning mode for at least the first 500 miles.)

If you're starting up after a total layoff of more than a few weeks, your first few trips should be very short. Use the first three weeks to get reacquainted with your bicycle. When I lived in a climate where five-month winter layoffs were the norm, my spring training began as follows.

- Week 1. No more than 3 days of riding and no distance over 5 miles. No riding on back-to-back days.
- Week 2. No more than 4 days of riding, with one longer ride of 7–10 miles.
- Week 3. Extend the long ride to 15 miles, ride 5 days if desired, and bring the total weekly mileage up to about 35.
- Week 4 and beyond. Increase mileage gradually, no faster than 10–20 percent a week. Even at 10 percent a week, you can double your mileage in 7 weeks; at 15 percent you can double it in 5. Repeated weekly increases of more than 15 percent aren't recommended.

This is conservative—more conservative than some people may need. But if you blow out a knee in the first month of training, you'll lose not only the time it takes to recover but much of your spring training as well. Be cautious those first weeks in March, April, or May, so you can be riding full steam in July and August.

BASE TRAINING

Your spring-training goal should be to gradually build up to a weekly mileage that will allow you to take longer day rides (including centuries) or easy weekend tours without additional training. If you like, you can do the buildup in stages, plateauing at one level for a few weeks before increasing to a higher level, again at no more than 10–15 percent a week. Once you've reached your desired weekly mileage, the process of maintaining it is what I call *base training*.

What is the appropriate mileage base? There's no easy answer because such factors as age, experience, and susceptibility to overuse injuries play a major role. But if your goal is simply to *complete* a long, single-day ride or a two-day self-contained

Rx: Hand and Arm Problems?

Tingling, burning, numbness, or a going-to-sleep sensation in the fingers or palms of the hands is caused by pressure on nerves. It comes from extended hours of leaning on the handlebars or from road shocks transmitted through the bike into your hands. Similar problems in the elbow can produce the same sensations in the lower arm. Because these problems can become increasingly severe over the course of a season or with the accumulated wear and tear of many years on a bike, don't just ignore them and hope they'll go away.

Shift hand positions frequently. To restore life to tingling fingers, periodically stretch the affected arm behind you, backward and upward as far as you can, opening and closing your fist several times. You can do this on the bike without missing a pedal stroke.

The first line of defense against these problems is padding, padding, and more padding—although some people, especially those with small hands, will find that an overly bulky cushion will itself make them uncomfortable.

Start with gel-filled cycling gloves; buy the cushiest ones you can find. If those aren't enough, try wearing an old stretched-out pair over a new pair. Padded handlebar covers also help. Cork-backed winding tape offers good padding, padded handlebar covers such as Grab Ons even more, and a homemade super cushion—made from a piece cut from an old closed-cell foam sleeping pad, wrapped around the handlebars and held tightly in place with strapping tape or handlebar winding tape—provides the most.

On the road, your arms should be bent, not locked at the elbows (see page 46), and you shouldn't have a death grip on the handlebars; just hold on tightly enough to keep control. If you see rough pavement coming, momentarily shift some of your weight off your arms to reduce the shock.

Other solutions include the following.

- Don't tilt your saddle too far forward. This throws weight onto your hands.
- Raise the handlebars.
- Buy a taller stem or one with less reach.
- Don't lean on your hands with your wrists bent backward (the way they'd bend if you were doing push-ups). This is the position that causes carpal tunnel syndrome in computer workers, and it can do the same thing to you on a bike.

Nerve pain in your hands is mostly a drop-handlebars problem. Switching to straight handlebars or a recumbent bicycle should produce a near-complete cure.

tour in reasonable comfort (as opposed to doing so quickly), you can manage quite well if your weekly mileage is at least 125 percent of the distance of the ride or tour. In other words, 125 miles a week of training will support a century ride or a two-day self-contained tour of 100 miles—probably with a comfortable margin of error. If you're young and have a lot of cycling experience, a comfortable saddle, and never-say-die knees, you may be able to get away with a lot less.

But just racking up the mileage isn't enough. You can accumulate 105 miles a week by doing 15 miles every day, but that won't prepare you as well for a 70-mile trip as doing less total mileage but getting in an occasional ride of at least 40 miles. You need to train for endurance and long periods of time in the saddle.

The Base Training Schedule table at right suggests schedules for weekly mileages of 50, 75, 100, 125, and 150. You could build schedules for other distances along the same pattern. Notice that the 125-mile week—roughly appropriate for a full century—has a long day of only 60 miles. Whatever length of day ride you're training for, there's no need to go the full distance in training; save that for the big day itself.

There is nothing magic about the precise daily distances, but these base-training schedules do follow a few rules.

1. Use a hard-easy pattern, with hard days followed by recovery days. This is important, especially early in the season. Recovery is part of training, although a short, easy ride the day after a particularly hard one can speed recovery by working the kinks out of your legs.

2. Take at least 1 rest day a week. Riding every day is the road to burnout, injury, and divorce.
3. For longer weekly distances, I've included 1–2 days a week of optional speed training. Do these only if you want to increase your speed. One workout is labeled "interval"; the other is labeled "pace." Interval training entails repeated short sprints of 2–4 minutes. Find a way to make it fun by charging hills, dashing to stoplights, or impulsively deciding to go as hard as you can for a mile. The speed part of these workouts should total about 10–15 minutes.

    Pace workouts are longer, not at a sprint but faster than your normal touring speed. The purpose is to increase the speed you can maintain over distances of 5–10 miles. In both types of speed workouts, don't be so engrossed in beating the clock that you forget about traffic.

    If you don't want speed workouts, there's no obligation. Take the speed days as easy ones, and do the mileage at your normal pace.

    Here are a few other important tips.

1. Be flexible. If there's a gale blowing, you're hosting a dinner party, or you just plain don't feel like cycling, take a rest day and adjust your schedule accordingly.
2. If you're not a schedule person in the rest of your life, don't force yourself to become one for cycling. Just try to get in 1 long ride a week, with easy days after hard workouts. As long as you keep your weekly mileage reasonably close to your target, you'll do fine.
3. Keep at least a minimal training diary. A wall calendar near where you park your bike is perfect. Jot down the distance pedaled, and keep track of weekly totals to make sure you're not increasing too quickly. If you develop an ache or pain, write it on the calendar with a brief explanation. If the ailment goes away on its own, this is reassuring; if it doesn't, the training diary may provide useful clues.
4. Don't pedal if you're sick, and don't try to make up for the lost mileage later. And yes, having a cold counts as being sick, at least for the first few days.
5. Begin all workouts with 5–10 minutes of easy spinning as a warm-up. Conventional sports-medicine wisdom recommends doing the same at the end of the ride, but unless you finish with a sprint or a big hill, this isn't necessary on the laid-back rides that provide the best training for touring. Do walk around a bit after getting off the bicycle.
6. If you shift training patterns even without changing your weekly mileage, do so gradually. This is particularly important if you're adding long rides, hills, or speed workouts. Don't make major changes here if you're also increasing your weekly mileage.

Base Training Schedule

Weekly Mileage	Daily Mileage						
	1	2	3	4	5	6	7
50	10	rest	10	5	rest	25	rest
75	18	rest	10	7	rest	35	5
100	24	rest	8 (I)	10	rest	50	8
125	23	10	10 (I)	12	rest	60	10
150	20	10 (I)	15	15 (P)	rest	75	15

I = interval training (optional)
P = pace training (optional)

7. Even if training for speed is one of your goals, do most of your training at an easy pace. This reduces overuse injuries and builds up endurance. Most cyclists defeat themselves by training too fast.

8. If you're new to athletics and aren't sure you know an easy training pace from a killer one, you can find out with a heart-rate monitor or by counting your pulse. For touring, at least 90 percent of your training should be at a low level, perhaps even as low as 60–65 percent of your maximum heartbeat, determined from the following equation.

$$\text{maximum heart rate} = N - (\text{your age})$$

For men, N is 220. For women, it's 226. If you're a 35-year-old woman, for example, your maximum pulse rate is 226 minus 35, or 191. A training pulse rate of 60–70 percent of this would be 115–133 (about 19–22 beats per 10 seconds). People vary, however, and target pulse rates are guides, not straitjackets. The most important information they'll give you is that your ideal training pace is slower than you probably think. Also, realize that target pulse rates measure level of effort, not speed. As you get in better shape, you'll go faster with the same effort.

Pulse monitors and charts of target pulse rates are racer gadgetry you don't need for touring. A cheaper and more natural approach is to develop an intuitive feel for how hard you're working. Are you gasping for breath? Slow down unless you're in the last seconds of a speed interval. Do you feel strong and able to go faster? Go for it, unless it's too early in the season. Are you chugging along at a good clip but are still able to maintain a reasonably normal conversation? That's probably your ideal long-distance training pace. The charts and gadgets will tell you these same things a bit more precisely, but the purpose of touring is to relax and explore, not to shave an extra minute off your time in a 10-mile time trial. You'll have more fun if you maintain the same attitude about training.

TRAINING FOR A TOUR

Once you've maintained your base training for a few weeks, you're ready to start preparing for a tour longer than a weekend.

This doesn't take any special training if the average daily distance will be no more than 25–35 percent of your weekly base-training mileage (40–50 percent if you've got a van to carry your baggage), and the terrain is gentle. Your base training should be sufficient. But if the terrain is strenuous or daily distances are longer, focus your training on preparing for the tour. You'll need to increase your mileage (as before, no faster than about 10–15 percent a week) and deviate from the hard/easy training pattern.

The key to this approach lies in phasing in a pair of

Rx: Sore Knees?

Knee problems are one of the most common cycling injuries, and the pain is likely due to overuse. Unless you have a preexisting condition or twist your knee in a fall, the most likely diagnoses are tendonitis of the big tendons above or below the kneecap or chrondomalacia, an inflammation of the back of the kneecap.

At the first twinge, ease off and downshift. If you're lucky, the pain was just a warning. If it continues, stop and take an anti-inflammatory, such as aspirin, ibuprofen, or Aleve. Do not take more than the total daily recommended dose, especially for ibuprofen and Aleve, without first consulting a doctor. Ibuprofen overdoses have been linked to kidney failure, and your kidneys are already being taxed by the dehydration that accompanies heavy exertion.

At the end of the day, ice the knee for 10–20 minutes. If it's swollen, hurts when you're off the bicycle, or hurts when you get on again the next day, you need a few days' rest or greatly reduced mileage. Then, try to eliminate the cause—candidates include too low a pedaling cadence, improper seat height (probably too low), poor cleat adjustment, or simply pushing too hard when you're not in shape. If the pain persists, of course, it's time to consult a doctor.

long rides on consecutive days. This toughens your legs and rear end for day-after-day riding, extending your comfortable touring distance significantly. At the beginning of this training schedule, a weeklong fully supported tour of more than 40–50 miles a day might be a strain. At the end, 60–85 miles a day should be within easy reach, depending on the terrain, even if you're carrying your own baggage.

The Focused Training Schedule has no speed workouts. They're not much use for self-contained touring, though you may want them for van-supported or organized tours if keeping up with faster riders is one of your goals. If so, do a speed workout on one of the short-mileage days, such as day 3 or day 4. Or invest one of these days in a hill workout.

On your long rides, try to duplicate the conditions you expect to find on tour. If you'll be touring in heat, train at midday. If you'll be touring in mountains, do your long rides in hilly terrain. (If no hills are available, try going back and forth over freeway overpasses. Dull, but it's a good workout.) If you're not used to either heat or hills, phase them in over the course of several weeks to let your body adjust gradually.

Training on the tour. Oddly, tours longer than one week require less training than shorter ones because you can do a substantial amount of training on the road. A transcontinental rider, for example, might start out at 25–30 miles a day, gradually building up to daily distances of 50, 60, 70, or even 80 miles. This doesn't work on short tours because it takes about a week for the training to take effect. Another way to train for a self-contained tour is to take a multiday organized tour sometime in the month beforehand.

Training with full panniers. If you'll be carrying your own baggage on tour, some people recommend doing at least part of your training with loaded panniers. In theory this is sound advice, but carrying around all that weight simply for the practice isn't my idea of fun.

Focused Training Schedule

Below is a 7-week schedule for doubling your training mileage and more than doubling the distance you can comfortably tour. It assumes that you begin at a weekly base of 75 miles, using the training pattern in the base training schedule table on page 67. Adjust the numbers proportionally if you start from a different base mileage, and feel free to stop before reaching week 7 if 150-mile weeks are more than you need. Because the focused training pattern is more demanding—both on the body and on the social life—than the base training pattern, I don't recommend substituting it indefinitely for base training. Save it for when you're planning a major tour.

Week No.	Daily Mileage							Weekly Mileage
	1	2	3	4	5	6	7	
Base	18	rest	10	7	rest	35	5	75
1	rest	12	10	7	rest	40	15	84
2	rest	10	7	10	rest	45	21	93
3	rest	13	5	10	rest	45	30	103
4	rest	13	5	10	rest	50	35	113
5	rest	14	5	10	rest	55	40	124
6	rest	16	5	11	rest	60	45	137
7	rest	20	5	20	rest	60	45	150

Rx: Overtraining?

Even if it doesn't result in specific injuries, excessive training can produce burnout and listlessness.

Avoid this fate by spending a few days off the bike or reducing your training schedule, especially with a reduction in hard workouts. Have at least one rest day in your weekly training schedule. On tour, vary your daily riding distances and be prepared to take a day off as often as once a week if your body so desires. Overtraining will ultimately lead to some form of injury, so catching this problem early is a good way to prevent injuries later on. In addition to burnout, symptoms of cumulative fatigue include

- unexpected weight loss
- loss of appetite
- a series of "bad" rides
- an increase in first-thing-in-the-morning resting pulse rate
- restlessness at night

TRAINING THROUGH THE WINTER

Spring training is much easier if you can do even a modicum of off-season training. That's also the only way to train for a spring tour.

If you live in California, the Pacific Northwest, or south of the Mason–Dixon Line, you can maintain a mileage base of 30–50 miles a week through most of the winter. But if the good weather is erratic, don't overdo it. Stay in spring-training mode: easy spinning, no hills, moderate distances. In three days of January thaw, you can't make up for the previous month of winter.

Cross training or using an indoor trainer can also extend the cycling season.

Cross training. Cross training simply means taking up another sport. Any aerobic activity will help, but the best ones are those that use your bicycling muscles. Hiking or backpacking are superb, particularly when they involve "putting on the brakes" by walking down big hills. Cross-country skiing is nearly as effective and has the advantage that the best conditions for it are pre-

cisely those under which bicycling is least practical.

Indoor trainers. As valuable as cross training is, athletes in any sport know that nothing trains you for a sport better than the sport itself. A number of companies sell devices that convert your bicycle into a stationary exercise bike. Some allow you to set the bicycle on rollers; others use the rear wheel to drive fan blades or magnets.

Rollers provide the most realistic simulation but can be scary because it's easy to steer off them and crash. Wear a helmet. Wind turbines and magnetic devices mount the bicycle on a much more stable stand, but some models, particularly of wind trainers, are noisy. Try muffling them with towels stuffed under the base.

Indoor trainers, sadly, aren't a panacea for the winter-training doldrums. They can provide a good workout, but indoor riding is boring. Watch television, listen to music, or (except on rollers, which probably require too much concentration) read a book or magazine. Put the book on a music stand, or search bike shops for a reading rack that hooks to your handlebars. Overheating is also a problem. Sit near a fan or keep a towel handy.

Even equipped with a reading stand, a TV, and a fan, you may find it hard to maintain the discipline to ride indoors through the entire winter. But you can still use an indoor trainer to get a head start on the spring or to practice increasing your cadence without the complications of terrain, wind, and traffic.

Exercise bicycles. Although health-club exercise bicycles are a good way to practice increasing your cadence, standard upright models aren't made for serious bicycle training. It's generally not possible to fine-tune the seat height, and the fat, cushioned seats are inefficient, forcing you into pedaling positions that feel almost bowlegged. For years, I figured that their primary use was in the weeks before you could comfortably get outdoors, giving you a head start on spring training. Putting in serious time on an exercise bike looked like a prescription for sore knees to me.

Then came a particularly dreary spring when the rains just wouldn't quit. Desperate for sun, I decided on short notice to do a 500-mile organized tour in a drier climate. I'd managed to log only 250 miles of training, plus as much time as possible on an exercise bike and other health-club equipment.

Rollers provide an indoor workout with much of the feel of "real" bicycling. They require con-centration, however, to keep from steering off course. Other types of indoor trainers replace the rear wheel with a mounting stand that holds the bicycle upright even if you're reading a book or watching TV. For an example, see the photo on page 44.

I was in good shape but had distressingly little bike-specific training. To my amazement, I not only survived but felt strong throughout the tour.

Exercise bike mileage, I realized later, is simply more intense than normal bicycle training (the same goes for indoor trainers). Because you can't coast, an hour on an exercise bicycle substitutes for much more than an hour on a regular bicycle—except perhaps when it comes to conditioning your posterior for days in the saddle. The new recumbent exercise-bike models are also easier on your knees. Stuff a wadded towel behind your back to fine-tune the leg position. Recumbent riding doesn't train quite the same muscles as those used on a conventional bicycle, but it's close enough to help a lot.

I still don't recommend spending large amounts of time on an exercise bicycle, but it's one way to put television-watching time to good use.

STRETCHING AND WEIGHT LIFTING

Stretching is an important but frequently over-looked part of training. It needn't be time consuming; 10 minutes on each of your hard workout days will help prevent injuries and make riding more enjoyable. Contrary to popular belief, stretching *after* your workout rather than beforehand will generally do the most long-term good.

Don't bounce when stretching. A sudden stretch makes the muscle think it's about to be hyperextended, and it protects itself by reflexively contracting. The bouncing toe touchers and other calisthenic stretches many of us were taught as children merely fight that reflexive contraction. They can also pull a muscle.

Proper stretches are static or isometric. *Static* stretching means stretching slowly until you feel a pleasant pull to the muscle (not pain). Hold that position for 10–15 seconds, trying to relax the muscle;

then cautiously extend the stretch farther, always being prepared to back off. *Isometric* stretches are similar except that, between cautious extensions of the stretch, you gently contract the stretched muscle (without allowing the stretched limb to flex) rather than relaxing it. Then you relax the muscle to gently extend the stretch, as in static stretching.

Isometric stretching is counterintuitive, but it allows you to get an even better stretch than you do with static stretching, and it represents a current revolution in sports training.

Certain once-popular stretches are now major no-nos. Toe touchers are one of these because they're hard on the back. Also taboo is the traditional "hurdler's stretch," in which you sit on your heels and lean backward to stretch the quadriceps (the big muscles in the front of the thigh). This does indeed stretch the quadriceps, but it also stresses the knee.

Stretching for cycling involves limbering up the upper body and counteracting the tendency of the leg muscles to become tighter and less flexible as they gain strength. For the upper body, use any gentle stretches that come naturally and feel good. What really matters are the legs. Some version of the following should form the core of your routine.

Calf stretch. Stand in front of a wall and lean forward, palms on the wall. Your feet should be flat to the floor, one well in front of the other, as though you were bracing to push as hard as possible against the wall. Shifting most of your weight to the forward leg, dip that knee until you feel a good stretch in the other calf. Do this with the trailing leg straight; then bend it a bit at the knee, too,

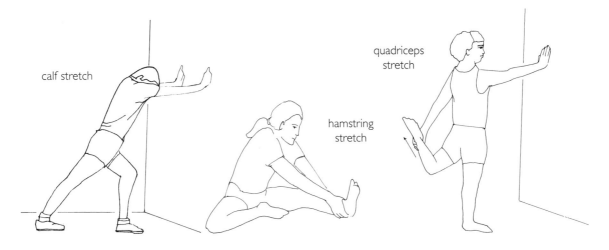

calf stretch

hamstring stretch

quadriceps stretch

Keeping the Fun in Training

Training should be fun. Don't turn it into just another chore. Find several low-hassle, traffic-free routes near home, vary distances, and don't always ride loops in the same direction. And don't be a fanatic about getting in the "right" mileage. If Tuesday's supposed to be a 10-mile day, it really doesn't matter if it's 7 or 13.

Whether you ride solo, with a small group, or with a club is up to you, but riding with friends helps keep training rides fresh and new. It also takes some of the misery out of headwinds by giving you an opportunity to draft. If you are a loner by nature, though, don't be afraid to train solo. Just make sure you have a repair kit and telephone money in case you break down.

When picking training partners, find people of approximately your own ability. You don't want to be always struggling to keep up, but neither do you want to be stopping to wait at the top of every hill. Don't be afraid to ride occasionally with people who are slightly better than you, though. You'll learn useful skills, and if you want to increase your speed, there are few quicker ways.

GREG SIPLE

feeling how that shifts the point of the stretch along your calf. Always do the stretch both ways. Another stretch that achieves similar results is to mimic standing on a steep hill, with your toe on a block of wood, rock, or other slightly elevated object, and your heel on the ground, calf relaxed. Do this and all other stretches one leg at a time for maximum control and least risk of overstretching.

Hamstring stretch. Sit on a flat surface with one leg extended, the other comfortably out of the way (don't sit on your heel; that's hard on the knee). Without locking the knee, lean toward the extended leg, feeling the stretch in the hamstring.

Quadriceps stretch (modified hurdler). Women will find this stretch less effective than men do, especially if they are already flexible. Stand on one leg, steadying yourself against a wall with one hand. Grasp your free leg by the foot or ankle, and push the hip forward. Don't yank the foot up toward your buttocks (that's hard on the knees). You'll feel the stretch in both the quadriceps and the front of the hip.

To learn more about stretching, check into the running literature (runners are far ahead of cyclists in this area), or talk to a health-club trainer.

Weight Lifting

If you've ever seen photos of bicycle racers, you may have noticed that those folks have *arms* as well as legs. That upper body strength comes from lifting weights, and it helps them control their bicy-

Commuting

Bike commuting is another superb way to extend the season as well as painlessly accumulate training mileage during the summer. Not only is it environmentally sound and economical, but a 5-mile commute can add 50 miles a week to your training.

Most touring bikes make good commuter bikes. And by happy coincidence, most of the modifications you make to adapt your bicycle for touring—thornproof inserts, fenders, luggage rack—are also useful for commuting.

Some hardy people manage to commute even through the winter. The biggest problems other than frostbite are snow and icy streets. You can buy (or make) studded tires or tire chains or, on the worst days, wimp out and ride a bus. If you live in a part of the country where they salt the roads, use an inexpensive junker bike until the spring rains have washed away the salt.

cles in crosswinds and to hold themselves above the handlebars for hours on end—the same things you're going to be doing. Strong arms and shoulders are also useful for hill climbing.

Although not essential, weight lifting can be helpful. All you need is a half-hour workout three times a week. Unless you're interested in racing, you needn't work on power lifts with the legs. Concentrate on strengthening the upper body with bench presses, lat pulls, curls, and triceps extensions. Also work on the abdominals, since this can prevent lower back pain. Incidentally, sit-ups are passé; *crunches* (imagine a halfhearted sit-up) are now in vogue. You might also want to strengthen your hands for gripping the brakes on long descents.

If you have access to weight equipment, hopefully you also have access to a trainer to show you the right way to use it and to recommend exercises. Remember that your goal is toning, not bulking up. That means you'll be doing larger numbers of repetitions at lighter weights—perhaps 2 or 3 sets of 15 exercises on each piece of equipment.

DOING YOUR FIRST CENTURY

Century rides and their shorter- or longer-distance cousins aren't races. There are no awards and no time clocks—although many cyclists like to use the stopwatch functions of their cyclometers to keep track of their times. (Personally, I never pay much attention to the time; my goal is to take advantage of the ride's route-finding to explore a new piece of rural countryside.)

In keeping with the tour mentality, these rides rarely have mass starts. Instead, cyclists arrive individually or in small groups, picking up their regis-

tration materials and setting out the same way—alone, with friends, or with whoever happens to be rolling out at the same time. Most cyclists are morning people, and century rides typically accommodate them by starting early to avoid late-afternoon heat and winds. Even if the start time ranges over a 3-hour window (say 6 to 9 A.M.), arrive early if you want the greatest amount of company on the road.

When choosing a century, get as much information as possible in advance. Bike shops and local cycling newsletters are good sources of ride schedules and application forms, but don't forget to ask the shop employees or experienced cycling friends about the ride's difficulty. Some tour directors delight in tackling the most difficult hills possible. If the route has *challenge* or some similar word in the name, it's likely to be this type of ride. In the western U.S., centuries often are rated for

RICHARD A. LOVETT

the number of feet of climbing. California's infamous Markleeville Death Ride, for example, often has a staggering 15,000 feet of climbing (and another 15,000 of descent). Any tour with more than 5,000 feet of climbing is too much for a beginner.

Whether you register in advance by mail or at the last minute on ride day, you'll generally have to check in when you arrive. You'll be given a pin-on number for you or your bike to prove that you paid the fee. Use it as instructed; it's your ticket to snacks, water stops, and other help along the route. You may also receive a souvenir water bottle or T-shirt, and possibly a ticket to a postride barbecue or picnic.

You'll also get a route map or *cue sheet*. The latter is simply a list of all major intersections, corners, and landmarks, with their cumulative distances from the start. Even if the tour director's cyclometer and yours differ slightly, the cue sheet is extremely helpful. Make sure you keep it where it's easy to refer to. There's no reason to get lost on a well-run century, but there's seldom a ride without at least a few cyclists who stray wildly off course.

In addition to cue sheets, century routes are often marked with arrows spray painted on the pavement using a system known as *Dan Henrys*, in honor of its inventor. Traditionally, these marks use a circle with a line coming out of its top to indicate right turn, left turn, or straight ahead; occasionally the circle is replaced by some other symbol. Even if you don't ride the tour, leftover Dan Henrys can

Dan Henrys for right turn, left turn, and straight ahead.

guide you to wonderful byways that you'd never have found by yourself.

Finally, try not to go out too fast at the start. If it's cool and calm and you're feeling strong, this can be difficult advice to follow. It's tempting to hop aboard one of the faster pace chains that are continually going by. But when you do so, you realize that you're going several miles an hour faster than in training.

That's the time to take your competitive instincts in hand and force yourself to slow down. If you want to draft, that's OK, but find a slower pace chain. Otherwise, you're setting yourself up for a spectacular "flame and die." Persuade yourself that half the other cyclists in that pace chain are going too fast (they probably are). If you drop off early and ride at your own pace, you're not being a wimp; you're simply being smart. Go easy in the first 20 miles so you can come on strong in the last 20.

Rx: Achilles Tendonitis?

The Achilles tendon is the big tendon at the back of the ankle. Stiff, inflexible calf muscles or overvigorous training can put too much stress on it, causing pain or inflammation. So can worn-out or overly flexible shoes. Generally, the discomfort is at its worst when you're off your bicycle, especially in the morning. As you ride, it moderates, misleading you into believing you aren't hurting the tendon.

Mild Achilles tendonitis may clear up on its own. But it can also get progressively worse, even producing a grating sensation every time you flex your foot.

Anti-inflammatories, ice, and reduced training or complete rest are the best treatment. Calf stretching can help prevent you from losing flexibility as the tendon heals, but keep it gentle. Foam heel lifts, available in drug stores, are also useful. They won't do you much good on the bicycle, but they'll take tension off the tendon when you walk, speeding recovery. They're thin, so you might need more than one; use the same number on each leg to keep your stride balanced. Try to avoid ones that look soft and cushy; they'll make your heel rub against the shoe, giving you blisters.

Tendons heal slowly, but mild cases can clear up in a few days. More severe ones can take weeks to months, and very severe cases (rare among cyclists) require surgery. So if you get a mild case, rest it now, before it becomes intractable.

BEYOND DAY RIDING

So far, you've learned the basics slanted toward touring, but with lessons on skills and equipment that would be the same even if you have no desire to progress beyond century rides or bike commuting.

Now it's time to specialize.

The prerequisites for the second half of this course are simple: a bicycle rigged for touring, enough training that you don't wind up deciding that your first outing is your last, and a lively sense of adventure.

The syllabus is equally straightforward. We start with organized tours—the easiest type of multi-day touring for the beginner—then progress to van-supported touring and credit-card touring, both of which can be done with relatively light loads.

That will be followed by a primer on tent camping—with heavy applications for bicycle touring—plus a discussion of how to carry overnight equipment by bicycle.

The Life on the Road and Challenges and Adversities chapters give useful information for all types of touring but assume that eventually you'll at least consider graduating to self-contained touring.

Self-contained touring is widely regarded as the most difficult form of touring, an impression fueled by the popular image of the touring cyclist, panniers bulging, straining to lug a 50-pound load up an endless hill.

With proper gearing, however, pedaling a loaded bicycle is only slightly more difficult than pedaling a stripped-down racer— just slower. If you have the patience, it pays you back in freedom. No other form of touring makes it so easy to quit for the night if you get tired, or the wind shifts against you, or you simply find a pretty place—whether you've reached your destination or not. With proper equipment, you can pitch a tent on any bare spot large enough to sleep on, boil or otherwise purify water from a mountain creek, cook dinner, and let the days unroll one by one. It's worth the extra weight.

As with Cycle Touring 101, you can mark your progress with a midterm and a final exam. For the midterm, pick a pleasant destination not too far from home and bicycle there for a weekend, camping or staying in a motel.

The final can double as a graduation exercise: hit the road for a week, either on an organized tour or on your own. If you've taken the time to prepare properly, you'll find that there's nothing "final" about this exam after all. It's the beginning of a whole new world of 2-wheeled adventure.

Cycling is a great way to see your neighborhood, the country, or the world—even if the road signs are sometimes incomprehensible. This cyclist is in Iceland.

ORGANIZED TOURS

6

SUMMER CAMP ON WHEELS

Historically, multiday bicycle touring was enjoyed predominantly in small groups or even solo. Then in 1973, a newspaper columnist at the *Des Moines Register* challenged another columnist to get back in touch with the "real" Iowa by bicycling across the state. The challenge was accepted, and the two invited their readers to join in.

Much to their surprise, 300 readers showed up. When they repeated the trip the following year, the number was over 2,500, and soon participation was being limited to 7,500. Now called RAGBRAI (the *Register*'s Annual Great Bicycle Ride Across Iowa), the ride has become an Iowa institution—one that easily leads to endless attempts at children's riddles. What has 15,000 feet but seldom takes a step? RAGBRAI. What is 450 miles long and works its way across the state like a giant mechanized caterpillar, eating everything that crosses its path? RAGBRAI. It has put the state on the map for cyclists throughout the world and has spawned scores of imitations throughout North America.

Thanks to RAGBRAI and its progeny, tens of thousands of cyclists hit the road each summer on inexpensive, weeklong tours or *event rides* sponsored by clubs, newspapers, state tourist departments, and a growing assortment of budget-minded tour companies. There's something for almost every level of ability, ranging from relaxed 30-to-40-mile-a-day family outings to mountain-and-desert challenges in some of the most rugged terrain in North America. Groups range from fewer than 50 to several thousand, with an atmosphere like an adult summer camp on wheels. Best of all, there are trucks to carry the riders' baggage.

Some tours allow riders' families to come along in RVs (although the number of RVs may be strictly limited). Ideally, these tours separate the RVs from the riders by forcing them to drive routes other than the tour route.

The typical tour package includes *sag wagons* (to carry riders or bicycles if either "sags"), route maps, water stops, group camping, and baggage transport. On the larger tours, there are even roving repair vans combing the course for cyclists who need assistance. Many tours offer indoor accommodations (seldom more than a gymnasium for "floor floppers"), and some provide meals. On point-to-point routes, there is often a modestly priced shuttle bus back to the start or to the nearest airport.

Usually, overnight stops are in very small towns, whose populations can be doubled or tripled by the influx of cyclists. For the locals it's frequently the most exciting thing since the last near miss by a tornado. For the cyclists it's an introduction to small-town hospitality.

These tours aren't races. There's no finish line, no time clock, no prize for being first except the dubious honor of being asked to help unload baggage.

A typical day begins before dawn with a "zipper serenade," as one by one, cyclists peek outside to see what the weather is likely to bring. After breakfast, riders flow from camp in small groups, often riding with different people each day or even from one hour to the next. On the smaller rides they quickly disperse, but on large ones the pack never thins, producing what one observer

described as an army to please the likes of Attila the Hun.

On the large rides, farmers quit work to sit on their lawns, taking a vicarious interest in being part of this whirring spectacle of people in motion. On tours that don't provide catered meals, community groups and churches compete to offer the most attractive dinners, while other groups turn each day's route into a succession of food stops ranging from bake sales to homemade ice cream, from pork burgers to watermelon. Unless you have an unusual ability to resist temptation, you won't lose weight, even at 70 miles a day.

On the Tour

Except for the fact that you'll be cycling every day for a week, life on an organized tour is similar to a century ride. All you need to carry is the minimum gear to get to camp: full water bottles, a tire patch kit, sunscreen, a spare tube, lunch money, and rain gear. You also need room for unwanted clothing, since you're likely to start early and shed layers as the day warms up. Fast riders and those who like to be first out of camp may want to carry a book as well, in case they beat the baggage truck to the next night's stop.

Know group riding etiquette, even on the smaller rides. Announcing "On your left" (when passing) or "Braking!" all week will get tiresome, but it's better than crashing. Signal all turns (and check behind for other cyclists), avoid swerving suddenly, and pull completely off the road, if possible, when stopping. Think twice before getting into tight, fast-moving drafting chains with strangers. Pace chains are probably the leading cause of serious accidents on this type of ride.

When hundreds or thousands of cyclists descend on a small town, the result has to be seen to be believed. Fairgrounds, high school football fields, and lawns of willing residents turn into mammoth tent cities that spring up overnight only to melt away with the dawn. On smaller rides, finding a good camping spot is seldom a problem, but on the large ones, it pays to be portable. If your baggage is light enough to carry a few hundred yards from the truck, you'll have fewer neighbors and a better chance of a quiet night's sleep.

Showers are generally available in school locker rooms, and that's where many cyclists go the moment they reach camp. If the hot water's gone, be patient. Water heaters recharge, and there's usually little demand for showers after dinner. Some rides—at least in the western U.S.—charter portable shower units designed for forest fire crews, making good on promises of hot water and short lines for as many as 2,000 cyclists. It adds a bit to the price, but for most people it's worth it.

Packing is different from packing for a self-contained trip. Because most of these tours have a one- or two-bag limit, a self-contained touring rig—which disassembles into too many pieces—is a disadvantage. Buy the largest duffel bag you can find. A heavy-duty nylon or canvas bag is adequate; make sure it has a sturdy shoulder strap. Waterproof material is also a plus. Some tours automatically move baggage indoors or under an awning if it rains, but don't count on it.

Think about trying to find your bag in a giant pile. Buy something distinctive. A green canvas duffel isn't a wise idea—too many other riders will have something similar. Many riders paste colored patches to their bags or tie on colored ribbons that flutter in the breeze. Be creative; one year's great idea will have a thousand imitators the next.

Realize that the bag is going to be thrown around, stepped on, and buried under hundreds of pounds of other baggage. Don't put anything fragile in it unless it's well padded. If you wouldn't trust it to an airline, don't trust it to the baggage truck.

In camp, you may want to use a flag, VistaLite (see page 137), or other easy-to-find object to help you find your tent after dark on a crowded football field. Folding lawn chairs are also nice for lounging around camp. Walrus and TravelChair both make comfortable designs that quickly fold into nylon carry sacks.

On tours with a one-bag limit, practice stuffing everything into your bag beforehand. If it's a tight fit, leave something behind. There may be no scientific explanation, but baggage seems to expand as the week progresses. If the fit is still tight or the bag is heavy enough to be unwieldy, add an empty gym bag to your luggage. Many tours enforce the bag limit only on the first day, not objecting if, having proved that you can compress your gear to a single bag, you later distribute it into two.

Your baggage will be similar to what you'd take on a self-contained trip, except you'll probably want more shirts and a couple of sets of street pants. For a fresh shirt each day in camp, put on the next day's cycling shirt after you shower. You'll have a clean shirt each evening, and one that's still reasonably fresh the following morning.

Don't count on visiting a self-service laundry midway through the trip unless you *really* enjoy waiting in lines. The same applies to pay phones. Don't rashly promise to call home every night, or you'll spend a significant portion of each evening waiting for a phone. If you must call, carry a cellular phone or use a pay phone before you reach camp, even if you have to pay a higher midday rate.

The biggest problem with living out of a duffel bag for a week is keeping things organized. If you're one of those people who throws everything around haphazardly anyway, you'll be right at home. Otherwise, invest in a collection of gadget bags so you can at least separate your toothbrush from your socks. Something larger, such as an extra sleeping bag stuff sack, will help keep dirty clothes from contaminating clean ones.

Finally, if food service isn't catered, eating can be a challenge. Restaurants and cafés are usually lined up out the door, and food lines for church and service club dinners can also entail long waits. Some people try to beat this by queuing up for dinner absurdly early; others wait until nearly dark, hoping there will still be plenty left over. Generally, the longer a ride has been running, the less problem there is with food lines. Even if a particular community has never hosted the tour before, tour officials have learned how to coach the locals on preparing more than enough food for adults who are going to eat like hungry teenagers—and have instructed them on how to serve it efficiently.

Unless everything's catered, make sure you take plenty of money. ATM machines can be days apart, and even though food prices are generally

Bigger, Better, or Lost in the Crowd?

Group size greatly affects the tour experience. Small rides are intimate, but there is relatively little sense of an event on tours with less than 100 riders. For some people, that's exactly what they want. You'll get to know your companions better, spend less time waiting in line, and be more able to get away from snoring neighbors at night. You'll also have a greater amount of individual service from the ride's support crews. On rides like this, the support personnel quickly get to know all of the riders and may even offer to sag you to the top of a particularly grueling hill if you're not in a mood to pedal there on your own. On larger rides, there's a different ratio of riders to sag vehicles, and sags are more likely to be reserved for those in the greatest need.

Midsized tours of 250–600 riders often offer many of the same advantages, with more of a carnival atmosphere thrown in for good measure. These tours are large enough to draw more attention from small communities, which may treat the riders to rodeos, fiddle concerts, drama productions, or exhibitions designed to show off their cultural heritages. With that many riders, you'll always have company on the road, without feeling lost in the crowd, but it's still easy to find your companions in camp.

Tours with more than 1,000 riders are more like traveling circuses. People who don't like crowds find them intimidating, but the large group size often brings out the best in small-town hospitality. The need for top-caliber organization can also mean shorter food, bathroom, and shower lines on these rides than on their smaller-scale cousins. You may also get top-quality professional entertainment. Some rides, for example, set up concert stages each night, importing bands from all over the nation.

For many cyclists, however, the main attraction of a big ride is simply being part of a mass, human-powered migration. Whether the route's across Iowa, Georgia, Oregon, or Québec often doesn't matter as much as the simple fact that you are going somewhere—and that you are doing so in the company of like-minded travelers.

In many respects, these rides are a microcosm of today's mobile society. Only 15 miles into a day, for example, you might meet someone you like. You chat for 5 miles, then by conscious choice or an eddy in the pack, you separate. You are alone again. You put down new roots, talking to the next rider of suitably matched abilities. Again, you are separated. People who meet on the road seldom ride a

dozen miles together.

Put that way, it sounds a bit depressing. But a bike ride, even if it's RAGBRAI sized, is a small universe. Even with thousands of people, after a few days you begin to meet some repeats. Somebody whom you haven't seen for three days calls your name with genuine enthusiasm. Another invites you to join him for dinner. "Small-world" stories abound.

This is the large tour at its best. It is a free-form existence with friendships that ebb and flow and regroup in surprising patterns until eventually you develop a kinship with the entire group that is nearly as strong as your kinship with specific individuals.

It is also a refreshingly simple life. All that you need to worry about is keeping the body and the machine running. There is no need for route planning. No need to worry about food or water. Usually, there are few cars; a contingent of state troopers may even police the route to aid in traffic control. If your body is up to it, the trip is relaxing and simple—life from the road shoulder, the opposite of life in the fast lane.

Whatever size tour you pick, however, you can be assured of three things: comradeship, the enthusiasm of the local populace, and a van to carry your baggage. What more

reasonable, you'll eat more than you might think. You might also have to replace a tire or want to treat yourself to souvenir T-shirts or cycling paraphernalia.

Choosing a Tour

New tours start every year, while old ones change format periodically. Some run the same route year after year; others try to avoid ever doing the same

route twice. Also, mailing addresses and phone numbers often change yearly, particularly for tours organized by bike clubs rotating leadership duties among their members.

Good sources of information are the ride listings in the backs of cycling magazines. Don't just check the current issues; go to a library and scan the previous year's listings as well. Even if they're out of date, important factors such as group size, mileage, registration fee, and time of year aren't likely to change dramatically from one year to the next. And the addresses should be current enough to at least forward to the proper place.

The tours you're looking for will show up as multiday events, ranging from two days to a week. A few will even be multiweek. Sometimes, though, it's difficult to distinguish camping tours from races with names designed to evoke images of the Tour de France. Ironically, the use of the word *tour* in a ride's name makes it more likely to be a race.

The Internet also helps, although finding the proper links can be frustrating. Look for a good topical listing of bicycle tours or *events*, or visit the home page of the National Bicycle Tour Directors Association for a calendar and links to several dozen major rides.

Another way to find tours is to contact bike clubs, bike shops, or the American Youth Hostels in the area you'd like to visit. If a full week is too much of a commitment, many clubs sponsor 2- or 3-day weekend rides. There are also a multitude of well-organized pledge rides run by such charities as the Multiple Schlerosis Society or the American Lung Association. If all else fails, read other cyclists' T-shirts, and don't be afraid to ask questions. I've learned about many good rides that way.

Several dozen well-established tours, mostly weeklong events, are listed in the appendix, along with their addresses, approximate dates, usual routes, and group sizes.

Preparation

Once you've chosen a ride, send a self-addressed stamped envelope (SASE) to the tour director for registration materials, or follow e-mail instructions on the organization's Web page. The SASE is common courtesy and can save a lot of time. Some rides may not answer you without one. Don't wait until the last minute; many tours fill months in advance.

If a ride is full, don't give up. There might be a waiting list, or registrations might be traded through classified ads or notices in bike shops. It's often possible to get on rides through late cancellations.

Once you get an application, feel free to contact the tour director to ask questions not covered by the brochure. What's the traffic like? How hilly is the course? Will it be hot, cold, or some of each? Does the tour guarantee the availability of hot showers? What kind of repair facilities are available?

Don't expect to be pampered. Most of these tours are organized *by* cyclists *for* cyclists. They aren't run by posh catering companies, and the workers—who may be unpaid volunteers—don't like to be treated like servants. The coordinators of a good ride should be well organized and prepared to help you in an emergency—but not to wait on you hand and foot.

Train adequately, and train early. For a week-long, 500-mile tour, train as you would for a century ride in the type of conditions you expect to encounter. If the course is hilly, train on hills—even if all you can find are freeway overpasses. If it's going to be hot, get used to heat.

There's more to preparation than simply putting in the miles. If you are going to have to ship your bicycle in a box, for example, it pays to learn the art of packing it (see pages 140–41) before 3:00 A.M. the day your plane leaves.

With a little preparation and the right attitude, you can expect to have one of the great adventures of your life and to make friends you'll keep in touch with for years to come. One of my favorite memories comes from a conversation overheard on a tour of the Oregon coast. After several days of headwinds and showers, August had finally asserted itself, the weather had cleared, and Oregon's normal fair-weather wind had scudded us effortlessly southward, beside an endless expanse of blue ocean. Returning from my shower, I overheard one of the other riders expounding his cycling philosophy to a friend. "Life doesn't give you many days that are perfect 10s," he said. "When you get one, you've got to take advantage of it for everything it's worth." There was a long pause. "Today was a 10," he finished.

I try to do at least one organized tour each year, and there's rarely one that doesn't serve up at least one perfect 10. Sometimes you get several, back-to-back. But I never fail to enjoy each and every one, for all it's worth.

7

VANS AND CREDIT CARDS: YOU DON'T HAVE TO CAMP OR CARRY A LOT OF WEIGHT

TYPES OF TOURS

If seeing the world at a bicycle's leisurely pace is appealing but you want more freedom to set your own itinerary than is provided by an event ride, credit-card touring may be the best way for venturing out on your own. It's an intermediate level between a fully supported organized tour and completely self-contained touring, allowing you to explore without having to carry 30–60 pounds of camping gear—or sleep in a tent. Another solution is van-supported touring, in which you travel with your own private support vehicle. Not only does the vehicle carry all of your baggage, but it can act as a private sag, carrying snacks, refilling water bottles, and even allowing you to rest and grab a ride if you get tired or simply don't feel like pedaling as many miles as your friends.

Even people whose primary interest is self-contained touring may occasionally want to shift to these lighter styles. Early in the season they offer ways to tour before you're well enough trained for heavy loads; in the fall they offer alternatives to long nights cooped up in a tent, and they're good ways to begin the sport with a minimum of specialized equipment.

Credit-Card

Credit-card touring draws its name from the assertion that you need only a credit card. That's an overstatement, however. You also need rain gear, a change of clothes, a jacket and tights, tools, and street clothes for dining out or exploring your destination by foot. What you don't need is camping gear, cooking equipment, or (frequently) lots of water bottles. All told, you'll carry no more than half as much as you'd carry on a self-contained tour.

For an extended credit-card tour—anything more than one or two nights—the best destinations are conventional tourist areas, where you have enough lodging choices to plan your accommodations around your desired route, rather than the reverse. Such areas also give you more day-to-day flexibility, allowing you to set out for a week without a complete set of reservations, confident that you can find *something* on relatively short notice. But don't make the notice *too* short unless you're traveling well off season. That could leave you searching desperately for a church couch or sitting up all night in a 24-hour restaurant or gas station.

Although areas with a lot of overnight accommodations are easiest for credit-card touring, more remote areas aren't out of the question—many small towns have motels. You won't find luxury, but you *will* stay warm and dry. Start by looking in travel guidebooks, but don't quit there. Some of these motels are too tiny to be listed—perhaps having only half a dozen units. Better sources of information are local chambers of commerce. When you find a motel, ask whether there's a restaurant nearby; that isn't always the case. After a full day's riding, you probably won't want to bike long distances after dark to and from dinner.

If you stay at expensive inns or B&Bs, credit-card touring is by no means a budget vacation. But if you don't need luxury, the price can be kept lower. I've done weekend tours with friends who've crammed as many as 9 people into one large suite. There's a charge for the extra bodies, but it's usually nominal.

Light Touring

When you first venture forth without the support of a van, organized tour, or inn-to-inn itinerary, the best way to gain experience is via *light touring*.

That term is often used as a catchall for any touring other than self-contained touring. But more technically, it refers to touring that avoids motel or van dependency without a lot of extra weight. On a light tour, you're prepared to camp but you carry only the bare minimum of equipment, remaining fairly close to civilization.

Plan the excursion either as a camping trip with motels as a foul-weather bailout, or as an inn-to-inn trip with camping as an option for greater route-planning flexibility. The difference is in intent, not equipment.

In both cases all you need in addition to your credit-card touring gear is a lightweight sleeping bag, a sleeping pad, and a minimal tent, tarp, hammock, or bivvy bag. You won't carry cooking gear, and you'll stick to warm enough climates that you won't need heavy clothes. By avoiding bulky clothing, you also avoid the need for both front and rear panniers, saving weight and equipment costs (panniers are luggage bags for bikes—see the next chapter).

All told, if you're careful about keeping down weight, you can do a light camping trip with only 6–8 pounds more equipment than needed for credit-card touring—even less if you can get away with a nylon tarp instead of a bivvy bag.

You can even do this with fairly luxurious accommodations; $150-per-night rustic lodges become inexpensive if you split the fee with enough people. If motels are too far apart at your planned destination, you can still manage a weekend loop by driving out the night before, staying in a motel, and reserving your room for a second night. In the morning, drive to a point halfway around your intended loop from the motel, bringing nothing with you but bicycles and day-trip necessities. Park, and pedal back to the motel for the night. In the morning, check your baggage at the front desk, pedal back to your car, and pick up your checked baggage on the way home. A similar approach would be to check into a centrally located motel and explore the neighboring terrain by a series of day rides.

Catered

If you really want to indulge yourself, sign up for a catered tour. Hundreds of organizations, large and small, offer such tours. Destinations can be as exotic and challenging as Vietnam or Baja, or as safe and familiar as New England or the antebellum South. None will be cheap, but you'll generally stay in better inns, dine with some degree of style, and have your baggage carried by van. You'll also be pedaling on routes that have been well scouted by trained guides. In general, expect these routes to be shorter and flatter than what you'd find on event rides, although some companies cater to experienced cyclists seeking indulgence only in the choice of accommodations. Many companies even offer high-quality rental bicycles, often for less than the cost of boxing and shipping your own.

Choosing such a tour is like choosing a cruise or a tour-bus vacation, and the outfitters will speak the travel-industry jargon of "destinations" and "departures." It sounds a bit alien to most cyclists, but the meanings are simple: the destination is where you go; the departure is the individual tour. Thus, a big touring company that revisits the same destination multiple times a year may boast 300 bike-tour departures to 65 destinations. The larger and more established organizations are more likely to offer a consistent package, but that doesn't mean the smaller outfitters can't do an excellent job.

To locate tours, search the World Wide Web for "bicycle tours" (these companies don't themselves refer to their products as "catered" tours) and scan the resulting list of hits to sort out the mix of club rides, event rides, and catered tours that such a search will locate. If you get lucky, you may even find Web pages that index dozens of tours by destination. Such index pages come and go, depending on the author's enthusiasm. You can also locate touring companies by talking to a travel agent or reading ads in outdoor or bicycling magazines. Sometimes you can find fliers in touring-oriented bike shops.

Van-Supported

With credit-card touring your route and daily distances are dictated by the need to reach a motel before dark. Van-supported touring gives you the option of camping without carrying heavy weight.

Your packs for van-supported touring will actually be lighter than for most forms of credit-card touring. You don't need to carry the next day's clothes, and if the van meets you occasionally during the day, you can also let it carry much of your tool kit.

The term *van-supported touring* is another misnomer: The support vehicle doesn't have to be a van. All you need is something large enough to carry everyone's baggage, with a bike rack capable of holding at least two bicycles.

There are two basic types of van-supported tours. In one, the van serves as a baggage truck, meeting you at each night's destination and giving

tired or aching riders a chance to hitch a day's ride. This approach is easy on the driver, who is free to spend the day sightseeing. Between overnight stops, the cyclists need to be prepared to fend for themselves.

The other approach is to have the van meet you every 10–20 miles to dispense water and snacks and give you a place to shed or retrieve clothing. Ideally, the driver plays leapfrog with the cyclists, giving them a head start between rest breaks, then checking up on them en route to the next stop. The biggest problem is finding a driver who's willing to spend a weekend, let alone a week, at this rather tedious pursuit. People who are willing to do it should be cherished as the golden resources they are.

If you can't find a full-time driver, rotate the job among yourselves. Obviously, the more of you who share the burden, the easier it will be. The first day will be the most difficult since no one is likely to *want* to drive. One approach is to divide

Van-supported touring can by done by car as well as by van. The hallmark of this type of touring is a vehicle to carry your gear and tend to riders' needs. Sometimes cyclists take turns driving.

Catered Touring Companies

The number of catered touring companies is staggering, as was their rapid growth when this type of touring hit the mainstream travel market in the late 1980s. In 1990, by one count, there were 135 such companies. By 1994 the number had nearly doubled to 249. Today, it would be hard to count them all.

Here are eight options, mostly in North America. All have been in business since at least the mid-1980s. Some offer hundreds of tours, catering to almost every conceivable taste. Others focus on specialized niches, either in popular regions or with tour packages designed to appeal to particular interests such as camping.

Prices (generally double occupancy) range from $150 a day to upward of $300. Expect meals to be regional foods, well prepared, with substantial portions, but on North American tours don't expect the type of gourmet dining experience you'd find in Europe. On this continent, the gourmet restaurants simply don't exist in the small-town byways that make for the best cycling. Vegetarians should ask in advance about menu options, but vegetarian cyclists are common enough that most companies make sure each meal has a veggie option.

Backcountry. This midsized Montana-based company (with about 100 departures a year) caters to multisport riders, combining biking with hiking, river rafting, or horseback riding. Most of its departures are to destinations in western North America, but it also runs tours elsewhere in Canada. Backcountry prides itself on small groups and individual attention to each rider. No camping trips. Average daily cycling distance: 20–30 miles. Bike rentals. Contact: P.O. Box 4029, Bozeman MT 59772; 406-586-3556; fax 406-586-4288; *www.backcountrytours.com*.

Backroads. Diversity is the watchword for the nation's largest cycle-touring company (in business since 1979). Its nearly 1,200 departures a year include both inn-to-inn and camping options, with destinations in most of the U.S., plus Europe, Asia, and South America. Backroads even offers a Turkish trip featuring snorkeling, sea kayaking, and sailing in the Mediterranean Sea. Also popular are winery tours in California and Europe. Average daily distance: 20–60 miles. Many tours offer short- and long-distance options each day for cyclists with differing abilities. Inn-to-inn trips always try to travel first-class, staying in the best lodgings that fit the route. Campgrounds on camping trips usually have hot showers. If not, solar showers are set up, weather permitting. Meals for inn-to-inn trips are in restaurants, either ordered from the menu or specially prepared for the tour. The emphasis is on regional fare, such as fine local wines in the Napa Valley, fresh lobster in Maine, or seafood in the Pacific Northwest. On camping trips, the guides do the cooking and cleanup. Bike rentals. Contact: 801 Cedar St., Berkeley CA 94710; 800-462-2848; fax 510-527-1444; *www.backroads.com*.

Bicycle Adventures. All of the 250 or so tours offered by this company are in the Pacific Northwest (broadly defined to include Hawaii, British Columbia, California, and Utah). Trips are 4 to 8 days long, with top-quality food featured strongly on the agenda. Some departures are designed for "single" riders—ones who are vacationing on their own, regardless of their marital status. All trips include some mix of activities other than cycling. Trips to Washington State's San Juan Islands, for example, include hiking on 2,400-foot Mt. Constitution, sea kayaking, or a whaleboat cruise through the islands in search of pods of killer whales. Average daily distance: 30–50 miles. Accommodations: B&Bs and country inns—generally small, quaint places (but with private baths) chosen for dramatic views, particularly across water. There may be an occasional camping trip. Meals: gourmet restaurants and picnic lunches. The gourmet emphasis means that breakfast isn't necessarily eaten at the inn; trips may include a few miles of prebreakfast pedaling. Bike rentals. Contact: P.O. Box 11219, Olympia WA 98508; 1-800-443-6060; fax 206-786-9661; *www.bicycleadventures.com*.

Butterfield & Robinson. Along with Vermont Bicycle Touring and Backroads, this company is the third of a triumvirate that makes up the "Big Three" of cycle touring. Specializing in high-end luxury since 1966, it has more than 200 annual departures to more than 40 destinations, mostly in Europe, but also in such exotic locales as Chile, Morocco, and Belize. North American departures tend to visit the Natchez Trace, Nova Scotia, and the Gulf Islands of British Columbia. The company's slogan is "Slow Down to See the World," and tours are designed accordingly, with the emphasis on culture, comfort, and not too much cycling. The Natchez

Trace tour, for example, stops for mint juleps one evening at a private home overlooking the Mississippi River. Also, because these tours are lower mileage than many other companies' tours, leisurely dining is a large part of the experience. Lunch, for example, may be served with silver and china while cyclists relax by a pool at an antebellum mansion. Or it may be a seafood and wine picnic on a rocky Canadian shore. Average daily distance: generally only 25–35 miles, with longer options for every day's route. Accommodations: the best country inns, chateaus, or villas available. Meals are at fine restaurants serving regional specialties, such as seafood and maybe even wild boar. Price includes bike rental. Contact: 70 Bond St., Suite 300, Toronto ON M5B 1X3, Canada; 800-678-1147 or 416-864-1354; *www.butterfield.com*.

French Louisiana Bike Tours. A small touring company that's happy to stay that way, French Louisiana specializes in Cajun country—cycling its back roads, sampling its food, and spending evenings in its dance halls. The company has been offering about 10 departures a year since 1986. Of particular interest is the Cajun Food and Music Tour, which includes a cooking lesson, dancing, and Cajun or zydeco music most evenings. Average daily distance: 30–50 miles, "adjustable" by hopping the van. Accommodations: B&Bs, with an occasional Louisiana plantation. Bike rentals. Contact: 3216 W. Esplanade #302, Metairie LA 70002, 800-346-7989; *www.flbt.com*.

Michigan Bicycle Touring. This regional company has been in business since 1978, offering tours principally in Michigan, a state that boasts more paved roads than any other in the nation. Most of the company's 100 or so offerings are weekend outings near Lake Michigan or Lake Superior, although 5-day tours are also available. Weekend tours consist of day trips from the same overnight base; 5-day trips are generally loops. Out-of-staters may be particularly interested in tours of the Upper Peninsula, which visit Mackinac Island, mountain bike through the little-known Huron Mountains (really just overgrown hills), or explore the rugged Keweenaw Peninsula, site of one of America's first great mining booms (for copper, in 1843). Some of these trips mix cycling with hiking or kayaking. Average daily distance: from 10–65 miles. Accommodations: B&Bs, country inns, historic hotels, ski lodges. No camping trips. Bike rentals; tandems available. Contact: 3512 Red School Rd., Kingsley MI 49649; 231-263-5885; fax 231-263-7885; *www.bikemot.com*.

Timberline Bicycle Tours. This midsized company runs about 100 departures annually, primarily in the western U.S., Canada, and Alaska. In general, Timberline tours tend to be more challenging than the industry average, with some having long days (80+ miles) over mountainous terrain. Although the company runs a traditional Banff–Jasper trip, for example, its hallmark Canadian Rockies Tour also takes in a substantial portion of southern British Columbia, covering 690 miles in 10 days, with 18,000–20,000 feet of climbing. Even the standard Icefields Parkway tour has a twist: it crosses the Continental Divide (twice) to loop through Kootenay and Yoho national parks along with Banff and Jasper. Average daily distance: generally 55–70 miles. Accommodations: historic hotels (especially national park lodges) and inns, if available. But mapping out good cycling routes comes first as long as there are acceptable places to stay, meaning that in small towns, Timberline tours sometimes stay in ordinary motels—adequate but not necessarily quaint or historic. The same rule applies to food as to lodging: if an extraordinary opportunity is available, the tour will take advantage of it. But good cycling won't be passed up if the best food options are simply good, hearty menus with lots of choices. Bike rentals are available, but this is one company that encourages riders to bring their own, especially on the more challenging trips. Contact: 7975 E. Harvard Unit J, Denver CO 80231; 800-417-2453; fax 303-368-1651; *www.timbertours.com*.

VBT Bicycling Vacations. The original inn-to-inn touring company (in operation since 1972) and still one of the largest, with more than 500 tours to 30 destinations all over the world. Originally called Vermont Bicycle Touring, VBT started in Vermont and still has a major focus on New England and the East Coast. The company views its experience and finely tuned operations as its greatest strengths. There are routes in Vermont, for example, that it has been perfecting for 28 years. The company tries to offer at least three length options each day, ranging from about 20–50 miles. Accommodations: country inns and small hotels. No camping trips. Bicycle rentals. Contact: P.O. Box 711, Bristol VT 05443, 800-245-3868; *www.vbt.com*.

the day's mileage among all the cyclists, with everyone taking 1 or more shifts. I've done this with groups as small as 3, rotating drivers every 10–12 miles.

Finding volunteer drivers usually isn't difficult after the first few hours; by then, somebody's likely to be happy for the rest break—except perhaps on long downhill runs.

In many ways, van-supported touring sounds idyllic. You can stay in motels and dine in fine restaurants, but after a while, being tied to the apron strings of the van may feel confining, continuously reminding you of your dependence on the internal combustion engine and all it symbolizes. Don't be surprised if the time comes when you wish to cast loose and strike out on your own, regardless of the weight.

Credit-card and van-supported touring both require a greater degree of self-sufficiency than you need for catered touring, organized tours, century rides, or training rides on familiar terrain. The rest of this book focuses on skills and equipment that will make you increasingly self-sufficient, while also introducing the most self-contained of all forms of bicycle touring, *loaded touring*. How much of this information you need depends on the type of touring you want to do. You won't need to learn much about bicycle camping, for example, if you never plan to spend a night outdoors. But you still need to know something about luggage racks and handlebar bags so you can carry sack lunches, rain gear, and a camera. Other skills, such as route-finding and map-reading skills, also benefit riders on virtually any tour.

LOADED TOURING: YOU CAN TAKE IT ALL WITH YOU

8

Loaded touring doesn't require a great deal of special equipment. Rather than viewing it as a whole new sport, think of it as bicycle camping; the main difference from car camping is the mode of locomotion. The first few times you attempt it, in fact, you'll probably want to make do with whatever camping gear you already have. If it's not too bulky or heavy, it will do fine for mild-weather touring.

But as you work your way further into the sport, you'll want better equipment, with *better* defined as lighter, more compact, more resistant to wind or rain—equipment that can turn an otherwise miserable evening into just another night on the road.

Much of the equipment is the same as that used by backpackers; except for panniers, you'll find it not in bike stores but in backpacking stores. If you're a backpacker, you've probably got most of what you'll need already.

If you've never backpacked—and don't intend to—don't let the comparison intimidate you. Bicycle touring is considerably easier than backpacking.

First, the weight is on your bicycle, not on your back. Equally important, cyclists can live off the land to a greater extent than backpackers can, resupplying themselves with food every day or bailing out into a motel if the weather turns especially foul.

Nevertheless, particularly on longer trips, good equipment is one of the keys to an enjoyable and not overly eventful outing. Even if all of your touring will be van supported or part of an organized tour, you'll appreciate good camping gear.

BASIC CAMPING EQUIPMENT

Tents

The classic tent is a two-person backpacking tent, either A-frame or dome. Some models, particularly dome tents, are freestanding—meaning you don't have to stake them to hold them upright. A freestanding tent should still be staked when possible, though, so a strong wind won't blow it away like a giant beach ball: I once saw one start to roll in an Iowa thunderstorm with a 12-year-old inside it. Freestanding tents are necessary only if you expect to camp where the ground is too rocky for stakes. That's a lot more likely backpacking than cycle touring.

A good tent is rainproof and allows comfortable air flow and escape of moisture from your exhalations. Traditionally this is done by combining an interior layer of breathable fabric—sometimes nothing more than mosquito netting—with a detachable rain fly. Your exhalations still condense, but they run down the inner surface of the fly to drip on the ground, outside.

Gore-Tex eliminates the need for two layers, reducing the weight slightly. But the reduction isn't as much as you might think, because Gore-Tex is heavy. Gore-Tex tents work best in warm environments and poorest in cool, damp climates where the temperature inside the tent can be below the dew point—which causes condensation even on Gore-Tex.

Two-person tents are the most versatile; larger ones obligate you to carry the weight around, even if you don't have enough people to fill them. Extremely large tents—anything designed for more than 4 people—aren't recommended. They are heavy and may not be sturdy enough in a storm. A group of my friends once took an inexpensive 8-person tent they called "the condo" on an organized tour. It stood 6 feet high, and the first strong wind smashed all the poles.

Too small a tent, on the other hand, isn't a good idea for rainy climates. When sitting out a long rainstorm, it's nice to have room to read comfortably or play cards.

An excellent way to shop for tents is by going on a large organized tour. Wandering around each evening's campground, you'll see almost every conceivable variety, with owners happy to talk about them.

Sleeping under the stars. In the right climate, or at least on a good evening, where rain, dew, and mosquitoes aren't likely, sleeping under the stars is a glorious alternative to being confined in a tent. Just throw your sleeping bag and pad on a tarp, gather everything else you need nearby where you won't lose it in the grass, and lie back, hoping for a truly spectacular celestial display. If the weather worsens, you could find yourself pitching a tent by flashlight, but in hundreds of nights of sleeping on the ground I've only had to do this a handful of times.

With a big enough tarp, you can fold it back over yourself as protection against dew or light rain. If you have the tarp to yourself, you can even roll up in it like a giant cigar, staying dry under less than ideal conditions. I once kept dry this way when an unexpected storm dropped half an inch of rain on me in the bottom of Death Valley.

Some people won't sleep without a tent because they're afraid of creatures, particularly snakes, crawling on them or joining them in the middle of the night. I won't say there's no such risk, but the only thing that's ever joined me was a friendly dog (it *was* a bit of a surprise). The much-repeated stories about snakes crawling into your sleeping bag might have a foundation in fact, but if it has ever happened, it must be rare. Skunks and porcupines present more realistic concerns—and ants, mosquitoes, or biting gnats can quickly drive you into a tent. You'll find a tent to be a summer necessity in most parts of the country east of central Kansas.

Bivouac bags. A tent alternative that is less chancy than sleeping under the stars is a bivouac sack, or *bivvy bag*. In its simplest form, it's a waterproof sleeping bag cover made of Gore-Tex or other waterproof, breathable fabric. For good weather, stuff your sleeping bag inside, and sleep under the stars. Under bad conditions, zip yourself in, away from the rain or bugs. Leaving a breathing hole is important to reduce condensation (some manufacturers also recommend this to avoid any risk of suffocation). Some models even have mosquito netting so you can leave a breathing hole without giving insects a route inside.

Bivvy bags are light, considerably less expensive than good-quality tents, and small enough to fit in a pannier. But the simplest ones aren't perfect substitutes for a tent. In cool weather, even with a breathing hole, there's likely to be some condensation, most of which will eventually be sponged up by your sleeping bag. In warm weather, you'll overheat if you have to zip up. And whatever the temperature, waiting out rain or a prolonged bug attack is even more cramped in a bivvy bag than in the tiniest tent.

A bivvy bag is a superb lightweight, waterproof backup for trips when you expect to spend most nights under the stars. Even if occasionally you do get condensation, it's not likely to soak all the way through your sleeping bag unless you don't take time to dry out the bag between uses.

Cyclists traveling in pairs can also carry bivvies, but the advantage is considerably reduced; for their combined price you can buy a tent that won't be much heavier than two bivvies. Of course, bivvy bags *do* give you the opportunity to put some distance between yourself and a snoring buddy.

Bivvy tents. In features and price, some bivouac bags are more like miniature tents than conventional bivvy bags. These fancy hybrids, called *bivvy tents*, have poles to keep the fabric off your face, and they give you a choice between mosquito netting and a storm flap. A lack of ventilation around your legs still makes them too warm for many climates, but for the cool evenings of mountains, deserts, and high plains, such bags are an excellent weight and comfort compromise for solo touring or for the odd person in a 3-person group. Think twice, however, about venturing into a wet climate with a tent so small you can't sit up in it. I took one of these to Iceland for three weeks; it was comfortable for sleeping, but squirming around changing clothes inside it quickly got old.

Hammocks. Another lightweight, 1-person alternative is a hammock. Bugs and rain may be problems with some models, but any hammock with *jungle* in its name probably has mosquito

Bivvy tents blur the boundary between tents and bivouac sacks. This model has mosquito netting and a hoop to allow a modicum of elbow space, but it's more a bivvy bag than a tent.

A Note about Tent Poles

When buying a tent for self-contained touring, you need to think about how easy it will be to carry. Many backpacking tents, particularly free-standing ones, have pole segments that are considerably longer than your rack. Although it's possible to strap these elongated tents in place, all that weight sticking out behind you (or to the side if you lash the tent crosswise) is destabilizing. It's a classic case of the tail wagging the dog, as the tent magnifies tiny wobbles into an uncontrollable shimmy. There are tricks for controlling this movement (see pages 99–101), but unless you're planning to use a baggage trailer rather than panniers (see page 102), try to avoid the problem by buying a tent whose poles fold into shorter segments.

netting and a waterproof cover. The biggest drawback is that hammocks limit you to campsites with suitably spaced trees or tree substitutes such as playground equipment.

Sleeping Bags

Any sufficiently warm sleeping bag will keep you comfortable. Inexpensive bags are heavy and bulky, though, so if you're going to upgrade your camping equipment, start here.

The best all-purpose sleeping bags are made from synthetics. Down is lighter, but you're in trouble if it gets wet. Wet down won't keep you warm, and it takes forever to dry. A damp synthetic bag, on the other hand, dries quickly in the sun; one that's been thoroughly soaked can be dried in a self-service laundry at low heat, perhaps with an old tennis shoe tossed in to help keep it fluffy.

A sleeping bag's quality depends as much on its design as on its materials. A well-constructed system of baffles should keep the insulating material from bunching up, without producing cold spots at the seams between compartments.

To stop drafts from creeping down your neck or back, a drawstring and Velcro closures at the head will allow you to pull the bag tight. Conversely, a double zipper at the foot allows you to *create* drafts if it's too warm.

Sleeping bags come in a variety of thicknesses,

often rated for temperature. The ratings are guides, not absolute predictors; a bag that's comfortable for one person may be too hot or cold for another.

A good sleeping bag, properly treated, will last for years. In long-term storage, it shouldn't be tightly stuffed in its sack, or eventually the fabric will compress and lose warmth. Put it in a large cloth bag or pillow case, tossing the stuff sack in with it, so you don't lose it. To help avoid mildew, air out the sleeping bag in the sun for a few hours before storing it, and use a storage bag that is either breathable or open at one end.

Sleeping Pads

What you put beneath you is at least as important as what goes above you. I learned this on my first attempt at winter camping (by car, not by bike). Sleeping under the stars on a 10°F night, I fell asleep quite nicely, bundled in a warm sleeping bag and a couple layers of clothes. Hours later, I woke up freezing, and added layer after layer of clothing before I figured out that I'd rolled off my sleeping pad. Within minutes of getting back on, I was peeling off the added layers as I started to overheat.

The lesson was graphic: you can sleep comfortably on a bed of ice *if* you have a good insulating pad beneath you. Without one, you'll get chilly, not to mention wake up stiff and sore, even at much milder temperatures.

The classic sleeping pad for most car campers is an air mattress. These also work for bicycle touring, but they're not ideal. Blowing them up every evening is a nuisance, as is fighting their tendency to scoot out from under you if you roll off center. And even though air mattresses are thick, they aren't the warmest things available: convection currents can quickly rob you of heat.

Better from an insulating perspective are closed-cell foam pads, such as the popular one made by Ridgerest. (Open-cell foams are softer, but they sponge up water.) Closed-cell pads are inexpensive, lightweight, virtually indestructible, and warm enough for any conditions you're likely to encounter. They aren't very cushy, though; getting used to sleeping on one takes a few nights, especially on hard surfaces.

A more comfortable choice is a softer, nylon-covered foam pad like the type made by Therm-A-Rest. These pads, which come in a variety of lengths and thicknesses, have an air valve that allows them to be inflated or deflated. Their spongy foam will self-inflate when you open the valve, but if you want them firm, it will take some lung power. Such pads are much thinner than air mattresses but are surprisingly comfortable. Unlike air mattresses, which are worthless if they spring a leak, the mixture of foam and air used by these pads means that, even deflated, they'll keep you reasonably warm. They're durable enough that the normal wear and tear of being lashed to your bicycle isn't likely to poke a hole in them. For added puncture resistance—and to keep the pad clean if you're bicycling on dusty roads—carry it in a light-weight nylon stuff sack. If a pad does spring a leak, it's patchable, although you'll need a Therm-A-Rest patch kit, not a tire patch kit.

These pads, unfortunately, are a good deal more expensive than the other options and a lot heavier than closed-cell foam. Store them inflated, so they don't permanently compress.

Groundsheet

A groundsheet fits between your tent floor and the ground. There are durable nylon tarps made specially for the purpose, or you can buy a disposable painter's drop cloth from a hardware store.

A groundsheet protects the bottom side of the tent floor from dirt or abrasion. It won't necessarily prevent leakage in a rainstorm; it might in fact do the reverse by trapping runoff between itself and the tent floor.

If rain isn't likely, I recommend a groundsheet simply to help preserve the life of your tent. In rainy weather its value is more debatable and depends on the abrasiveness of the surface on which you are camped. You may keep drier by doing without it. At a minimum, tuck the edges well beneath the tent to reduce their tendency to channel moisture beneath you. For some tents you can buy a custom *footprint*, which is a groundsheet shaped exactly like the tent floor, held in place by elastic loops that attach to the poles. It's lighter and more compact than a conventional groundsheet, has no protruding corners to trap rain, and costs about $30.

ThermaLounger

Are you the type of person who likes to get into camp early, sit back, and read a book? When car camping you can carry a folding lounge chair, but by bicycle that's impractical. The same people who make the Therm-A-Rest pad have invented the ThermaLounger, a contraption of staves and nylon into which you can insert the pad to convert it to a portable lounge chair (see photo below).

A pair of straps, one on each side, pulls the

The ThermaLounger converts your sleeping pad to a comfortable chair.

ThermaLounger into a V, which you adjust by loosening or tightening the straps. It's not light (about 1½ pounds), but it has the same addictive comfort as a beanbag chair and rolls up into a package not much larger than the pad, which can remain inside for sleeping or transport.

For long-distance, self-contained touring, this product probably isn't worth the weight. But for short-mileage overnighters or organized tours where limited baggage space prevents you from bringing a full-size lounge chair, it's perfect.

Pillow

If you really want a pillow, purchase an air pillow or carry a small conventional one with you. But even for van-supported touring, I merely stuff extra clothing into my sleeping bag stuff sack—perhaps the clothes I'm going to change into in the morning. Putting them in the sack isn't necessary, of course, but it reduces the risk of poking a zipper tab in your eye as you sleep.

Cooking Equipment

Cooking equipment is optional; you may prefer to eat at cafés or snack in general stores. If you decide to carry a stove, the ideal ones for bicycling are the same as for backpacking: compact, one-burner, fueled by white gas, such as the popular MSR WhisperLite.

Look for a stove with a good windscreen, and compare specifications on how long it takes to boil a quart of water. The specifications will probably be based on ideal conditions—laughable in a windy camp at high elevation—but they're the best comparative guide to how long you're going to have to wait for dinner.

Some stoves have built-in flint-and-steel sparkers. They're convenient, but don't rely on them; carry matches as a backup.

White-gas stoves must be primed. Consult the owner's manual for instructions, and heed warnings about not using your stove inside a tent, where a flare-up might cook you along with your dinner.

The only utensils you need are a large pot (about 2 quarts), a stirring spoon, a pocket knife, and perhaps a pancake turner and a nonstick frying pan. A second, smaller pot is useful for side dishes, particularly those that can be reconstituted from hot or cold water while your main dish simmers. Gloves or a washcloth are adequate pot holders, although an aluminum *pot grabber* is a useful, lightweight accessory.

Sometimes you can dispense with the stove and cook over wood fires, but fires aren't always possible, and it's hard to keep soot from migrating from the pot onto everything else you're carrying with it.

BAGS

As explained earlier, bicycle bags are called *panniers* (*PAN-yers* or *PAN-ee-ers*, depending on what part of the country you're from). Occasionally, the general public refers to them as "saddlebags" because they bear some resemblance to horse-packing equipment.

Whatever you call them, panniers (or a trailer, as discussed below) are the one piece of specialty bicycle camping equipment you need for self-contained touring. You could get by with a backpack, but that's brutally hard on your back, puts your center of gravity too high, and is dangerous to both you and the equipment if you fall. Even if all you can afford are cheap panniers, get the weight on the bicycle.

Panniers come in pairs that are carried either in front or back. The principal difference between front and rear ones is size: front panniers are usually smaller. You can get color-coordinated sets of front and rear bags, with matching handlebar bags, but unless you're worried about not being able to match colors later, you needn't buy all of these initially unless you're planning to start self-contained touring with a several-day trip.

If your first self-contained tours are weekend outings, a gradual way to acquire panniers is to buy rear ones first, adding front ones when you need them. Or buy a small set of panniers first, using them as rear panniers for light touring or credit-card touring and transferring them to the front if you later buy full-fledged rear ones.

Pannier designs change from year to year as manufacturers introduce new features to secure the pannier ever more firmly to the rack. But the basic idea hasn't changed for years. At the bottom of the pannier is a spring-loaded hook; at the top, a pair of clips. The hook fastens to the bottom of your rack, while the clips go over the top. A nylon strap serves as a handle to ease installing and removing the bag, while some kind of tensioning device allows you to adjust the spring to pull the bag off easily—but not so easily that it bounces off when you hit a bump.

Front and rear panniers are either top loading or side loading. Side-loading models are more convenient, especially for rear panniers, allowing you easy access even if your tent, sleeping bag, and pad are lashed above them (see pages 97–99). Nevertheless, top loaders are popular, perhaps because they are more waterproof. A well-designed side-loading bag, though, should be more than adequately waterproof for most conditions, especially if it has good storm flaps around the zippers.

Rear panniers should be tapered on the front side so your heels will clear them at the back of the pedal stroke. Don't buy ones that won't give you enough room: there are few things more irritating than having to kick them out of the way every few minutes to keep your heels from going bump-bump-bump against them. Obviously, this will be a bigger concern if your shoes are size 13 than if they're size 7.

Side pockets are also useful. They add to the pan-

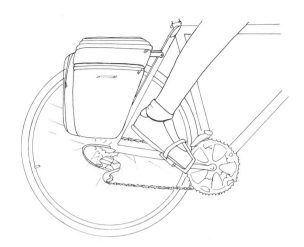

Make sure there's enough room between the pannier and your heel.

niers' price but are worth it because they make it easier to organize your gear. A major plus is an external pocket big enough to hold a water bottle (upright so it can't leak). Beware of pockets on top of the main compartment; they can bulge high enough to get in the way of your tent and sleeping bag. Also, make sure the various pockets aren't designed so they'll spill their contents when opened—a major nuisance with some pannier designs.

The main compartment should be a single unit to carry large or odd-shaped items, such as spare spokes, cooking pots, or a backpacking stove.

You should be able to use any rear pannier in front if it's not so big that it drags on the ground. Specially designed front panniers, however, are smaller and simpler, with fewer pockets because presumably you've already got plenty of pockets in back. Top loaders aren't as much of a nuisance in front as in back.

One nice front-pannier feature is an elasticized-mesh exterior pocket into which you can drop things such as sunscreen or sunglasses for easy access. Before buying, test the elastic to make sure it isn't so loose that things will bounce out on the road. Mesh pockets also can be used for holding wet clothing as it dries. Be leery of packs on which the elastic is replaced with a zipper—such pockets can be difficult to get into if the main compartment is full.

Reflective tape on any pannier, front or rear,

Side-loading pannier. Note the plethora of pockets. These add to cost but are very convenient, especially the rear one, which can hold a spare water bottle. Note how the zippers are protected by storm flaps. These are important for keeping your gear dry.

Front panniers with mesh pouch.

could literally be a lifesaver. Look for it on the back and sides of rear panniers and on the front and sides of any panniers you plan to put in front. Straps to compress the pannier to eliminate extra volume and increase stability are also useful.

Some panniers are designed more for moutain-bike touring than for road touring; the difference lies largely in the fabric's weight. Mountain bike bags are made to be durable enough for narrow, brush-lined trails. They'll work on the road, but you don't need their extra weight or expense.

Handlebar bags. Handlebar bags are controversial. They are extremely convenient places to stash everything from your camera and wallet to a snack, but they're also destabilizing, raising the center of gravity of your front wheel, and sometimes vibrating enough to make your front end shimmy at high speed. I find that the advantages outweigh the disadvantages for self-contained touring, but it's a closer call for light touring, especially on a racing bike with sensitive steering. Also, I'm short and use a small frame. Taller riders sometimes report that the stability problems are more significant on larger frames.

The size of a handlebar bag is up to you. I want one big enough for my camera and snacks, such as a bag of cherries from a roadside fruit stand. Extremely large bags will tempt you to load too

much weight into them, at risk of destabilizing your bicycle. But it's a trade-off because they're also more likely to have 1 or more convenient external pockets for your tire patch kit, chain lube, and other small, frequently used tools.

Handlebar bags should mount firmly to your handlebars to reduce vibration. They also need to be easy to remove for boxing your bike for airplane trips or for simply carrying the bag with you by hand. In the past, handlebar bags mounted with complicated systems of hooks, rods, and shock cords that could take five minutes to attach. Today's better bags use a single large plastic clip, detaching and reattaching literally in a snap.

Map pouches. Map pouches are clear plastic compartments that hold a map on top of your handlebar bag, folded in reading position and always dry. They are one of the principal reasons handlebar bags are worth getting; make sure yours either comes with a pouch or has a way to add one.

Map pouches have another use. If you want to lather up with sunscreen, on the move and one-handed, squirt a small puddle of it onto the top of the pouch. Now you can put the sunscreen back in your handlebar bag, freeing a hand for rubbing in the lotion. That little trick eliminates one of the great excuses for getting sunburned: *I knew I was burning but was waiting to do something about it until the next time I stopped.*

If you don't use a handlebar bag, you can still benefit from map pouches that attach to your handlebars with Velcro or nylon straps. These handy waterproof pouches flip forward, out of your way, when you're not using the map, or back atop your handlebars when you need a quick look at it. They typically have larger windows than bag-mounting pouches and are particularly useful in century rides and organized tours where you're traveling light but need to refer to a route map or cue sheet. Their biggest drawback is wind resistance. If you have a bike with a short frame, don't get a pouch so large that it rubs against the tire.

Rack packs. There are a variety of bags, smaller than panniers, that mount on your rear rack. For van-supported touring, organized tours, or century rides, such bags combined with a handlebar bag or small front panniers may be all you need to carry your rain gear, spare tube, camera, and wind jacket.

Rack packs have lower wind resistance than do

Handlebar bag with map pouch.

rack pack

panniers because they don't stick out to the side. Since they're fastened only on the bottom, though, they have a tendency to wobble when you pedal hard. Hooking bungee cords over the top solves

this problem and gives you a place to lash clothing too bulky to fit in the bag. Just don't let the clothing rub on your tire.

LOADING UP

A full touring rig consists of front and rear panniers, a handlebar bag, and a "stack" of tent, sleeping bag, sleeping pad, and anything else that won't fit in the panniers lashed to the rear rack with bungee cords or nylon straps.

The weight should be distributed with less in front than in back. The conventional rule of thumb is a 40-60 split, but if you're carrying a lot of weight in a rear stack, you'll probably find the division comes closer to 30-70. The precise split isn't critical; before front panniers came into widespread use, many cyclists, myself included, carried heavy loads for long distances with no weight in front except a handlebar bag. Front-heavy loads are also possible—and with low-rider front racks a few people prefer them—but bulk

Going in European Style

American pannier manufacturers have focused mostly on designing nylon panniers with a plethora of pockets. European designers, led by German bag maker Ortlieb, favor single-compartment bags, whose simpler design makes them easier to make waterproof.

Ortlieb bags are made of a rubberized material similar to that used for canoeists' dry bags. Like watersport bags, they're top loaders that roll down from above to seal off leaks. Properly closed with four or five tight rolls of fabric, they're impressively waterproof, capable of withstanding a garden hose at high pressure or days of drizzle. Not surprisingly, they're gaining popularity in damp parts of North America such as the Pacific Northwest.

Ortlieb's bags use ingenious spring clamps that won't pop loose from the rack unless you release them by pulling on a nylon strap. It's a good design, although it's set up for European racks and may take a bit of adjustment to fit some American ones.

The single-compartment design has advantages and disadvantages. On the plus side, the enormous compartments of Ortlieb's larger bags are big enough to hold hiking boots, a bivvy tent, and a spare tire—all in a single bag. They also offer greater packing flexibility. On the other hand, the bag's waterproof seal only works if the bag is fairly full. Otherwise, water leaks in around loose rolls of fabric. That means it's important not to get a bag bigger than you need.

Another problem is what I think of as the "duffel-bag syndrome." Large single compartments are a nuisance when rummaging for small objects. You'll need to invest in ditty bags to keep your tools and toiletries from scattering. Ortlieb's newer designs reduce this problem with strap-on, roll-top side pouches—not as convenient as zippered pockets but a compromise that preserves the company's reputation for bone-dry waterproofing.

© ORTLIEB

problems usually make such a rig impractical.

More important is keeping each set of panniers balanced, side to side. With practice, loading this way becomes second nature, but check yourself the first few times by hefting each pair of bags, one in each hand. To keep from being fooled if your arms aren't equally strong, do it twice, reversing hands.

Similarly, the bike is easier to handle if the weight is concentrated low and close to the frame. It also helps to pack symmetrically. That means that if you depart from the heavy-items-low-and-inside rule by putting a water bottle in an accessible external pocket on one side, match it by carrying another water bottle or something equally heavy, such as your tool kit, in the corresponding pocket on the other side.

There are two basic ways to stack your sleeping bag, tent, and other large items: lashing long items either crosswise or lengthwise. Lengthwise produces the least wind resistance, since the edges of the stack aren't sticking out to the side, but it's also the least stable because the lashed-on items can jiggle from side to side.

More likely, you'll find that you have to lash crosswise, wind resistance or not. When lashing this way, it's also easier to add extra equipment to

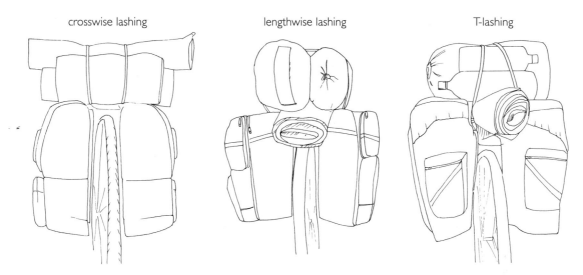

| crosswise lashing | lengthwise lashing | T-lashing |

Rear-rack-loading methods. Note differences in accessibility to main compartment between top-loading (left and right) and side-loading panniers (center).

the stack, such as a 2-liter soda bottle converted to a spare water bottle. Just slide it beneath the bungee cords, behind the sleeping bag.

A third approach, which helps if your panniers are so full that they bulge well above the rack, is to lash items in a T shape. Flat, narrow items, such as a groundsheet or a fully deflated Therm-A-Rest pad, can run lengthwise on top of your rack, eating up the extra space between the panniers and giving you a flatter surface on which to lash your tent and sleeping bag crosswise.

A few cyclists carry extra gear in a backpack or dangling from their handlebars. This is destabilizing, dangerous, and uncomfortable. Leave unnecessary gear at home, get larger panniers, or lash the extra material to your rack. Avoid long items that wag behind you or hang out so far to the side that they might snag on a bush or get clipped by a passing car.

GETTING RID OF THE SHIMMIES

The first time you hop on your loaded bike, you're likely to be dismayed to find it unstable, shimmying uncontrollably even at fairly slow speeds. Because this is so common, start each tour by testing your loading job, riding around a large parking lot or a

quiet side street. This helps, but don't be surprised if additional shimmy problems surface later, the first time your speed exceeds some magic number—for example, 15, 20, or 25 mph. Don't panic; just pull to the side of the road to look for possible causes.

Shimmies can come from a variety of sources, and tracking them down is more art than science. Don't assume, for example, that a shimmy in the front wheel comes from problems in the front; it may be a manifestation of problems in the rear. Be patient; small adjustments can make the difference between a rig that shimmies unnervingly at 15 mph and one that's rock steady at 35.

Here are some of the most likely sources of instability, and their probable solutions.

- *Handlebar bag is overloaded.* The less weight in your handlebar bag, the less mass there is to vibrate. Store tire irons and a tire patch kit in it, but the bulk of your tool kit should go elsewhere. Nor should you weigh it down with water bottles.
- *Weight distribution in panniers is uneven.* Remove them and check for balance. Shifting a couple of pounds from one side to the other may be all you need to do.
- *Too much weight is too high.* Repack with the heaviest items as low in your bags as possible.

Similarly, heavy items should be at the base of the stack, rather than bouncing on top of it.

- *Stack is lashed too loosely.* Before leaving home, test your bungee cords to make sure they're the right length. If your cords are still too loose, find a different place to hook them, or cross them diagonally for a tighter stretch. If this doesn't work, carry a pair of nylon straps as a backup. Such straps are also useful insurance against destroying a bungee cord by accidentally winding it up in your gear cluster. The best straps have metal teeth and a metal roller that allows you to yank them extremely tight. Because the metal adds extra weight, you won't find these in backpacking stores. Check the camping section of a discount store such as Wal-Mart. Use these in addition to bungee cords, not as replacements. Bungee cords are useful for securing items that tend to flap or for holding cycling shorts, towels, and other wet clothing while it air dries.

- *Weight distribution of stack is off center.* This will cause the same type of problems as do unbalanced panniers.

- *Stack isn't sitting on a firm, flat surface.* The stability of the stack is much influenced by the surface on which it's built. When strapped down, your sleeping bag and tent should make firm contact with the rack; when in the T-shaped lashing described earlier, with tightly compressed equipment sitting firmly on the rack.

- *Sleeping pad isn't completely deflated.* If a Therm-A-Rest–style sleeping pad is beneath the sleeping bag, as in the T-shaped lashing, it's hard to make a firm base for the stack if the pad isn't fully deflated. This is a 2-step process. First, open the valve and roll the pad up as firmly as you can, kneeling on it. Then, close the valve, unroll the pad, and roll it again, tighter, stopping to open the valve to bleed off additional air just before you finish. Lash the pad to the bike with the valve closed to keep it from self-inflating.

- *Sleeping bag isn't tightly enough stuffed (that is, stuff sack is too big).* Usually you can solve this by tightening your straps. If that doesn't work, you may need a compression stuff sack. The simplest of these use laces to take up unwanted volume. Another design, made by Seattle Sports, has straps, buckles, and an air

valve to allow you to kneel on the bag to compress it extremely tightly. Its down side is a $50 price tag and the fact that the bag is made of a heavy (highly waterproof) fabric that adds about a pound to your load. But compression bags give you packing flexibility by allowing you to carry a larger sack than would otherwise be shimmy-proof. This is particularly useful on tours to remote destinations, where rare supermarket stops periodically fill your panniers with so much food that you need a dry place for dislodged clothing.

- *Wrong lashing configuration.* If you've lashed your tent and sleeping bag lengthwise, try lashing them crosswise. Or shift to the T configuration.

- *Not enough straps.* Two straps will hold your sleeping bag, tent, and pad in position, but it may take more, run at different angles, to shut off all possible jiggles.

- *Loose items in stack.* Spare mountain bike tires are particularly hard to carry. They're hard to lash down firmly, too big to put underneath your sleeping bag, and heavy enough to have

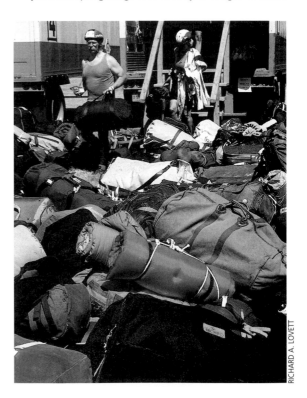

RICHARD A. LOVETT

a substantial effect on weight distribution. Get them as low as possible, possibly even like earmuffs strapped to the sides of your panniers.

- *Spoke reflectors.* A shimmy that comes only at very high speeds, especially in light touring, might be caused by your spoke reflectors. Since these are good protection at night, it can be hard to choose between removing them or living with the shimmy.

OTHER PACKING TIPS

Every experienced cyclist has a preferred way of packing; it won't take you long to develop your own. What matters isn't so much *where* you put things as whether you can *remember* the location and not have to unload half of your equipment each evening in search of your toothbrush.

Here are a few tips, developed mostly by the grumble-and-learn approach.

- *Think in terms of accessibility.* The least accessible place is the bottom of your rear panniers, so use that for things you don't need immediately: tomorrow's clothes, dinner makings, your stove, exposed film.
- *Your handlebar bag is the most accessible place*—and the only one you can reach without stopping.
- *Front panniers are highly accessible.* I use one for rain gear, a wind shell, and tights; the other for lunch makings and snacks. I fill extra space with anything else I might want quickly, such as camera lenses.
- *What do you do with your bicycle when you get off it for a rest break?* Do you usually prop one side against a wall, fence, or tree? If so, the other side (for most people, the left) will be more accessible. Alternatively, do you more frequently lay it down on its side? That means you probably put the right side up to keep grit out of the chain and derailleur. That's a bit hard on handlebar-mounted mirrors, but it means the right panniers are the accessible ones. Pack accordingly.
- *With small panniers and a lot of bulky clothes,* conserve space by putting your sleeping bag in a larger stuff sack than necessary. Then stuff your warm jacket, spare T-shirts, or other clothing in with it. Stuff these clothes in ahead of the

sleeping bag if you're not likely to need them on the road, afterward if you might.

- *Sharing a tent, you can split the weight* if one of you carries the poles and stakes, while the other carries the rest. Just make sure the poles and stakes are nicely bagged so you don't lose any.
- *To keep your sleeping bag dry even in a downpour,* line the inside of the stuff sack with a garbage bag. Some people put the garbage bag on the outside of the stuff sack instead, but that means it won't be long until it's poked full of holes. You can also line your panniers with plastic, but this isn't as necessary.

LIGHT-TOURING RIG

Without much baggage, you can dispense with various parts of the full touring rig. A pair of front panniers used in the rear, for example, may be all you need for a weekend of credit-card touring. The same panniers combined with a rack pack and handlebar bag might keep you going inn to inn for a week. Some people do such tours with front panniers only.

For van-supported touring, you might need nothing more than a handlebar bag or rack pack for your map, rain gear, and camera. A single rear pannier, if lightly loaded, can also work without destabilizing you or damaging the rack from the unbalanced load. I carry it on the side closest to the traffic, trying to use the extra bulk to encourage drivers to pass me with adequate room.

As mentioned in the previous chapter, for weekend self-contained touring you can often get by without front panniers, using the old-fashioned touring rig of rear panniers, stack, and handlebar bag.

WHAT TO CARRY

An equipment checklist for loaded touring is on pages 104–6. It is designed for a one-week trip under varied weather conditions. Abbreviate it for shorter trips or lighter styles of touring.

Don't be intimidated by the number of items. Many are accounted for by first-aid materials, tools, and spare parts. If you tour frequently, you can assemble these in advance as separate kits, storing them between uses. Just remember to replace anything you've used.

Towing It

Panniers put the weight of your baggage directly on your bike, altering its handling and increasing wear and tear, particularly on your rear wheel. Some people prefer to get the weight onto its own wheels.

Like every equipment choice, this one has its pros and cons. Trailers give you more room than panniers for bulky objects, and save the need to purchase expensive racks for full-suspension mountain bikes. But they can't carry as much weight as you can put directly on the bike frame.

Another tradeoff involves on-the-road repairs. By taking weight off the bike, trailers reduce your risk of flat tires and broken spokes on your rear wheel—the two biggest nuisances of heavy touring. But they have their own wheels and spokes—and their tiny wheels won't use the same spares as your bike. There's also the risk that the mounting hardware will break—although that's a lot less serious than an unfixable bike breakdown, since you could always leave the trailer and pedal off to civilization without it.

There are two basic types of trailers: one-wheeled (leading brand B.O.B, $275) and two-wheeled (leading brand Burley, $275).

The B.O.B. looks unstable, but it tracks nicely along behind you, bouncing over rocks and chuckholes. If you miss an obstacle, the trailer probably will, too, and it's vir-tually impossible to run it off the road unless you first do the same with your bike. Its teetery balance means that learning to drive it takes practice, but it's no worse than heavy panniers. Fully loaded, however, it does have a tendency to fall over or jackknife when you park. When possible, prop bike and trailer against a long wall. When I tested one with too much weight on steep, rolling hills, it became frighteningly "whippy" on downgrades, snapping the front end of my bike back and forth with every minor wobble. When I cut back the weight, it became perfectly stable. How much weight you can carry depends on your bike and your body mass. At 5'6" and 136 pounds, I max out at about 50 pounds.

The Burley is larger and easier to learn to use. Its wheels, though, won't track behind yours, so it's possible to drop one into a chuckhole you think you've dodged, or off the lip of the pavement. You have to steer pretty close to things to do this, however, and when I deliberately dropped a Burley's wheel off a 2-inch pavement lip, it pulled back onto the road without any difficulty. I did run it over a curb on a sharp corner, however; make wider-than-normal turns until you've figured out what you can and can't do. It's also possible to flip a 2-wheeled trailer (a scary thought) but the only person I know who actually did this says that Burley's clamp is so well designed that the upside-down trailer just dragged along behind him, without affecting his balance. Parking, the same beautifully hinged clamp allows you to simply lay your bike down on its side, with the trailer still standing—a major advantage.

The Burley's chief oddity is that it uses an angled hitch that attaches from the side. There's enough spring in this that the trailer will surge behind you noticeably with each pedal stroke unless you have a nice even cadence that delivers fairly equal power across the entire pedal stroke. That's good cycling style anyway, however; the Burley will just encourage you to practice it. It's most difficult if you like to stand on the pedals to power up steep hills.

Recommendations: For mountain biking on rough, narrow trails, the narrow B.O.B. is the only way to go. For a major trip on rough gravel, I'd also choose it over panniers or a two-wheeled trailer. On roads, I still prefer panniers, but if you want a trailer, the easier-to-drive-and-park Burley probably has the advantage. Tandem couples and others who want to carry more weight than a trailer alone allows might try combining one with front panniers. Also, both the one- and two-wheel designs allow you to lash equipment to a rear rack, and may leave room for a small set of rear panniers.

Forgetting something isn't the end of the world. Even something as vital as your sleeping bag can be replaced in a small-town discount store.

First-aid kit. Unless you're going somewhere really remote, you don't need an extensive first-aid kit; many problems, such as chafing, develop slowly enough that you can buy what you need from drugstores along the way. Do carry things you'll use regularly or might need in an emergency, such as water-purification tablets, assorted bandages, prescription medications, bee-sting remedies, and anti-inflammatories like aspirin or ibuprofen.

If a pill bottle is too bulky, transfer the pills to small, inexpensive waterproof containers.

Tool kit and spare parts. Because bike stores appear less frequently than drug stores, your repair kit will be more extensive than your first-aid kit. Not all bicycles will require everything on the list, however.

Some of the tools are ordinary household items; others are specialty ones. The most convenient Allen wrenches, for example, come linked together on a key-chain ring or folded up like a multibladed pocketknife. Similarly, a set of bike-repair socket wrenches comes in a Y-shaped tool with a different socket on each end.

Not all of the listed tools are for bike repair; some, such as safety pins and ripstop tape, are for your tent, panniers, and other equipment.

Every rider in your group should have a minimal tool kit: Allen wrenches, tire patch kit, spare tube. But only one rider needs to have everything. The complete tool kit sounds heavy, but much of the weight is accounted for by two items: wrenches and pliers. If you keep those light, you can get the weight down to 2 or 3 pounds, not counting the spare tubes or spare tire.

Spare tire. The heaviest and bulkiest spare part on the list is a tire. Your group should always have at least one of each size that might be needed. It's even better for each person to have one, especially those whose wheels differ from the standard 26 inches—for which tires may be difficult to come by in small towns.

When on a van-supported tour, carrying spares is no problem. But on self-contained trips, tires can be cumbersome. The simplest way to carry one is to coil it up, being cautious not to kink it. Here's how.

1. Hold the tire horizontally in front of you, or put it on a flat surface.
2. Pull the far edge toward you, over the top of the near edge, letting the tire twist naturally into a three-looped shape like a set of eyes and a nose

(if you're a history buff, think "Kilroy Was Here!"). The loop forming the "nose" crosses above the others.
3. Adjust the size of the loops until they're roughly equal. Then, raising the tire off the flat surface, fold both "eyes" downward, one at a time, into the "nose." Congratulations! You have reduced a large, unwieldy tire to an easily manageable triple ring.
4. Check to make sure there are no kinks; then tie the ring closed with string. You can carry it in a pannier or on your rear rack as part of the stack.

Practice this at home, before you hit the road, until it feels natural enough that you can do it easily. Coiled tires can be stored at home indefinitely.

You could also buy folding tires that come in boxes, but they're more expensive, can't be found in every bike store, and may be harder to install than ordinary tires are. They also eat a lot of space in your panniers and are most common in narrow, racing-tire widths. Once you've mastered the art of coiling a tire, there's not much reason to buy one pre-folded.

Other cyclists have carried spares by stuffing them inside the spokes of their front or rear wheels. It's ingenious, but I'd be afraid of causing a high-speed shimmy.

Water bottles. Most bikes come equipped with two water bottle cages. You can and should mount a third on the front of the down tube, behind the front wheel. Two more bottles can go in the exterior pockets on most rear panniers, one on each side, easily accessible for swapping with empties.

If you need more water than that, bury extra bottles in the main compartment of your panniers or lash a plastic 2-liter soda bottle to your stack. These bottles, and the similar mineral-water bottles, make excellent water bottles because they

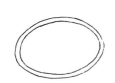  

Coiling a tire.

Carry lots of water.

don't leak and can be refilled time and again. Gallon jugs of distilled water can be lashed to the stack (with a bit more difficulty), but because their tops pop off easily after they've first been opened, they're good only for one-time use. Don't open one until you've emptied enough other bottles to hold its entire contents.

Water bottles come in 16- and 24-ounce sizes. Larger is nice, but the 24-ouncers won't fit the extra cage on your down tube and may not fit your pannier pockets. Since you'll want to rotate bottles rather than always having to pour water from one to another, think through your rotation system before buying too many 24-ouncers.

Camelbak. This company makes backpack-style "hydration systems" containing large, collapsible water bags. A drinking tube arcs around your neck to allow you to sip, hands free. "Sip" is the name of the game; if you're accustomed to stopping every few miles to slam a whole water bottle, you'll

CAMELBAK

be frustrated by the system's slow water flow, which gives you a mouthful easily enough but takes patience for a large drink. They're great for racers. The biggest advantage touring is that the chin-level nozzle prompts you to drink regularly—important in hot weather. The biggest drawback is that if you take a Camelbak on a multiday tour you're stuck with it for the duration.

Camping and Cycling Equipment

Tent
Sleeping bag
Sleeping pad
Groundsheet or footprint
Panniers
Handlebar bag
Rearview mirror
Water bottles
Flashlight, with spare bulb and batteries
Pocketknife
Bungee cords or nylon straps
Maps
Towel and washcloth
Nylon cord (25–50 feet)
Lock and cable
Headlight and taillight
Food (approximately 1-day supply)

Clothing

Helmet
Cycling gloves
Cycling shoes
Cycling shorts (at least 2 pairs)
T-shirts or jerseys (at least 2)
Underwear and socks
Tights or leg warmers
Wind shell
Rain gear
Elastic band to secure flapping pant leg
Warm jacket or sweater

Tool Kit

Tire patch kit (2)
Tire levers (set)
Small amount of talc
Pump
Allen wrenches

Chain lube
Screwdrivers (Phillips head and flathead)
Crescent wrench (6-inch)
Socket wrenches
Needlenose pliers/wire cutters
Small Vise-Grip pliers
Chain tool
Spoke wrench
Freewheel remover
Tire gauge
Presta-to-Schrader valve adapter
Duct tape (small amount wrapped around pencil
    stub)
Ripstop nylon tape
Safety pins
Plastic ties
Pedal wrench (if bike is shipped in a box)

Spare Parts

Inner tubes (2)
Spare tire
Spokes (6)
Toe clip strap

Chain link
Brake and derailleur cables
Extra cyclometer battery
Miscellaneous bolts and nuts

Cooking Equipment (optional)

Stove, fuel, and matches
1½- to 2-quart pot
Small pot
Frying pan
Pancake turner
Plate, bowl, and/or cup
Eating utensils
Can opener
Stove maintenance kit
Sharp knife (pocketknife OK)

Personal Items

Sunglasses
Sunscreen and sun-blocking lip balm
Toothbrush, toothpaste, and dental floss
Soap and shampoo

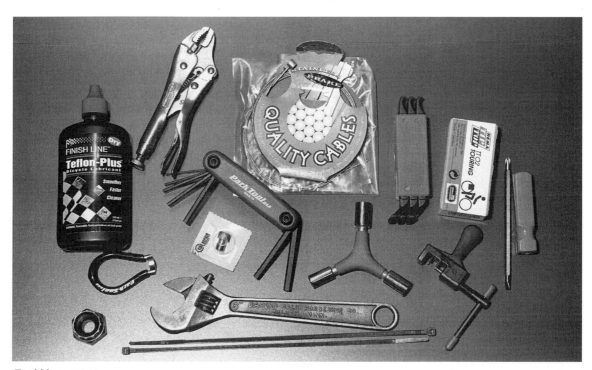

Tool kit contents.

Complete camping gear for the solo cyclist (larger groups can share community items). Note that clothing has been kept to a minimum. This is not as unwieldy a load as it looks because most items will fit the panniers or, like the helmet and shoes, be worn on the road. Total weight, without food or water, is about 30 pounds. This equipment was carried in the touring rig shown in the photo on page 89.

Comb
Nail clippers
Toilet paper

First-Aid and Emergency Materials

Matches (regular and waterproof-windproof)
Telephone change
Insect repellent
Aspirin or ibuprofen (for inflammation)
StingEze (insect bite painkiller)
Antihistamine
Talcum powder, Chamois Butt'r, or other antichafe product
Water purification tablets
First-aid cream
Tweezers
Elastic bandage
Adhesive bandages
Butterfly bandages
Sewing kit with needle

Additional Items (as needed or desired)

Camera and film
Writing tablet and pens (2)
Playing cards
Reading material
Warm gloves
Bandanna or ear warmers
Waterproof helmet cover
Camp shoes
Swimsuit
Water filter
Spare eyeglasses or contact lenses
Eyeglass repair kit
ThermaLounger
Day pack (for hiking)
Compass
Snakebite kit
Hand lotion
Petroleum jelly
Long pants
Stocking cap
Ben-Gay

Shedding Ounces

A full touring rig, complete with food and water, will weigh about 50 pounds. If it were a backpack, that might be unmanageable. But bicycles have wheels and can be equipped with low gears. That makes a lot of difference. A friend who once did a student-budget crossing of North America notes that by the end of the trip, weight had become so insignificant to him that he was saving money by purchasing peanut butter in 5-pound containers. And when photographer Vera Jagendorf and I did the first edition of this book, we toured mountainous eastern Oregon with a 7-pound tripod, five camera bodies, assorted lenses, and what seemed like enough film to keep Kodak in business for a month. I could barely lift my loaded bike off the ground, but we nevertheless did as much as 4,500 feet of climbing a day.

Still, it's more fun to go as lightly loaded as possible. Even if you don't mind the weight, it's nice to get rid of unwanted bulk. Entire books have been written on this subject by long-distance hiking trekkers such as Ray Jardine and Ryel Kestenbaum. I've found that a considerable amount of weight can be eliminated by purchasing better equipment—but that doing so costs about $10 an ounce. Here are a few suggestions for getting the biggest bang for your buck.

- At the end of each outing, sort through the items in your pack, noting whether you used them. If the answer is *no* and they aren't vital spare parts, tools, rain gear, or other safety equipment, consider leaving them behind next time.
- Get an inexpensive postal scale or diet scale and weigh everything in your pack, item by item. You may get some surprises. Toiletries, for example, can add up. Do you really need that entire 4-ounce bottle of hand lotion, or can you just take an ounce of it in a 50-cent squeeze bottle? Can you replace bath soap, shampoo, and dish soap with a similar squeeze bottle of a multipurpose liquid soap sold for backpackers? A few changes like this can produce a couple pounds' savings.
- Invest in lightweight tools designed for use on the road. Look for multiuse tools such as needlenose Vice-Grip pliers/wire cutters.
- Consider replacing your sleeping bag. Bag designers are always creating lighter, warmer designs. I recently shaved 18 ounces off my load by upgrading the summer-camping bag I'd been using for 15 years. And the new, lighter one was warmer. Similarly, don't carry a beefier bag than you need. On unexpectedly chilly nights, a stocking cap can allow you to stretch your sleeping bag a few degrees below its normal temperature range. That said, don't go overboard with this; shivering all night is a good way to ruin an outing.
- Upgrade your tent. For most bicycle touring, there's really no need to carry more than 3 pounds of tent per person, and you may be able to go even lighter.
- Ditch the stove, pots, stove fuel, and cooking utensils, and eat most meals in cafés. It's a good way to meet the locals. An occasional cold dinner in camp won't kill you, either. If you're a caffeine addict, you may be able to substitute instant iced tea (chilled overnight) for your morning java.
- Don't carry too many changes of clothes. T-shirts, for example, weigh about 8 ounces apiece; a week's supply weighs more than your share of the tent. Instead, carry multiple weights of clothes that can be worn in layers appropriate for all expected conditions. Hand wash them whenever the opportunity arises.
- Check your equipment for heavy items scavenged from household or car-camping use and replace them with specialty backpacking equipment. Shifting from a D-cell to an AA-cell flashlight, for example, saves a lot of weight. So does replacing that fluffy cotton towel with a quick-drying polypropylene one designed for backpackers.
- Don't forget the weight of your panniers. There's no reason to carry heavy mountain bike models unless you'll need the added protection against scrapes and thorns.

LIFE ON THE ROAD

9

On organized rides or other catered outings, once you've chosen a tour, all other decisions are made for you by the tour director. Pick tours based on the entry fee, the size of the group, and your interest in the area.

On van-supported and self-contained tours, however, not only do you get to choose the destination, but you also have full control over the route. That may be a bit intimidating at first, but once you learn a few basic skills, the added flexibility is one of the great benefits of designing your own tour. If the weather's unpleasant, you're under no obligation to pedal a preset distance to the next camp. If a side road looks inviting, you're free to explore. You can even take a day off to go hiking or linger at a pleasant village, campground, or seaside resort. Or if you get a dream tailwind, you can run with it all day, milking it for all it's worth.

Picking good bike routes is part planning, part luck—with an element of "winging it" with on-the-road decisions based on your developing familiarity with the region you're touring. These spontaneous decisions, in fact, are a major part of the touring experience, contributing much to the freedom of the road, especially if you're fully self-contained, able to camp along the way if a "shortcut" proves longer or more rugged than expected.

CHOOSING A DESTINATION

The first step is choosing a destination. The best ones have low traffic, plenty of places to camp, small-town hospitality, and compact topography that doesn't force you to travel interminably on straight, flat roads. Good options are

- islands
- coasts and lakeshores, if there are back roads to keep you away from the heaviest traffic
- spectacular mountain country, such as Glacier National Park and the Canadian Rockies, where the scenery is worth the cost in hills and RVs
- gentle farm country with plentiful back roads

Other areas like deserts and high plains can also be rewarding but aren't good places for your first outings.

To preserve the spontaneity, plan your routes only in general terms and try not to schedule too tightly, especially if you have an airplane to catch at the end. Many things can slow you down, and it's nice to have a day's grace. The best way to tour is without a fixed return date, but that's a luxury few can afford.

Point-to-point routes and loop routes each have their advantages. Point-to-points allow you to cover more terrain but complicate the transportation problem at the beginning and end. Loops allow you to leave a car at the start but almost certainly mean that part of the route will be upwind.

A good compromise if you're touring close to home is to go to the start by train, plane, or bus and bike back home. Then, if you run out of time, you might even be able to prevail on your spouse or a friend to come get you. The disadvantage, of course, is that this limits you to places close enough to home that you can pedal all the way back.

Planning around Wind

Most people have been taught that the average airflow across the U.S. is from west to east. This is true enough to be important in planning cross-country trips, but local wind patterns may be considerably different. Where I live, for example, fair-weather winds are northerly, and storm winds come from the south.

To get this information for a region far from home, call the National Weather Service at the nearest sizeable town or log onto the Internet to peruse climate information for your destination. But be careful to get the right statistic. I once was told that the average June wind in western Nebraska was 10 mph from the northwest. Such gentle breezes weren't my image of Nebraska, and when I got there I found that the statistic I'd been given must have been a monthlong average. Midafternoon winds alternated between 30 mph out of the northwest and 20 mph from the southeast.

Terrain features radically modify wind patterns. Deep valleys can trap and funnel wind into a gale that can either blow you up slope or ruin a good downgrade. In the mountains on hot summer afternoons, the wind often blows uphill from both sides as hot air rises out of the valleys. This is so common that it's rare to get a tailwind on an afternoon downgrade, regardless of what direction you're going.

Wind is almost always stronger in the afternoon than in the morning. If a day dawns windy, hit the road early to avoid gales later.

WHERE TO SPEND THE NIGHT

If there's one question that noncyclists most frequently ask, it's "Where do you spend the night?" With credit-card touring, the answer is obvious: motels, inns, or B&Bs. But on a self-contained camping tour, the options are wide open: state parks, national forests, church lawns, highway rest areas, and the yards or guest bedrooms of local residents—all are possibilities.

Campgrounds

The first few times you do self-contained camping tours, you'll want to avoid worries by heading for a state park, reserving a campsite in advance, if possible, so you know it'll be waiting for you. But the principle advantage of self-contained touring is the freedom you have to avoid a reservation-bound schedule. As a practical matter, scheduling reservations for anything longer than a weekend trip can be difficult—especially given the vagaries of wind, weather, and the whims of your own body. After a few shakedown excursions, it's time to take the plunge and go without reservations, learning to spot the camping opportunities as they arise.

The fundamental rule in choosing campsites is safety—with comfort and cost close behind.

Established campgrounds, whether commercial or in parks or forests, rank high on the first two scales, especially since they often offer such amenities as running water, swimming, and scenery. Public ones are the least expensive, though some private mom-and-pop operations may offer inexpensive "cyclist's specials." Large private campgrounds sometimes charge for sewer and electric hookups as though you were an RV.

Camping in such places by bicycle is different from camping in them by car. By car, if a campground says it's full, it's full, and you have to drive on in search of another place to spend the night. By bicycle that could be a catastrophe, and campground managers know it. Even when a campground is busily turning away your 4-wheeled cousins, it will probably find room for you.

Even better, some campgrounds, especially in state parks along popular cycling routes, offer special bike-only sites, which you'll wind up sharing with however many other cyclists happen to be passing through. Other parks might send you to a picnic area or some other place that would be verboten for automobiles. These quiet areas often make ideal campsites.

In general, the quietest, most spacious tent sites are usually in the more primitive public campgrounds. But it's a trade-off; private campgrounds and developed state parks are more likely to have showers.

For another good source of campgrounds, try the national forests. Expect the camping to be primitive, with drinking water (probably) but pit toilets rather than modern bathrooms. When these campgrounds fill, though, there's not likely to be a bike-only site or a grassy picnic area for overflow; the only level, brush-free spots are usually the designated sites. But before you give up, cruise slowly around as though you're looking for a site. If your party is small (four people is a bit large), there's a

good chance someone will invite you to share one. It's a great way to meet some interesting people, often ones who'd love to be doing what you are— or who did it when they were younger.

Municipal Parks

In farm country, especially in the Midwest and Great Plains, small-town municipal parks are another good option. Generally, the smaller the town the more likely it is to permit camping and the less likely you are to be hassled by kids. The best choices are usually towns of 200 to 1,500 people—small enough for hospitality but large enough to have nice parks. On Friday and Saturday nights, opt for the smallest towns you can find; even there, cruising teenagers can be a nuisance. They're not likely to be dangerous, but they can ruin a night's sleep.

Municipal park camping is a great way to meet the local people. By the time you've pitched camp, half the town will know you're there. If the day's still young, don't be surprised if several of them come by to visit or talk to you while you're buying groceries. Grade school kids may also come by on their bikes. Whether their attitude is awestruck hero worship or feigned nonchalance, being the center of all that attention will do as much as a good night's sleep to put the spring back in your legs.

Not all towns allow this type of camping. The closer you are to a big city or a major tourist area, the more suspicious the locals will be of you—and the more concern you should have about being hassled. If in doubt about safety or legality, ask someone in authority. But expect that the answer won't vary widely from town to town; if it's legal in one, it's probably legal in neighboring ones as well.

Nontraditional Campsites

Campgrounds and municipal parks are the most conventional places to camp, but they aren't always available. Once you start getting creative, though, the choices are almost endless.

In ranch or farm country or in a tiny crossroads too small to have a park, you can always ask to pitch a tent on someone's lawn. There aren't many rural or small-town folk who'd turn you down. The biggest obstacle is working up the nerve to ask, especially at a farmhouse surrounded by big dogs. If walking up to a door and knocking seems too brazen, try hanging out at a general store or café, chatting with the customers. You don't have to specifically ask to camp on their lawns. Just ask about campsites in general; if nothing else comes to mind, someone's likely to volunteer.

If the café or general store has a lawn (not uncommon in the tiniest towns), the same approach may get you permission to camp there. You'll probably also get access to the bathroom, at least during store hours. I've used this technique with gas stations and taverns, too, but their normal clienteles don't make quite as good company as what you'll find at cafés and general stores. Regardless of the type of store, I express my gratitude by eating there or stocking up on groceries.

Churches are another good source of accommodations. Their well-maintained lawns are ideal for camping, and the pastor may be glad to help. Ask for permission at the church office. If that's closed, one of the nearby houses is often the pastor's home. On a rainy night, you might even be invited to sleep indoors on the floor of the church's social hall.

In a slightly larger town, try asking the police. They may simply direct you to the nearest state park, 20 miles away, but more likely they'll give you useful suggestions, possibly including permission to camp in a park where it wouldn't otherwise be allowed. I've even had the police offer to "send by an extra patrol" to make sure nobody's bothering me.

If night catches you in the middle of a national forest or on public range land, the solution is even easier. Wheel off into the woods, out of sight of the road so that any unpleasant individuals who happen to drive by won't know you're there. To be safest, don't let anyone see you leave the road, don't light a fire, and use your flashlight sparingly. If no one knows where you are, you're unlikely to be bothered.

In sagebrush or scrub desert, look for gullies or piles of jumbled rocks to hide in or behind (don't camp in a gully, though, if there's any threat of a flash flood). Another way to get out of sight is by camping under a bridge. But don't camp in such places if they're cluttered with beer cans—they may be favorite drinking sites of local rowdies.

Abandoned buildings or houses under construction also offer tempting places to spend the night, especially if its raining. Use them only as a last resort. They're obvious enough camping spots that you may have unwanted company. Furthermore, abandoned-looking buildings may not actually be abandoned—and at a construction site the owner may stop by in the evening to inspect the day's progress.

Other tempting but illegal places are national parks (except in established campgrounds), Indian reservations, and private land of any kind. If you're attentive to other possibilities, there's seldom a need to trespass.

On highways, roadside parks provide camping possibilities, often with bathrooms and drinking water. These will put you on display to any passing motorist, though, so be prudent. Don't camp here if the road is heavily traveled or within an hour or so's drive of a major urban area unless you have enough company from RVs or people napping in their cars to make you feel safe. Many roadside parks have prominent "No camping" signs or rules limiting the duration of a stay to no more than a few hours. Don't worry too much about these; the police aren't likely to chase cyclists out in the middle of the night.

Finally, if good camping spots are few and far between, talk to any cyclists you meet coming from the opposite direction. It's always fun to meet your fellow two-wheeled travelers, and each encounter is a heaven-sent opportunity to learn the lay of the land.

Hostels

Because of the prominence of the American Youth Hostels organization (AYH), and because of the word *youth* in its name, hosteling is most commonly associated with college students. But you'll be equally at home even if your hair is graying. I've stayed in hostels a number of times, and the average age of my companions has usually been 30–45.

The difficulty with hostels is finding them. AYH can supply you with a list of member hostels, but many small-town hostels—which are the ones you're most likely to be dealing with—are unaffiliated. The best way to learn about them is by word of mouth. Ask the locals, and especially ask any other touring cyclists you meet along the way.

AYH's book of hostels is available by contacting its national office (733 15th St. N.W., Suite 840, Washington DC 20005; 202-783-6161; hiayhserv @hiayh.org) or visiting the organization's Web site, *www.hiayh.org*.

Spending the night in a hostel is relaxing. Count on running water, a stove (with or without pots and pans), and often the company of other cyclists. Some hostels have beds, others merely offer floor space. Either way, you'll usually need a sleeping bag. Some hostels provide gender-segregated dormitory-style accommodations; couples may have to split up for the night. Other hostels give you individual rooms or put everybody in one big (or little) one.

Inns and Motels

When credit-card touring, you'll spend all of your nights in motels and inns. Occasionally you'll stay in such places on self-contained tours—perhaps to avoid inclement weather, perhaps because you *really* want a shower.

Checking into a motel by bicycle is usually straightforward, but once in a while a clerk will object to bicycles in the room. If so, ask what the concern is. If it's a vague comment about "dripping grease on the carpets," you can offer reassurance that your well-maintained machine won't do that. If all else fails, ask point-blank whether the motel will accept responsibility if your bicycle or any of your equipment is stolen. The answer will undoubtedly be no, but that may get you access to a locked storeroom.

Even when you aren't hassled about bringing the bike indoors, don't create ill will for future cyclists by tracking mud on the carpet or leaving scuff marks on the walls.

ROUTE PLANNING: YOU SAY THERE'S A BIG HILL AHEAD?

Good maps and map-reading skills are important on even the most spontaneous tours, greatly reducing the element of luck in both the planning stage and in making those mile-by-mile decisions.

There are three basic types of maps available: bicycling maps, highway maps, and topographic maps. Don't rely solely on one map or one type.

County maps are also useful, but they can be hard

Sampling Local Life

Touring is more than pedaling from place to place. It is a process of learning about the land and its people. After a few days on the road, it can also become a new, relaxing way of viewing life.

Part of that lifestyle is pausing—not just for the grand attractions that would catch the attention of any tourist but also at small, intimate places passed up by motorized tourists: mountain streams, small-town museums, off-the-beaten-path wildlife refuges. Sometimes you may find yourself chatting with a general-store proprietor who's lived in the same small town all her life or taking a siesta at a tiny roadside park—in itself an experiment in a lifestyle quite different from both normal work and the average vacation. Learning to mix these with pedaling is a formula for cycle touring at its finest.

to find and a weeklong tour can cross quite a few counties. You can usually manage without them.

Bicycling Maps

Bicycling maps are highway maps on which some roads have been color coded by a scheme, such as green, yellow, and red for "good," "mediocre," and "deadly." They might also show hills, campgrounds, prevailing wind directions, ferries, hostels, and so forth. Don't expect them to include every paved road; farm lanes are often too numerous.

The ideal map would state shoulder widths in feet, with the color codes used only for traffic volume. You could then make your own trade-offs between the two. A high-traffic road with a 10-foot shoulder, for example, is safe but a lot less pleasant than one that's shoulderless but with low traffic. Unfortunately, many bike maps combine such information into the color codes according to trade-offs that may not be clearly stated. Familiarity with the map will gradually give you an understanding of its makers' priorities, but it's still frustrating.

Highway Maps

Cycling maps are a luxury. You can navigate almost as well from highway maps, learning to pick potential bike routes at a glance. Because these maps often show more detail than bike maps, they're useful even if you have a cycling map. Here are some route-finding tips, but don't expect them to work every time. Even the most experienced cyclists are sometimes surprised.

- Look for roads that have been bypassed by freeways or other main highways.
- Avoid roads that are the shortest routes between major cities, even if you never get close to either city.
- Look for the secondary roads, often designated as "other paved" in the map legend and identified on the map by gray or light blue lines. These are often your best choices—just make sure they're paved. In lightly populated areas, though, don't automatically rule out the main highways. I've ridden U.S. highways that carried only a few cars an hour.
- Does the road follow the pattern of the river drainages, or cross from one to another? One way you're likely to be on flat bottom land; the other will be hilly.
- If the road parallels a main river, how closely does it follow the water? The farther away it is, the more likely it is to bounce along the bluff rather than stay on the floodplain.
- Curvy roads deter high-speed traffic, but when they wind all over the place, there's usually a reason, often big hills. In forested country, winding roads might also be heavily vegetated, with limited sight distance. Ride them only if you're comfortable with such conditions.
- Coast and lakeshore roads could be flat or could bounce from headland to headland—it can be hard to guess from the map. On summer weekends, heavy boat-trailer traffic can make them dangerous.
- Some maps use shading to indicate topographic relief. Elevations, if given, also tell you a lot about the terrain.
- Look for national forests. These usually occupy upland terrain—or at least hilly land. If several tracts of forest lie in more or less parallel north-south strips, it's a good guess that each is a mountain range.
- Are the roads in an area parallel, with only a few wiggly connecting links? The parallel roads may be following valleys, while the connecting links cross the intervening ridges. For an

example, look at a map of eastern Tennessee.
- Know the area's overall topography. I once used such knowledge to good effect on a tour that began by following a wickedly hilly coastline. Inland, I knew, was a range of low mountains, backed by a long, flat valley. Near the end of my trip, I crossed the mountains to use the valley for a quick, easy return to my starting point.

Topographic Maps

Topographic maps are the best source of detail about terrain. The U.S. Geological Survey (USGS) maps identify the site of virtually every windmill, cemetery, church, and hamlet. They also show you every significant ditch, gully, and hill. (If you don't know how to use them, read a book on backpacking or talk to a friend who does a lot of hiking.)

The DeLorme Mapping Company of Freeport, Maine, has been publishing a beautiful series of state-by-state topographic atlases. Available in bookstores, they're too big to carry on the road but are great for planning. Benchmark Maps publishes a competing series that many find easier to read.

Another good set of topographic maps is put out by the federal Bureau of Land Management (BLM). These maps, which also distinguish public land from private (useful for picking campsites), cover only regions with a lot of public land, generally in the rural western U.S.

BLM or USGS topos cost several dollars apiece, and since each one covers only a small area, the costs quickly adds up. Buy only the ones you need.

Asking the Locals

Don't be too proud to ask the people you meet for route advice. There's no better way to get up-to-date information.

Ironically, however, there's also no better way to be seriously misled. People usually are pretty good about knowing whether you should turn left or right at the next intersection, but don't rely too strongly on their distance estimates or descriptions of hills or road conditions. Half the time, the advice will be wrong.

The reason is simple: by car, the difference

between 10 miles and 20 isn't really that much. Similarly, noncyclists just aren't tuned in to the details (such as a 5-mile gap in the shoulder) that can make the difference between a good route and a bad one. This particularly goes for information about road surfaces. People usually know whether a road is paved or not, but "bad" gravel to a driver may be hard-packed dirt—bumpy perhaps, but passable even on a narrow-tire road bike. "Good" gravel may be so loose it's a problem even on a mountain bike.

If crude estimates are all you need (for example, is there a town with a general store in the next 5–20 miles?), none of this matters. If you need better information, discreetly ask more than one person and weigh the credibility of the answers. The most reliable ones come from other cyclists; the next best from truck drivers or farmers familiar with the back roads. But even then you can get misled. I've asked farmers the distance from their farm to the nearest town—something I'd expect them to know—only to have the answers be wrong by nearly a factor of 2.

Inaccurate Maps

The same caveats go for maps. Plan with a safety margin that allows for major errors. A friend and I once set out on a four-day trip we intended to be mountainous but not overly taxing. Based on 3 maps and a telephone conversation with a ranger at a park along the route, we expected no more than 2,000 feet of climbing a day, probably less. Instead, we found that all of our maps lied, the park ranger had badly underestimated the elevations, and only the BLM topos (which we didn't consult until afterward) revealed the awesome truth: our 240-mile loop had an incredible 20,000 feet of climbing—the most macho thing either of us had ever done by bicycle.

Our maps had omitted the highest pass in the region (a 3,000-foot climb) and had placed a town on the wrong side of a hill. Two other towns turned out to be ghost towns, with no sources of food or water.

Neither of us, before or since, has ever encountered such a succession of map errors. But the experience reinforced a lesson we both already knew: never trust too much to the accuracy of a map.

Farm Lanes

Farm lanes often provide the best cycling, but they can be exceedingly bumpy, dead-ending, or unpredictably turning to gravel. Sometimes, farm-lane navigation is best reserved for people who not only enjoy route-finding challenges but also have fat tires to see them through the occasional mistakes.

That said, there's much to recommend these quietest of back roads, which can wind so intimately through the landscape that they pass between a farmhouse and the barn that goes with it. Also, the route-finding itself carries a sense of pioneering adventure. One of the most rewarding tours I've ever taken involved navigating the back roads of central Michigan, stair-stepping southeast as I chose my route based on the quality of the pavement and the volume of traffic. Not only did I reach my destination, but much of the time I was on roads that weren't on the map.

This type of navigation is difficult to teach, but it's a skill some people find to be almost intuitive.

Begin by knowing the terrain. Don't expect farm lanes to cross major rivers—or even minor ones. In rolling terrain don't be surprised if these roads go straight over whatever's in their way, making them considerably hillier—and steeper—than the main thoroughfares.

The quality of farm lanes varies. Some states are good about marking dead ends; others aren't. In Wisconsin, virtually all farm lanes are paved; in neighboring Iowa, most are gravel. Elsewhere, road surfaces can differ from county to county.

In some parts of the country, farm roads follow the compass lines in a nearly perfect grid, 1 mile apart. But in California's Central Valley, the grid is not complete, and the roads aren't always spaced the traditional distance apart.

The best way to get this type of information is by asking local cyclists or stopping at a bike shop. You can also watch the farm lanes for a few miles before leaving the main roads to try them, noting how complete the grid is and what fraction of the roads are paved. Signs also help; if some roads are marked as dead ends, you can hope the others go through. A sign saying a road leads to a town is cause for hope that the pavement will continue at least that far.

Keep track of your progress on the highway

map. If the road you're following isn't shown, towns, county lines, lakes, and rivers make good landmarks. Knowing where you are will help you find campsites, know which way to turn at intersections, and locate main roads when needed.

Not Getting Lost

If the roads are laid out on a geometric grid, it's easy to keep track of direction as long as you remain alert. But if they wiggle and you don't have a good sense of direction, your first realization that you're going the wrong way may be when you come to a town you weren't expecting.

Sense of direction is a skill not easily learned. But there are a few ways to keep yourself headed the right way.

- Learn to tell directions from the sun. You can do this pretty accurately with a watch with an hour hand. Hold it flat, with the hour hand pointing toward the sun. As long as you're north of the tropics, south will be about halfway between the hour hand and the numeral 12. With a digital watch, try to imagine where the hands would point on an old-fashioned clock. Even if you don't have a watch, guessing at the time will probably aim you close enough to the right direction.
- If there's a numbering system on the farmers' mailboxes, keep track of the numbers. They probably go to zero in the middle of the county or at one of its corners, like house numbers in a city.
- Carry a compass.

Map Sources

Since information that shows up on more than 1 map is more likely to be accurate, it's a good idea to get several maps. Here are some possible sources.

- state tourism or transportation departments (best sources of bike maps)
- gas stations
- convenience stores
- tourist information centers
- bike shops
- chambers of commerce
- auto clubs
- backpacking stores (for topos)
- specialty map stores
- Adventure Cycling Association

Adventure Cycling Association, a national organization formed to promote touring during the U.S. Bicentennial, has mapped 25,000 miles of long-haul routes across the country, dividing them into segments that many people find perfect for 7- to 10-day trips. The maps tell you precisely what to do at every corner, have contour lines, and show the locations of bike shops, campsites, hostels, and general stores. See the appendix for additional information.

FINDING YOUR WAY THROUGH CITIES AND TOWNS

Bicycle touring and cities don't mix. Plan your route to stick to the smallest towns possible, giving a wide berth to anything bigger than 50,000 people—preferably smaller. Sometimes cities can't be avoided, especially at the beginning and end of a trip, when you might need access to public transportation. Here's how to make those encounters brief and reasonably pleasant.

- Get a map. A bike map might have inset maps of major cities, with recommended routes. Otherwise, get a city map in advance from your travel agent or an auto club, or buy one at a convenience store on the city's outskirts. In smaller towns, look for maps posted in gas stations. A few minutes here can save a lot of wasted energy later.
- Time your trip to avoid traffic. Sunday morning is best. Avoid weekday rush hours.
- Don't be afraid to ask directions. The biggest problem cycling through a sizeable town isn't getting into it—it's getting back out on the right road. If you're looking for a little blue line on the highway map, note the name of the first town it goes to and ask for the road by that name.
- Talk to local cyclists. They may even offer to lead you.
- Off peak, main thoroughfares are often safe and can be the quickest ways through town.

Guarding against Things That Go Munch in the Night

When bicycle touring, you can't store your food in the safety of your car. Like a backpacker, you're open to the possibility of having it eaten by anything from a mouse to a bear.

The traditional backpacking solution is putting your food in a spare stuff sack and hanging it in a tree, high enough and far enough from the trunk that even a bear couldn't reach it. Most cyclists are much more cavalier. You won't encounter bears in a city park; there the problem is more likely to be rodents. I carry a length of nylon cord to hang my food in a tree, but I rarely use it. More often, I put my leftovers in my panniers, operating under the assumption that mice can't climb spokes. So far, it's worked.

To be safe, I never keep food in my tent, nor do I eat there. It's one thing to have food stolen from my panniers; it's another to have a raccoon gnaw through the wall of my tent. If you *are* camping in bear country, hang your food in a tree, and don't sleep too close to it.

- Be flexible. If one road is dangerous, a better one may be nearby. Residential streets can be a gamble, though, possibly leading to endless cul-de-sacs and stop signs.
- Marked bike routes can be both helps and hindrances. Seeing the signs might reassure you that you've picked a good route, but if the route turns a corner, you don't know whether or not to follow. Trust your own route finding.
- Parkways often provide pleasant, scenic throughways and are favorite places for bike paths. But auto commuters are aware of their advantages, too, so watch out for traffic.

SHOWERS, SANITATION, AND LOCKS

Baths and Showers

At the end of a hard day, most of us want a hot shower. On tour that can sometimes be a tall order. If you absolutely *must* shower every night, stay in motels or commercial campgrounds. Some state parks have showers, but to know which ones you'll need a statewide brochure with a facilities checklist.

Nevertheless there are ways to get showers on most days, especially if you don't mind taking them midday. Most commercial campgrounds will sell you one at a reasonable price, but for an even cheaper shower, go to a municipal swimming pool. State park campground showers could also be available to cyclists, sometimes with no fee. And occasionally in a café or general store, one of the locals will greet you with the offer of a shower. As a last resort in a showerless wilderness, bathe in a creek or take a minimal sponge bath with the contents of a water bottle.

Laundry

You can wash dirty clothes in self-service laundries, sinks, and even in creeks (but don't use soap, even if it's biodegradable, in a creek). Wet clothes can be dried in laundries or, if you don't mind looking like a traveling clothesline, slipped under the bungee cords or straps holding your sleeping bag to air dry as you pedal. Mesh exterior compartments in your front panniers also work well.

Sanitation

If you're a backpacker accustomed to urinating in the woods and digging cat holes every morning, bicycle touring is luxurious: few areas are so desolate that you won't see bathrooms several times a day. But even in civilized country, bathrooms can be impossibly far apart by bicycle. When there's no alternative, wander off into the bushes or, in farm country, a field of tall corn.

Under these circumstances, the rules of backpacking sanitation apply. Urine is no problem, but if you take a slightly longer visit, dig a hole 6 inches deep—and bury the toilet paper, too. Women should bury their toilet paper when they urinate, or carry it away in a plastic bag.

Locks

Many touring cyclists rarely lock their bikes, even if they leave them unattended for an hour or longer. Similarly, on large organized tours, thousands of cyclists leave their machines unlocked overnight.

I like to be a little more cautious than that. Bike theft and equipment pilfering are rarely problems in rural areas or small towns, but they can be if your route carries you through a major tourist area. Bike shops along the popular Pacific Coast route, for example, all seem to have tales of cyclists who've lost everything and had to replace it. And bicycles are stolen occasionally on organized tours, perhaps by professional thieves from nearby cities.

For a lock, I prefer a lightweight cable, padlocked to the metal rails beneath my saddle, accessible but out of the way (as in the photo on page 53). The U-shaped locks popular in cities are overkill for touring, and too heavy. If you lose the key, lighter locks have the advantage that even a small-town police station will have bolt cutters sufficient to get you back on the road.

If there's nothing to lock your bike to, make it more difficult to steal by passing the cable through the wheels or locking several bicycles together.

Even the best lock guards only your bicycle. The best defense against losing equipment from your panniers is never to let your bike out of sight. When eating in a café, choose a table near a window, where you can keep an eye on your bike. At night lock it, and sleep close by. You might be such a heavy sleeper that someone could carry you away with everything else, but a thief won't know that.

If you do leave your loaded bike unattended for long, try to find someone to keep an eye on it. Or park it in a well-traveled place where a potential thief won't know you're not nearby, watching. If you go hiking, though, there's seldom any alternative to leaving your bike at the trailhead. Lock it securely, cross your fingers, and enjoy your hike—but don't leave your camera or wallet behind.

FOOD

The first time I toured, I was amazed by how much I ate. By trip's end, I was wolfing large pizzas without assistance and eating every high-calorie snack I could get my hands on—and had lost 4 pounds.

Cycling all day burns calories—lots of them—although how many is an open question. Such factors as equipment efficiency, wind direction, tire inflation, and whether or not you're drafting make good estimates hard to come by. For level-terrain riding without panniers, I've seen numbers ranging from 30–50 calories a mile. For mountain terrain, one organized tour, the Cycle Oregon, plans a 7,000-calorie-a-day diet for a 450-mile week. That's about 75 calories a mile, plus normal base metabolism (about 2,000 calories/day). And that's without panniers.

If you're bicycling to burn off calories as part of a diet regimen, the vagueness of these numbers is frustrating. But the bottom line is that on tour you'll be using 5,000–10,000 calories a day, maybe more. It's possible to gain weight, but difficult.

The ideal source of those calories is the subject of jibes between health-food addicts and the junk-food contingent. If you're looking for a diet to give you maximum athletic performance, consult one of the many detailed books on this subject. But the basic rules for eating on a tour are simple.

- The best energy foods are high in carbohydrates. Pancakes and spaghetti are classic ways to begin and end the day.
- Don't radically change your food choices simply because you're on tour. Eat foods that you know you like—ones that like you, as well.
- Remember that you're not trying to set speed or endurance records. So what if your lunch isn't ideal?

When you get home, though, beware—it's easy to gain a lot of weight before your appetite readjusts.

When to Eat

Another thing that changes is your eating schedule. Not only will you be eating a lot, you'll be eating frequently. Otherwise you may encounter the "bonk," a mild version of what marathoners call "hitting the wall."

Bonking comes on suddenly. One mile you're feeling fine; the next you can't concentrate and feel as though you're pedaling through molasses. If you're a racer who has to keep going no matter what, bonking is bad news. When touring, it's merely unpleasant.

Since bonking occurs because you've run out of energy, the solution is simple: stop and eat something, particularly something high in carbohydrates. In a few minutes you'll probably feel almost as good as new.

With practice, you'll learn your limits and how to avoid bonking. Regardless of how many pancakes I have for breakfast, I know I'll bonk after 40 miles—less with panniers, considerably less in hilly terrain. I carry a snack and eat it or stop at a general store *before* I hit those limits.

Beyond that, your eating pattern is up to you. Some cyclists snack all day long and never eat a real meal; others want to sit down and relax three times a day. Here's my usual meal plan; yours undoubtedly will be different.

- Dawn. Eat a cold breakfast, so I don't spend the cool morning hours in a café or waiting for water to boil. Pita bread, bagels, or granola are excellent starters. Toaster pastries such as Pop-Tarts carry well, can be eaten cold, and are high in carbohydrates.
- Midmorning. A second, "real" breakfast at a café, usually a stack of pancakes.
- Late lunch, 2:00 P.M. This can be anything from a sandwich to a milk shake to the lunch special in a café. Sometimes I graze on snacks from a string of general stores and convenience stores.
- Late afternoon snack.
- Dinner. Sometimes cooked in camp, sometimes another café meal.

Whether you eat in cafés or cook your own meals, there's no need to carry a lot of food—seldom more than a 24-hour supply. If there's any kind of civilization around, you can resupply at least daily.

Camp Cookery

Cooking is optional. You can travel all the way across the country living off general stores and cafés. But a stove substantially increases your range of menu choices.

Buying stove fuel in quantities smaller than a gallon can be a problem—one you'll encounter even on short trips if they begin with an airplane flight, where carrying fuel is illegal. But the problem is easily solved once you're on the road. You can buy fuel by the pint from a camping store, and some gas stations, particularly in camping country, have white-gas pumps. You can also beg or buy fuel from fellow campers.

A gourmet backcountry chef can do wonders with a single-burner stove or a wood fire. Most people, though, are at a loss dealing with anything more complex than spaghetti or pancakes. Freeze-dried backpacking dinners offer easy options (just add boiling water to a foil pouch and wait a few minutes), but they're expensive and difficult to obtain on the road. You'll eat better at a fraction of the cost by buying food in supermarkets. Here are some suggestions.

- *Packaged rice or noodle dishes.* Designed as side dishes for use at home, these make good main courses on the road. Check the cooking time before purchasing (some take 20 minutes), don't believe the stated number of servings, and add cheese to make them heartier.
- *Ramen stew.* Start with one or more packets of ramen noodles; add dehydrated soup mix, vegetables, and cheese. Quick and tasty.
- *Pseudo-falafel.* Start with bulk falafel powder from a supermarket. Mix to a paste, form into thin patties, and fry in vegetable oil at low heat. Serve with pita bread. It's not deep fried, but this falafel bears a reasonable resemblance to the real thing. Carry the oil in a small plastic bottle, sealed in a plastic bag to guard against leaking.
- *Burritos.* Warm them in your skillet or fry lightly in oil, quesadilla style. Use cheese, a tomato (you can carry one a few miles if you're careful), and any other vegetables you want. Packaged meat will also travel safely for a couple of hours. Or use refried beans, either from a can or as a powder obtained in health food stores, reconstituted with boiling water.
- *Soup or noodles in a cup.* Although they're bulky and easily crushed, these just-add-water products form an excellent meal starter, particularly on nippy evenings.

Space-Age Pots

If you're really trying to cut weight, titanium cookware offers a way to shed as much as a pound, compared to stainless steel. The weight savings compared to aluminum aren't as substantial, but titanium cooks better and dodges worries from persistent allegations regarding health risks from aluminum cookware. Titanium's not cheap, however: expect to pay about $100 for two small pots and a frying pan.

Single-Burner Cooking

Cooking a hot three-course meal for two people on a single-burner stove can be a difficult logistical exercise in pot juggling. But it's possible without too much wasted time and with a minimum of dirty dishes. Here's my two-pot approach for soup; a main dish with vegetables, noodles or rice, and protein; and a hot beverage.

1. Start with soup, boiling enough water in your smaller pot to reconstitute a package of Nile instant soup or Cup O'Noodles for yourself and your companion. Meanwhile, mix ingredients for the main course in your larger pot. This pot and your spoons are the only dishes you'll need to wash afterward.

2. Cook the main course while you're eating your soup. Stir frequently to avoid sticking. If you're fortifying it with cheese, add that at the end to reduce the mess.

3. Use your leftover soup cups for bowls. Boil more water in the small pot while eating the main course.

4. Finish the meal with hot chocolate, coffee, or tea, again served in your leftover soup cups (OK, so the tea may have a slight pasta flavor—remember, you're camping).

5. To really get the most from your soup cups, use them again in the morning for coffee, tea, hot chocolate, or instant oatmeal. Save the cups overnight, however, only if temperatures will dip low enough that you're not worried about food poisoning.

An excellent reference for preparing tasty dishes with a minimum of equipment is Don Jacobson's *One Pan Gourmet: Fresh Food on the Trail* (Ragged Mountain Press).

WATER

Water, at 2 pounds a quart, is the heaviest and most important thing you'll carry. Count on going though upward of a gallon a day—twice that in hot weather.

How much you'll need to carry at any given time depends on the distance between water sources, but at a minimum you should have three bottles (five if you're carrying heavy baggage), refilling them at every opportunity. If water sources are more than three hours apart (or temperatures are over 80°F), you could need even more than that.

Dehydration is insidious. Drink *before* you feel thirsty. The sensation of thirst develops slowly: by the time you feel it, it's well past the time you should have been drinking. The tepid liquid in your water bottles may be unappetizing, but if you're working hard, drink at least one bottle an hour even in cool weather. Drink steadily over the course of the day. Your stomach can only absorb about a quart of water an hour, so when you're sweating hard, you need to make maximum use of your stomach's absorption capacity by making sure there's always some water "in the pipeline."

If your water supply is limited, drink it; don't pour it over your head. Ounce-for-ounce it will do you more good inside you.

To tell if you're drinking enough, pay attention to your bladder. Drink a lot in the morning, even if it means visiting the bushes several times in the first few miles. On the road, start drinking when you realize it's been awhile since you felt any bladder pressure.

If you never need to urinate as the day progresses, you're dehydrating. Similarly, urine color in the morning is a valuable indicator of whether you've recovered from the day before. If it's dark, you probably haven't.

More urgently, a sensation of chills on a hot day is a not-to-be-overlooked warning sign of dehydration. Rest and drink, immediately.

GROUP SIZE

The cycling experience varies dramatically with group size. Large groups give you a wider variety of companions and also ease van-supported tours by providing a larger pool of drivers. Decision making, however, can become cumbersome. Large groups also have fewer choices of campsites and more chance of friction between people with different riding styles or preferred times of day for pedaling. Someone is bound to be dissatisfied with the daily mileage.

For self-contained touring, groups of two or four can be ideal. That gives you companionship and the ability to draft in a headwind without making your group so large that finding campsites is difficult. And because less of your energy is devoted to group dynamics, you'll have more opportunity to talk with the locals and get a feel for the culture you're visiting. A group of four is usually better than three because a foursome can split into pairs if people's riding paces vary. Threesomes can be awkward if you're not good friends, since it's easy for one person to feel left out.

Going Solo

The ultimate form of self-contained touring is going solo. It's not for everyone, but if you like your own company, it's one of the most rewarding ways of travel. Since there's no group, there are no group dynamics to worry about, and solo touring puts you in the closest possible touch with the landscape and the people who inhabit it. You can stop when you want, ride when you want, and do however many miles a day you want.

Special Concerns for Women

by Vera Jagendorf

As a woman with thousands of miles of touring alone, with other women, and with men, I find that two concerns are greater for women than for men: safety and bathrooms.

Safety is what everybody first thinks of. When I spent a 2,500-mile summer traveling through the western U.S., mostly solo, one question people constantly asked was "Aren't you afraid?" My response was always the same: "There's no reason to be. Everyone has been friendly and helpful."

The potential dangers aren't all that different from everyday life. Obviously, if you find yourself being threatened in the middle of nowhere, you're at a loss. But that can happen in everyday city life, too, and is probably more likely there than in the rural areas or small towns you'll be visiting.

As anywhere, the most important deterrents to hassles are awareness, avoidance, and confidence. It's when you show fear that you open the door to more than a verbal taunt. And somehow, after climbing a big pass or traveling hundreds of miles, it's hard not to do anything but exude an aura of *I can take care of myself just fine!*

Even verbal taunts are rare. When I traveled alone, women tended to react to me with mild bewilderment; men usually gave me instant respect. Even the "Hey, baby" macho types were no problem. What I was doing seemed to strip them of that *I'm-better-than-this-female* attitude. Awed out of their pretense, they became ordinary people, more likely to offer a beer than a catcall.

Being on a bicycle piled with gear itself arouses people's curiosity, encouraging them to talk to you when they'd never do so otherwise. Being a woman makes you even more of an oddity. You're also more obviously nonthreatening than a man. That brings out the best in people, making them want to show off the friendliness of their towns, while they travel vicariously through your story.

People will want to help you, inviting you in for showers and meals. Once, when I was traveling with another woman, a rancher let us sleep in an empty house. Other people invited us to camp on their lawns. Men get such offers, too, but as a woman you'll get them more frequently—probably daily, or close to it.

If you're traveling alone and are at all friendly, many people will want to buy you lunch or an ice cream cone or give you some other such invitation. Don't let city-bred sensibilities scare you away. There's nothing wrong with going into a restaurant with a stranger, especially if afterward you're going to be camped in a campground with dozens other people. You'll find out a lot about the town and the people.

Bathrooms. Men can relieve themselves on the side of the road and not look like they're doing much but staring at the scenery. Women are likely to want more privacy. But if the biggest plant around is a sagebush and the nearest town is 10 miles away, you have to learn to be quick or not to care. If you need more decorum than that, you should avoid touring in remote desert areas.

RICHARD A. LOVETT

It's also not as lonely as it sounds. Riding solo, you personify a deep American wanderlust, a dream shared by many people in the towns you pass through; you'll find that many will want to talk to you. You may also meet other cyclists along the way, solo or in small groups, joining them for anything from a few miles to several days, perhaps even making lifetime friends with people you'd barely have spoken to riding in a group.

Riding solo, expect to cover more terrain than in a group, even though you don't have a drafting partner. In a small group, when one of you has a flat, everyone stops. When one of you is tired, you all take a rest. Traveling solo you avoid that, as well as being more likely to ride at odd hours or late into the evening.

The downside is that your pack is slightly heavier, since there's no one with whom to share community gear, such as stove, pots, tool kit, and tent.

The risk factor is real but greatly exaggerated. If you crash or get sick, you won't have a companion to render first aid, but in rural country, people are usually extremely helpful. If you do get hurt, the chances are that the first person to come along will help you out.

When it comes to traffic, you might actually be safer than in a group. To begin with, you won't be tempted to ride two abreast. However companionable, that's more dangerous than single file. Secondly, when drivers encounter a group of bicycles, they often pass all of them at once, even if they shouldn't. Riding solo you're less of an obstacle and therefore may be less likely to be crowded.

The precautions to reduce the risk of being mugged or harassed are similar to those that apply to women, which are discussed at right on page 121.

CHALLENGES AND ADVERSITIES: WITH PROPER PREPARATION, BOTH CAN BE FUN (ALMOST)

10

HILLS AND MOUNTAINS

Bicyclists use the word *hill* indiscriminately to describe terrain ranging from freeway overpasses to full-fledged mountains. Often, they reverse the meaning of the word *good*. If someone tells you that the Continental Divide in Colorado is a "good hill," it's likely to mean it took her all day and she thought she was going to die before reaching the top. With practice, though, even "good" hills aren't so bad. Climbs test your stamina; descents are exhilarating but require more skill.

When approaching a daunting climb, resign yourself to taking however long is necessary to reach the top. If it's a mountain, it might be hours, so pace yourself accordingly.

Before the going gets steep, downshift to a gear close to the one you think will be appropriate. You can shift one or two gears easily enough on the hill, but it's hard to make big jumps when you're grinding to a halt.

Try standing up occasionally to vary the rhythm. Because your optimum cadence standing is lower than sitting, *upshift* one gear before you stand. But be cautious about charging up long hills this way; it's easy to injure a knee, and some touring bikes—especially when loaded—are unstable when ridden this way.

While sitting, choose a gear that lets you keep up nearly the same cadence you'd maintain on the level. This takes practice; even experienced cyclists often climb hills in gears that are too high. Sliding

backward a bit on the saddle also helps, particularly on steeper stretches. You'll find yourself doing this automatically; it changes the leverage of your pedal stroke and gives you more hill-climbing strength.

If the hill is too steep to climb any other way, flatten it out by "tacking" up it in a series of broad, sweeping S-curves. It takes forever, and you have to be particularly alert for traffic, but sometimes it's the only way other than walking.

On long hills, playing mind games can help get you to the top. "I'm going to take a break at the next milepost" or "in 20 telephone poles" or "when the sun comes out from behind that cloud"—any of these converts the climb into a series of smaller, less daunting goals.

Rest breaks. When you take a break—and only macho racer types feel they've been defeated by a hill if they do—shift into your lowest gear before you halt. Stopping somewhere other than in the middle of the steepest pitch in sight also helps make it easier to start back up.

Rest before you get seriously tired; numerous short breaks are preferable to one long one—if you stop for more than 5 or 10 minutes, your legs may start to stiffen up, especially if it's cool.

I ride frequently with a friend who is a master of the short rest break, stopping as often as twice a mile for 30–60 seconds. Riding with her, I reach the top feeling fresh and energetic and without spending a great deal more time than I would have if I'd been more macho.

Machismo is your worst enemy. It can hurt your knees or increase the chance of painfully sore muscles. If you have trouble forcing yourself to stop until you're about to collapse, remind yourself that you'll be pedaling again tomorrow. Frequent rest breaks allow you to cover more distance a day with greater comfort.

Descents

The fun part starts when you finally reach the top.

If the descent is "slow" and you want to go faster, hunch forward, bending low over the handlebars in a "tuck." Pull in your knees and elbows to reduce air resistance further, but keep your head up to see what's happening far in front of you.

Loose flapping clothing or equipment will slow you down. Zip up, tuck in, and button down for maximum speed. You might want to do this anyway since the downgrade may be chilly. Also, check your equipment to make sure nothing is in danger of getting into the spokes. If that happens at 40 mph, you'll regret it.

And 40 mph is the operative phrase. Depending on aerodynamics, your terminal velocity on a long, steep hill will be somewhere between 30 and 55 mph. What speed is safe depends on your confidence, your bicycle, and the wind direction. If your wheels aren't perfectly round, they could shimmy at high speeds. Spoke reflectors may also be destabilizing, and some bicycles respond differently to headwinds than to tailwinds.

Most people find that 40–45 mph is the maximum speed at which they feel safe. Cyclists have been known to tuck in behind trucks and ride the draft at 65 mph, but this is insane—think about what would happen if you blew out a tire.

If the hill is steep enough that your natural coasting speed is too fast, do the reverse of a tuck, holding your shoulders high and wide apart, leaving your jacket partially unzipped. This can knock several miles an hour from your speed. In loaded touring, the wind drag of your panniers will slow you down more than their weight is likely to speed you up.

You may also need your brakes. Because your weight shifts forward on the downgrade, you won't get much stopping power from the rear brake without locking the wheel. You might not even be able to come to a full stop with the rear brake alone, so you *have* to be confident about using both brakes.

If all you're trying to do is hold down your speed, either brake will suffice; the best approach is to alternate between them, letting one cool while you use the other.

If you must brake a lot, stop occasionally to let your rims cool, especially if you're carrying heavy baggage. It's rare, but enough of a temperature change from hot rims can pop a tire when the air expands inside it. Radical climate changes can have the same effect; I once met a California cyclist who blew a tire after dropping 6,000 feet from the Sierra Nevada into the blistering heat of the Sacramento Valley. Such events could be due more to improper tire installation than to temperature change, but I wouldn't run down big hills on overinflated tires regardless.

Blowouts are more likely from running over something sharp or letting a piece of baggage get in your spokes, skidding the wheel. If it happens, don't panic. It's usually the rear wheel, which is easier to control. Brake to a halt, using the unaffected wheel as much as possible. Try to go straight, especially for those first important seconds when you're shedding most of your speed.

Sudden blowouts are uncommon, so don't let the fear of one intimidate you. One of the great joys of a downgrade is speed—as long as you're not going so fast that you're on the verge of losing control.

Technical Descents

If a downgrade is smooth, broad, and reasonably straight, you can often just put down your head and "let 'er rip." But if the downgrade is winding, rutted, or full of gravel, it's much more "technical," requiring skill and judgment mixed with caution. Ruts, even ones that are hard to see, can grab your front wheel and wrench it sideways; gravel can appear suddenly as you round a bend and cause a skidding crash.

Avoid gravel patches if you can. If you must cross one, do so by going straight, without braking hard when you're on it. On curves, don't go so fast that you couldn't stop if you found the lane to be unexpectedly blocked.

You can negotiate technical descents even if you're not used to them by inching your way down. With practice, descending even a series of full-fledged switchbacks is a wonderful exercise, with mind and body working in perfect harmony as you lean right, then left, then right again, easing your way down the mountainside. You might be surprised to find that your hands become so tired from braking that you have to stop to rest them. It's a good opportunity to enjoy the view.

If there isn't a good shoulder, don't get too close to the edge of the road. Crosswind gusts are common on hills and can knock you 2 or 3 feet sideways before you have time to react. Rounding right-hand bends with limited sight distance, ride well out into the lane to increase the distance you can see, as well as the distance from which others can see you. On left-hand bends, riding well out in the lane allows you to ride faster by reducing the tendency of a crowned road surface to throw you in the wrong direction. Just don't ride so close to the center that you lean into the path of an oncoming car.

Wind Chill

Descending a hill generates wind. Simultaneously, you're inactive, not producing much body heat. Combine that with sweaty clothes from the ascent, and on long hills you've got a recipe for a good case of the shivers. On loaded tours, you'll generally have plenty of clothing with you. On day rides, organized tours, or other low-baggage outings, anticipate this need and carry enough clothes for descending in whatever conditions you're likely to encounter, particularly in mountain country. On day trips, turn back early if a climb takes you to altitudes that are chillier than anticipated.

If you do get stuck facing a descent with inadequate clothing, resign yourself to descending more slowly than planned. That cuts the windchill until you get to lower, warmer elevations. In mountains, the warm-up can happen in only a few miles. Temperatures change with elevation at about 3–5°F for each 1,000 vertical feet, depending on climate. If you get cold anyway, turn around every now and then and pedal vigorously back *up* the hill for a minute or two. That should warm you up enough for another mile or two of descent. But don't work so hard that you start to sweat, or you'll just get colder later.

Cold hands are another potential problem. Long-fingered gloves will solve most temperature woes; if you don't have such gloves, don't let your hands get so cold that you can't control the bike.

Mountain Weather

Just because the calendar says it's summer, don't count on "summer" weather in the mountains. I've encountered July 4 snow at 8,000 feet in Wyoming, and subfreezing mid-August nights in the high desert (4,000 feet) of eastern Oregon. Afternoon thundershowers are the norm in the Rockies from mid-July through mid-September, as well as in the Southwest, where the summer rainy season is locally called the "monsoon." The Appalachians are lower but are still high enough to generate potentially uncomfortable weather.

If you're going overnight, be prepared for chilly temperatures, and listen to weather forecasts (or ask the locals). Mountain weather forecasting is difficult, but it's at least possible to learn whether you're in a warm trend or a cool one—or whether a major storm system is approaching.

Hiking guidebooks frequently warn about the rapid changeability of mountain weather, but the reality's a bit more complicated. The weather can indeed change quickly, but not instantly. And it usually follows a pattern that with practice can be anticipated. The thunderstorm that suddenly rolled over the top of a nearby peak at you, for example, was probably preceded by clouds that, over the course of a few hours, converted a sunny dawn into a partly cloudy midmorning and a gray midday. Most people who get caught by surprise have failed to observe the signs of degenerating weather until the storm is virtually upon them.

Make a habit of keeping an eye on the clouds, watching the direction from which they're moving, so you can see what type of weather is headed your way in the next few minutes. In most of the western U.S., summer days should dawn clear; if there are puffy clouds at dawn (even tiny ones), they're going to build with remarkable speed— possibly spitting lightning at you by as early as noon. Plan accordingly. Even if it's clear at dawn, don't venture above treeline in the afternoon unless you have a clear line of vision in the direction from which the clouds are coming, and an easy bailout to lower terrain. By bicycle, you can flee more quickly than a hiker can—possibly even out-running the storm—but don't cut it so close that you wouldn't have time to fix a flat.

In the Pacific Northwest and the Canadian Rockies, thunderstorms are less common (although not unknown), but cold, soaking rains can settle in for 24 hours or longer at a time. These are generally preceded by bands of increasingly thick, high clouds that will start appearing 12–18 hours in advance. When it's still warm and sunny, it's tempting to shrug these off—and if they're far away to the north or south, the storm may indeed bypass you. But if there's a darker stripe of clouds behind them, particularly along the western or southwestern horizon, it's a good sign that a massive Pacific Ocean storm is bearing down on you and will arrive in a few hours.

Traffic

On an upgrade, cars usually present no problem. Drivers sympathize with your sweaty efforts, and you're going slowly enough that it's easy to maneuver out of the way.

On downgrades cars are more dangerous. You're going faster, so you won't meet as many of them, but that same speed makes it harder to get out of the way. Take enough of the lane to discourage cars from passing you on blind corners.

If a car does pass you with insufficient sight distance, slow down immediately to let it get by quickly. If a car pops into sight coming from the opposite direction, the driver passing you will have to choose between hitting it head-on or hitting you.

Even on straight roads, slowing down when a car passes is a good idea. Many drivers just don't understand how fast you're going, and it's not uncommon for them to start pulling back in the moment their front bumpers reach you. Trucks and long RVs are particularly dangerous. After hearing of a cyclist killed this way by the rear wheels of a logging truck on a 40 mph downgrade, I decided that the moment a long vehicle starts to pass me, the safest thing to do is to brake hard—until I'm going as slowly as the driver probably thinks I am. Being able to shy away from a long rig that cuts in too soon is yet another reason for keeping a safety cushion of ridable pavement between you and the edge of the road.

In some parts of the country, cars are almost uniformly courteous, even if they have to follow you downhill for miles. Reward that courtesy by looking for the first good opportunity to pull over.

Rolling Hills

In many states, mountains are conspicuously absent but hills are plentiful, forming rolling terrain in which you climb the same 50–100 feet several times a mile—an endless roller coaster that's every bit as exhausting as the Continental Divide.

If you have good knees, stand up on the pedals at the base of the hill, upshift, and "pop" the hill in a few swift, strong pedal strokes (this won't work on self-contained tours, when the weight of your panniers will hold you back). When you reach the top, sit back down, shifting to a gear where you can find a proper, fast cadence. Then use the downgrade to build up momentum for the next hill, repeating the process again and again and again. It's great fun—unless you run out of energy before you run out of hills. Pace yourself accordingly.

POOR VISIBILITY: FOREST AND FOG

Wooded areas are cool, shaded, and often threaded by scenic, little-used roads; in short they can be perfect for cycling. Take care, though, to make sure you're visible despite sharp corners or dense vegetation.

As with blind curves anywhere, keep your ears open to what's going on behind you, and ride well out into the lane to be visible from a greater distance. If a car comes up behind, move over to be safe, but don't encourage the driver to pass unless there's enough visibility.

Logging trucks. In most places, weekends present the most dangerous traffic conditions as thousands of urbanites flood to the hinterland. In logging or mining country, the usual cautions can be reversed: the greatest threats are on weekdays. Pedaling through such a region on a workday, keep your ears open and give the trucks the road if necessary.

Warning pennants. Carrying a slow-moving-vehicle triangle is one way to make yourself more visible under poor conditions. A different kind of high-visibility symbol is a warning pennant on a tall fiberglass wand. These orange flags are eye-catching and may give motorists advance warning of your presence over the top of hillcrests or around curves obscured by dense vegetation. They're useful even in the open, and in a crosswind from the

right they bend sideways into the traffic lane, encouraging cars to give you a wider berth as they dodge the flag.

These pennants aren't stylish, and they increase your wind resistance. There may also be compatibility problems with rear panniers. But the biggest drawback is that the pole, mounted by a bracket to your rear frame, may droop backward—right at eye level for any cyclist close behind. If you use one, mount the bracket at an angle that minimizes this, or tape the wand to your rack to give it a second support point.

Fog. Fog is extremely dangerous; wait it out if you can. If you absolutely must ride in it, use lights and reflectors but assume you're invisible. Yield to everything that moves—or looks like it might.

DESERTS

Deserts and semiarid country present unique challenges, along with some of the most beautiful scenery in the nation, but they're not good choices for your first tour. The heat, big hills, and long distances between outposts of civilization make them places to graduate to after you've developed your skills under more forgiving conditions.

The biggest of these difficulties is the sheer, raw distances. You can avoid heat by cycling at dawn or dusk or picking a season when the temperature is moderate. Hills can be inched up in low gear; dry air can be overcome by drinking plenty of water. But scenery unfolds slowly over the distances, in

rare cases (such as parts of the Great Basin) so slowly that you might spend 24 hours or more between resupply points.

Van-supported touring eliminates most of these problems by giving you a mobile snack shop and water-supply point. Organized tours frequently tackle such country, setting up temporary tent cities on ranchers' hay fields or rural school grounds. With self-contained touring, though, you need to be comfortable with heavy loads. Part of the weight will be clothing; even if it's hot at midday, a desert can be cold at night. But most of the excess will be water, especially if towns are far enough apart that you might need to camp on the open range.

Precisely how much water you'll need depends on the temperature and your body's water efficiency. The latter can vary widely. On one journey through 24 hours of hilly, semidesert mountains, I carried more than 2 gallons of water and used it all. My companion drank only two-thirds as much.

Don't ration your water—it's a myth that doling it out in tiny sips will make it go further. All it will do is make you miserable earlier. A better way to reduce your water use is to dress sensibly. Wear a light-colored helmet and a loose, light-colored shirt. Going without a shirt not only risks sunburn but dehydrates you faster as the wind sucks moisture from your body. Being highly visible is as important as heat reduction, especially if you're in an area where long, straight roads and dancing mirages can hypnotize drivers into reacting slowly.

If you'll be riding in midday heat, some of your training should be in hot weather. Some people, stupidly, try to train their bodies to use less water by not drinking on training rides. It doesn't work, it *does* run the risk of serious medical complications, and it teaches you nothing about how much water you actually need. Drink what you need, and keep track of the amount so you have a good idea of how much to carry on tour. Also, do your first desert touring in areas where the towns are close enough that you'll never have to carry more than a few hours' supply.

At each town, ask whether the next one shown on your map really exists, and find out whether it has a store. Highway maps are littered with tiny hamlets where nothing remains but the name and one or two buildings.

Not all arid areas are stark rock and cactus. The high desert of eastern Oregon, for example, is a land of sagebrush, ponderosa pine uplands, and frequent snow-fed rivers. But it's still desert cycling, with blazing midsummer sun, challenging hills, and long, unpopulated distances.

Thorn Country

Thorns, commonly associated with deserts, are even more of a problem in semiarid regions that don't quite qualify as desert. A simple warning: some things out there can eat your tires. The two I'm most familiar with are sandburs and goatheads. Both will puncture tires even if you have thorn-resistent inserts. In dry country, never ride through grass, even in a well-watered city park. In extreme situations you can pick up a dozen or more sandburs all at once. Some types are even reputed to grow in tar strips, so steer clear of anything green and carry more than 1 spare tube.

LIVING—OR AT LEAST DRINKING—OFF THE LAND

In some areas, much like a backpacker, you can reduce the amount of water you carry by drinking from streams. This is particularly appealing in the mountains, where creeks run clear and cold, but it can also work in semidesert country if it is well laced by creeks fed by distant mountains.

Anywhere, though, you must first purify the water by one of three basic methods. The most surefire way is to boil it for 5 minutes, a nuke-'em-dead approach to bacteria, viruses, and *Giardia* (a nasty single-celled parasite that has become the bane of backpackers). But even boiling won't do any good if you suspect chemical contamination.

A second approach is to use water-purification tablets. Lightweight and portable, these are perfect for emergencies and should be a normal part of your first-aid kit. The label will tell you how many to use, depending on water temperature and clarity. Make sure you also treat the lip of your water bottle by splashing a little of the water onto it after the tablets have dissolved. Don't forget the drinking nipple. Then let it stand for the length of time recommended by the label—usually about 20 minutes.

If boiling or using pills is too time-consuming, or if you don't want to drink chemical-tasting water, backpacking water filters offer a high-tech solution that gives you a quick drink with all the flavor of a mountain creek. These filters use a hand-operated pump to force the water though a very fine filter, sometimes combined with activated carbon. They're expensive, so take time to check out the various designs before you buy. Don't get one that requires three hands, and look for a pump handle that's comfortable to use, quart after quart.

Touring in the mountains, I prefer water filters because they allow me to camp on the spur of the moment beside a creek or in a remote, primitive campground. They aren't light, weighing about as much as a full water bottle, but a party of three or four people needs only one. And the filter can save you far more than its own weight by reducing your load of water.

Be aware, though, that filters clog easily. Avoid muddy water, or strain it with cheesecloth before filtering it. Also read the manufacturer's description to see precisely what the filter removes. Most filters are rated to remove *Giardia* and bacteria, but they won't remove viruses, such as the one that causes

Backpackers' water filters are a handy way to resupply on water between towns. Don't use them with muddy water, however, or they'll clog with silt.

hepatitis. It's important, therefore, to choose the water sources that are the least likely to be contaminated. Iodine and other water-purification tablets do kill viruses when used according to instructions.

A new backcountry concern is a single-celled parasite called *Cyrptosporidium*, which exploded into the national spotlight in the early 1990s when it sickened 400,000 people in Milwaukee, Wisconsin, killing more than 100. Increasingly, *Crypto* is found in backcountry water. Boiling kills it, and any water filter that removes *Giardia* should also be good against *Crypto*. Water purification pills, however, won't work.

"Need water." If you're brave and outgoing, there's another way to avoid carrying large amounts of water. I once met a cyclist who went all the way across Nevada with only a couple of water bottles—and a cardboard sign reading "NEED WATER." When he ran low, he hung the sign on the back of his equipment rack. The first RV, he said, always stopped.

If you don't have a sign, you can also flag down an RV by holding out a water bottle and waving it. But if you're so far off the beaten path that there aren't any RVs . . .

BRIDGES, TUNNELS, AND FREEWAYS

Bridges

Most bridges are no obstacle, but occasionally a wide, comfortable shoulder vanishes at the start of the bridge, forcing you to share a lane with the traffic, even on a busy road.

As with any narrow road, the best defense is usually to be assertive. Or take a sidewalk if one is available.

Where to ride in the lane depends on its width. If it's roomy enough for both you and the traffic, stay well to the right. If not, wait for a gap; then enter the bridge far enough out into the lane to force cars coming up from behind to either follow you or cross the centerline to pass. Most drivers will understand. If they don't, let them get angry; don't invite someone to sideswipe you by moving to the side if there isn't room.

Gusting crosswinds with weird eddies or backdrafts around pillars or railings can also be a prob-

Narrow bridges can be frightening. "Take the lane" sufficiently to force cars to cross the centerline to pass you.

lem. Be alert, ready to steer whichever way is necessary. This is another reason to be assertive in your choice of lane position: if you need to steer sharply to the right to keep your balance, it's nice to have room.

Some bridges have odd road surfaces, such as an open steel mesh that gives you a disconcerting view of the water below—sometimes *far* below. Unless you're acrophobic, the worst problem with these meshes is that they're slippery when wet. But small objects can also drop through, so make sure your bags are tightly closed.

Tunnels

Tunnels, even short ones, are dangerous. Inside, it can be dark enough that you're riding blind, and usually there's no way to get out of the traffic lane if you need to. A tunnel presents all the hazards of a narrow bridge—in the dark. If you have a support van, you can let it follow you, emergency lights flashing, or even carry you through.

That's the bad news. The good news is that as long as the tunnel doesn't bend, you're probably more visible than you think, beautifully silhouetted against the exit. Furthermore, drivers are likely to be as uncomfortable about finding you inside as you are about being there. Most will react with exaggerated caution.

To ride through anything but a short tunnel, begin by putting on your night-riding equipment: a reflective jacket, headlight, and taillight, if you have them. You're mostly worried about cars behind you, but remember that you're in big trouble if an oncoming driver doesn't see you and decides to pass someone else.

Treat the tunnel as you would a narrow bridge, waiting for a gap in the traffic and then pedaling through as briskly as safety allows. Some tunnels have sidewalks, but they're usually narrow, slanting, and dangerously close to the wall. Use the traffic lane instead, far enough out from the edge to be clear of rocks and debris. You'll also be more visible here than if you hug the wall. The worst mistake you can make is to crash—that *would* make you difficult to see.

Some tunnels have warning lights and signs proclaiming "Bicycle in Tunnel," which you can activate by pushing a button. These are reassuring, but don't rely on them too strongly; never underestimate the ability of spaced-out drivers to cruise ahead, uncomprehending.

Freeways

It might surprise you, but bicycles are sometimes permitted on freeways, particularly in the rural western U.S., where freeways can be the only paved roads. In some states, all but the most urban freeways are open to cyclists, but even if a state isn't that liberal, you may be allowed to use freeways to cross major rivers or for other short distances where there are no reasonable alternatives.

To find out if you're legal on a particular section of freeway, check the "prohibited" sign at the entrance ramp. If bicycles aren't mentioned, they're probably allowed. If you're using the freeway to cross a river, you'll sometimes get after-the-fact reassurance from a sign telling you where cyclists must exit.

Although freeways have wide shoulders that safely separate you from the traffic, riding them is no fun. They're noisy and smelly, and occasionally some driver who doesn't know you're legal feels honor bound to yell at you. There is also an endless succession of tire retreads, broken fan belts, hubcaps, and other debris, forcing you to keep alert. It's particularly easy to get flats from tiny pieces of wire in steel-belted tire fragments.

The biggest problems on freeways are interchanges. The difficulty doesn't come when you're getting on and off; then, the nice wide shoulder allows you to do your own thing unimpeded by the traffic. Instead, the problem arises when you're already on the freeway and want to go straight, through an exit. To do that, you have to cross the exit ramp without knowing which of the cars coming up from behind might suddenly veer into the exit lane without signaling.

Unless there's a big gap in the traffic, reduce the time spent inside the exit lane by crossing it at right angles, much as you would a railroad track. Follow the exit ramp until you have some room to maneuver. Then turn sharply left, aiming for where the shoulder resumes on the other side of the exit. Signal your intention as a left turn, don't veer into the traffic lane until you're sure you can get across safely, and don't loiter. Crossing an entrance ramp is similar, but here you can breathe easier because at least you don't have to guess which cars are coming your way.

Another problem with freeways is narrow bridge shoulders covered by pebbles and litter that force you out into the traffic lane. Although the traffic lanes are usually wide enough to share with cars, drivers don't expect you to be there and can't be trusted to be alert. Wait for a big gap in the traffic, especially one that's clear of trucks, and again, don't loiter. Luckily, narrow stretches of shoulder like this don't occur on all bridges, especially ones that are specifically intended as bike routes.

GRAVEL

Most cyclists who don't have mountain bikes won't venture onto gravel. But many gravel roads can be handled perfectly well on a loaded touring bike with 700 x 35c or 26 x 1.4-inch tires. The biggest problems are washboard surfaces, loose stones,

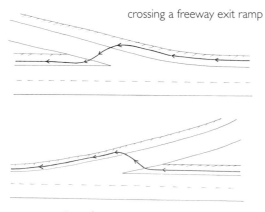

crossing a freeway exit ramp

crossing a freeway entrance ramp

Fixing a Flat Tire

Tools: tire levers, tire pump
Parts: tire patch kit, tube (possibly)
Time: 10–20 minutes

Every experienced cyclist has a method for fixing flats. Here's mine for conventional tubed tires. (It's not as complex as the number of steps makes it look.)

1. Move safely off the road, avoiding grass or weeds where you might lose tools or a valve cap. Lay down the bicycle, chain and derailleur side up.

2. Remove the wheel. (Most brakes have quick-release levers or other ways to loosen or unhook the cable to allow them to open wider than usual. Ask your shop to demonstrate; loosening the brakes makes it easier to remove the wheel.) Remember what gear you were in. Putting the wheel back on is easiest if you shifted to the smallest cog before stopping—but that means a tough start when you're ready to go, especially with a full touring rig. An intermediate gear is probably the best choice if you're sure you can remember it later.

3. Sit down, with all of the necessary tools within easy reach. Hold the wheel off the ground to reduce the chances of getting grit inside it.

4. Deflate the tire as far as possible; then use tire levers to remove the tube.

    Tire levers come in sets of three, but you usually don't need all of them. Each has a smooth tip on one end, bent upward at about 30 degrees. The other end is slotted and serves as a handle. Starting on the part of the rim farthest from the valve stem, carefully insert the nonslotted end of the lever between the tire's sidewall and the rim, with the bend turned so the handle slants away from the wheel. Push the tip of the lever beneath the lip, or *bead*, of the tire; then pry toward the wheel until the handle almost touches the spokes. This should cause a short segment of the tire to pop over the rim. Gently run the tire lever around the rim, holding the handle near the spokes so the tip won't gouge holes in the tube. Most likely, a single pass will free the entire side of the tire.

    If that doesn't work, start over, but this time hook the slotted end of the tire lever beneath a spoke. This will hold the gap between rim and tire open while you repeat the procedure with a second tire lever, a few inches away. Try the run-it-around-the-rim trick with the second lever —or hook it under a spoke and use a third (see drawing). If that still isn't enough, the lever in the middle is no longer needed; use it to extend the gap, leapfrogging around the rim as far as necessary. The entire procedure only takes a few seconds once you get used to it.

5. Starting at the side opposite the valve stem, pull out the tube. It's not necessary to remove the other side of the tire (see photo page 133). If you remove the tire completely, set it somewhere clean to avoid picking up grit that will cause a new puncture.

6. If you're in a hurry and have a spare tube, you may not want to bother with a patch. Get your spare tube, and skip to step 9. If the tube has already been patched several times, you might wish to discard it even if you're not in a hurry; multiply-patched tubes are prone to slow leaks.

7. If you decide to patch, pump air into the tube and try to locate the hiss that marks the hole. If you're not sure you've found it, spit on the suspected site and look for bubbles. If you still can't locate the leak, immerse the tube in water and look for the trail of escaping bubbles. Be patient; a slow leak may produce only one bubble every few seconds.

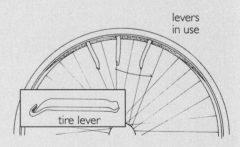

levers in use

tire lever

8. Patch the hole. Your patch kit should contain patches, glue, and a small piece of sandpaper. First, sand the surface of the tube near the hole to help the patch stick. Sand thoroughly, until you see black rubber.

    Make sure the tube is dry; then spread glue over it on an area slightly bigger than the patch. Don't worry if you cover too large an area; it won't stick to the inside of the tire or rim if

You needn't take the tire completely off the rim to get at the tube. Leaving one side of the tire still hooked inside it—as the back side of the tire is here—reduces the opportunities for grit to get into the rim, creating new punctures.

you use talc, as described below.

Let the glue dry until it loses its glossy sheen. Unlike most other glues, tire patch glue will still bond when dry—but won't bond if it's too wet. The patch probably has a flat side and a rounded side. Pull the backing paper off the flat side, and press the patch onto the tube. Once the patch is in position, press on it firmly to produce a strong bond. Squeezing tightly with your fingers will work most of the time, but if you can do so without picking up grit, it's better to lay the tube against your saddle and rub the patch firmly with the tip of a tire iron.

9. Now check the tire, trying to find the cause of the flat. There may be a thorn or piece of glass still poking through, waiting to cause another flat. Being careful not to cut your finger, run your hand around the inside of the tire, feeling for the cause. Many flats, especially those with small side-by-side punctures (often called *snake bites*) are caused by pinches, particularly when you hit a big bump with underinflated tires.

10. While inspecting the tire, also inspect the inside of the rim. Flick out any grit, and make sure that the plastic or cloth "rim strip" that covers the heads of the spokes, keeping them from poking holes in the tube, is in place and intact.

11. If you completely removed the tire to inspect it, slip one side of it back onto the rim. Then insert the tube inside the tire and smooth it into place around the rim, beginning with the valve stem—this is easier if you first pump a little air into the tube. A friend of mine always lines up the valve stem with the manufacturer's label on the tire. That way, when he gets a flat, he can use the hole's distance from the valve stem to identify what part of the tire he needs to inspect.

    While installing the tube, try to avoid pinches or wrinkles, and work symmetrically from the valve stem to keep the stem from being pulled to one side. I divide the tube into quarters, beginning with the valve stem, then moving to the side directly opposite it, followed by the points between. This allows me

to distribute the tube evenly. With practice, this will become automatic.

12. Snap the tire back over the rim, again beginning at the valve stem and working symmetrically away from it. Do this with your fingers if they're strong enough. If you can't do the job by hand, carefully insert a tire lever under the wall of the tire, this time with the curved side facing inward, and lever the tire into place one section at a time. You may need to use two tire levers, one on each end of the obstinate section of sidewall. Be very careful not to pinch the tube.

13. Look the tire over before inflating it. Most tires have a thin line showing just above the rim; it should be a uniform distance from the rim, without suspicious bulges. Check both sides, beginning at the valve stem. If the stem doesn't look right, push it firmly into the tire and then pull it back again, wiggling it as you do so to help settle it in place.

14. Inflate the tire partway, and examine it again. If it looks OK, deflate it; then pump it back

(continued next page)

Fixing a Flat Tire
(continued from previous page)

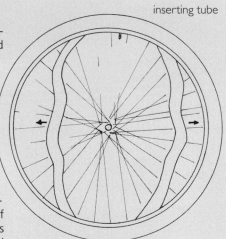

inserting tube

up again. This inflation-deflation-inflation approach gives unwanted wrinkles a chance to smooth out. You can now fully reinflate the tire, but it may be easier to maneuver it past the brake blocks if it's not yet fully inflated.

15. Remount the wheel, making sure it lines up straight in the brake blocks. This is usually no problem in the front, but the rear wheel may rub the chainstays. Some bikes have a pair of set screws in the rear drop-outs (the slots from which the wheel "drops out"), preset to line up the wheel automatically. Other bikes aren't so nicely equipped, and you have to twist the wheel around a bit in the drop-outs until it spins freely.

Mounting a rear wheel is confusing the first few times you do it, but it merely takes a bit of thought. First, insert the end of the axle into the chain loop. Pull the derailleur up and back, so it's out of the way, and as you slide the wheel into the drop-outs, let the chain settle into the gear it was on when you removed the wheel. Except for the gearing, the cahin and derailleur should wind up looking like those in the drawing on page 19.

16. If you released your brakes, reconnect them!

and sand, where your tires can bog down all the way to the rims. Nevertheless, on a good gravel road you can still cover 6–10 miles in an hour. On hard-packed dirt you can make even better time.

The trick to riding gravel is to take it easy, seeking out the smoothest, most rock-free path you can find, often following the tracks where repeated traffic has knocked most of the loose stones out of the way. Sometimes, you'll need to cut back and forth from one track to another, passing through loose gravel in between. Do so gently to avoid skidding the front wheel, but not so slowly that you run out of momentum in the middle. Similarly, avoid sharp turns. If you have no choice but to make one or if you feel unstable for any other reason, pull one foot out of the toe clip and hold it to the side, ready to brace yourself if you slip. Meanwhile, coast or brake lightly for a controlled speed reduction.

Downhills are more difficult because you need the brakes, increasing the chances of skidding. Don't be surprised if a speed that felt safe on the level is too fast downhill.

As on the level, find a smooth surface, watching well ahead for patches of loose rock. Use both brakes for maximum control, with your hands in the down position if you have drop handlebars.

Since going downhill shifts your weight forward, your back wheel will skid more easily than on the flat. Nevertheless, do part of your braking in the rear because a rear-wheel skid is easier to control than a front-wheel skid. To reduce the chances of a rear-wheel skid, transfer weight by sliding as far back on the saddle as is practical (this probably won't be necessary with full panniers). With practice you'll learn to tell by the feel of the brakes if you're getting close to skidding.

Going up a steep hill, stay in the saddle to keep from losing rear-wheel traction, and don't accelerate hard in a low gear. That can spit gravel backward—cool if you're a kid but not much use otherwise.

Gravel roads usually have little traffic, which you can hear or see coming from a long way off. That helps because it allows you to find the best place to ride, even if it's on the wrong side of the road. Gravel also provides a good opportunity to ride side by side, one in each wheel track. Just don't get too close, and beware of traffic on blind summits.

If the road is crowned, keep close enough to the center that the crown doesn't make you veer gradually but inexorably toward the ditch. Expect slow going in rolling terrain. Gravel roads often climb steeply over every little hill in their paths.

CONSTRUCTION ZONES

Construction zones are an irritant. Sometimes you get through easily enough, but often you wind up riding on gravel or very bumpy surfaces, dodging construction equipment, or sharing a narrow lane with one-way traffic.

The worst construction zones are those where a flagger stops traffic as a pilot car shuttles it through one direction at a time. When you encounter one of these, ask the flagger if a bicycle really needs to wait. You may not have to.

Shuttling through with traffic is easier on a downgrade because you can come closer to keeping pace with the cars. Some cyclists like to follow at the back of the line to avoid blocking traffic, but I prefer starting in front because it gives me a head start.

On rare occasions you won't be allowed to pedal through at all. If so, you'll probably be shuttled through in the back of a pickup. Even in situations where you are permitted to pedal through, the construction crew will often be happy to offer you a lift.

Bridge out. Closed bridges can force you to detour miles out of the way. More often than not, though, the bridge will be passable, especially if you're willing to dismount and carry your bicycle. The real question is how paranoid the construction crew will be about breaking their liability insurance rules by letting you pass.

Much more rarely, you might encounter bridges on which bicycles are prohibited. Usually this means there's a safer alternative nearby, but on one memorable occasion, I was denied passage of a Mississippi River toll bridge because the insurance carrier was concerned about the risk of ice prior to some arbitrary date in the late spring. The fact that it was 60°F didn't matter; I had to find another bridge.

If you're self-contained, such setbacks are a nuisance, but on day rides or credit-card tours, they can be calamities. In unfamiliar terrain, plan your route with an eye to what would happen if a critical bridge were closed, trying not to schedule such crossings too late in the day.

HITCHING A RIDE

Sometimes you encounter situations where you either can't ride or really don't want to. Perhaps it's because of mechanical breakdown, or truly abominable weather, or being caught by night without adequate lights. Maybe you're just tired. The only solution is to stick out your thumb.

It's amazing how easy it is to catch a ride. I've only had to hitch twice, but both times, the first van or pickup truck stopped immediately. Other cyclists report similar success. Sitting by the roadside with a bicycle, you are obviously nonthreatening—and obviously in need of assistance. The bike, even though it is bulky, is an asset: it proves your bona fides, and it's best to stay with it, rather than chaining it to a tree and trying to walk.

Similarly, it helps to be wearing your helmet as you hold out your thumb. It's one of the signs of a serious cyclist, subtly helping to prove that you aren't a bum. You might still wait a long time for a ride, but it's more likely to be because you're on a back road where there are no cars than because no one will stop.

AVOIDING CONFRONTATIONS

A loaded touring bike weighs 80 pounds, has a comfortable cruising speed rarely more than 15–20 mph, and is powered by frail muscle, bone, and sinew. Automobiles weigh a ton or more, can accelerate from 0–60 in seconds, and are driven by people who sometimes carry guns and have been known to use them on each other. With those odds, why pick a fight?

Many rude motorists are ordinary people who aren't used to dealing with bicycles. A shouted "Hey!" to get their attention if they're about to cut you off is reasonable, but other than that your best reaction is to get out of the way, congratulating yourself on your defensive cycling skills and forgetting about it.

People who harass you by shouting obscenities, telling you to get off the road, deliberately cutting closer to you than necessary, or—as was popular in one place I lived—leaning out the passenger window and barking like an angry dog are harder to be so philosophical about. Keep a cool head, even if they throw things or deliberately run you off the road. Ignore them if possible; pull off the road if not. Get the license number if the behavior warrants it and get a description of the driver in case the car owner claims someone else was driving.

Part of keeping a cool head is not letting the driver know how much he or she shook you up—that just adds to the sport. And don't wave your fist, curse, or flip the finger. You don't want a driver to stop and get out of the car, waving his fist in return.

These confrontations—rare unless you provoke them—seldom escalate to violence. If an angry driver does stop, keep your distance so he isn't tempted to throw a punch. Calm yourself *now*, prepare to apologize even if you weren't wrong, and think about escape routes. At the same time, a no-nonsense, I-can-take-care-of-myself attitude can do a lot to keep the situation from escalating further, even if you actually know nothing about fisticuffs.

If, instead of stopping, a motorist comes back at you for a second pass, let him have the road. Don't wait for the third pass. Look for people—a gas station, general store, occupied farmhouse, whatever—and head for help.

In camp, avoid harassment by staying in established campgrounds or somewhere so secluded that nobody can possibly find you. If you choose the latter approach, avoid fires and make sure your bike reflectors aren't visible from the road.

Once in a great while, when camping in a city park you could be hassled by kids. This isn't likely to be more than an annoyance—cruising teenagers honking at you every time they pass by or preteens dashing through camp, displaying their courage by thumping on your tent. The best solution is to let them have their fun.

RAIN

Rain is seldom welcome, except perhaps in August, if it's a light drizzle holding down the temperature when it would otherwise be unbearable. But riding in rain is usually unpleasant.

A good rain suit helps, as do fenders, and it helps to have clothing that will keep you warm when wet. Being wet is uncomfortable; being cold and wet will quickly rob you of energy and trap you into a cycle of alternately freezing and wearing yourself out pedaling hard enough to keep warm.

Even if the temperature isn't all that cold, getting overchilled can be dangerous, impairing both your coordination and your judgment. Hypothermia isn't usually as serious for cyclists as it is for hikers and backpackers, simply because you're close to civilization. But don't venture out onto long, lonely stretches without clothing to keep you warm enough even if it gets wet.

Camping in Rain

Camping in rain, your comfort depends on the quality of your equipment. A good tent won't leak except under extreme conditions. To avoid camping in a puddle, stay out of low spots that might flood. If you're using a groundsheet, tuck it completely underneath the tent so it won't trap rain running off the fly. Digging trenches around the uphill side of your tent to "ditch" it is an environmental no-no, unnecessary with modern waterproof tent floors.

You can buy waterproof covers for your panniers and handlebar bag or toss a tarp over your bicycle in camp, but with high-quality panniers this isn't necessary. Just make sure they're properly closed, with the storm flaps folded down over the zippers. Bicycles are made under the assumption they'll occasionally get wet. Check the lubrication of your chain in the morning, but otherwise your machine should weather a storm more easily than you do.

Thunderstorms

Take thunderstorms seriously. Not only do they entail strong winds and rain so hard that neither you nor the drivers can see the next bend in the road, they also involve lightning.

Start thinking about your options from the moment you see the storm. On the High Plains, it could be hours away, but so could the next town. In other parts of the country, towns may be closer, but haze can cut visibility, reducing your warning to less than an hour.

The best places to wait out thunderstorms are cafés or general stores. In farm country the farmers will almost certainly be happy to let you seek refuge in a barn. I've done this more than once, always having an interesting conversation with the farmer in the process.

When the storm gets close enough that you can hear the thunder, count the number of seconds between the flash and the boom. Sound travels at 5 seconds a mile, so you can determine how far away that particular flash is. The leading edge of the storm, of course, may be closer.

Thunderstorms can travel at up to 30 mph, so if the flash is only 5 seconds behind you, the storm can be on top of you in as little as 2 minutes. It's long past time to take shelter.

Caught in the open, you're in a potentially life-threatening situation. Find a place where you're not the tallest thing around—a road cut, a string of telephone poles, anything that's more likely to draw fire than you. But don't stand too close to an isolated pole or tree—if it gets struck, the electricity will fan out into the ground.

If you're caught totally in the open, you may have been told to lie down in a ditch, getting as low as possible. But Great Plains cyclists, who should know as much as anybody about lightning, say that it's better to squat on your heels as low as possible, touching the ground with only your shoes. If you avoid puddles, the sole material will serve as insulation, protecting you better than lying flat. Keep well away from your bicycle, whose metal will attract stray currents from any nearby strike.

Thunderstorms usually don't last long. Most of the lightning and the wind fury come in the first few minutes, with the danger declining after that. I've known thunderstorms to last as long as 24 hours, dumping 10 inches of rain in the process, but such monsters are rare. More likely, the storm will be gone within an hour, followed by sun, a rainbow, cooler air, and gentle breezes.

Hail

Hail stings. Big hail is dangerous. It usually comes in major thunderstorms, where you'll already be wanting to seek shelter from lightning. If hail catches you in the open, wear your helmet. If it's big hail, hold something over your head, such as your sleeping bag or a raincoat, spread wide so that the hail bounces off it rather than you, protecting your fingers as best you can.

When you're camping, a well-staked tent will protect you from fairly substantial hail; I've personally weathered hail as large as Ping-Pong balls. If you're worried about larger hail punching holes through your tent, hide under your sleeping bag and pad. Nevertheless, if you get enough advance notice of the approaching weather, it's best to seek shelter.

To avoid wind damage in any severe storm, guy out your tent and stake it firmly. If I'm seeking indoor shelter, I usually put my bicycle carefully inside the tent so the weight will keep it in place even if it collapses. Another short-notice alternative is to flatten the tent, stake the corners, and put the bicycle on top of the fly; you can do this in 2 minutes. Ideally, of course, it's best to break camp and

This Colorado hail storm dropped an inch of stones the size of chick peas in 5 minutes.

carry your gear indoors with you, but you don't always get enough warning.

Showers

Scattered showers are another story altogether. They usually don't move as quickly as thundershowers, aren't as violent if they catch you, and are often small and slow enough to dodge by adjusting your pace or zigzagging though the back roads.

The art to dodging showers is keeping track of which way the clouds are moving and how fast. With long experience, this becomes nearly subconscious—you simply *know* it, without knowing why you know.

NIGHT RIDING

Riding after dark is best avoided, but if you're forced into it, you have two concerns: to see and to be seen.

The latter is the most immediately important. Your helmet, wind shell, panniers, and bicycle should have reflectors or reflective tape on the back, front, and sides. For a rear light, a flashing red strobe like that made by VistaLite is highly visible, relatively inexpensive, and runs for a long time on a pair of AA batteries. The light is designed to replace your rear reflector, but when touring with bags you'll have to mount it to the back of your rack rather than to the reflector bracket behind your seat post, where it would be blocked by your sleeping bag. That takes a special bracket not easy to find. Don't leave the light mounted to the bracket when you're not using it. Its weight causes vibration that can fatigue the bracket metal, eventually causing it to snap.

Ankle-mounted, strap-on lights are attention getting but again aren't useful with panniers, which block them from sight. You could put the light on your elbow, but then it doesn't move up and down with each pedal stroke, robbing it of much of its effectiveness.

Most states require a headlight, but that isn't as critical for safety as a taillight because oncoming traffic is less likely to pass close to you.

Headlights designed to meet minimal legal requirements will help protect your from cars but won't do much to help you see. On a dark country lane, you can manage with a battery-powered headlight strapped to your handlebars or even with a flashlight taped to them as a rough-and-ready substitute. But in traffic, oncoming car headlights will periodically ruin your night vision, and most lightweight bicycle lights don't illuminate enough to compensate.

Generator-powered lights, run by a magnetic drive or a small dynamo that rolls against your tire, are brighter but sap enough energy to slow you down appreciably. Their brightness depends on speed, with the light shutting off completely if you stop. Some backpackers' headlamps are also bright enough to illuminate the road surface well in front of you, but strapping one to your helmet is potentially dangerous in a crash. You might, however, be able to rig it to your handlebar bag.

The best headlights, which are favored by bike commuters, use large rechargeable batteries to produce a dramatically bright beam. Unfortunately, battery life and weight are problems. One manufacturer rates a 44-ounce battery pack at 4 hours, a 29-ounce at 2.6 hours. Rechargeable batteries must be recharged, preferably after each use. On camping tours, that can be impossible, although on a credit-card tour, plugging a battery pack in at night is easy.

Ironically, that ability to recharge makes these heavy lights easiest to use for credit-card touring, when you're supposedly traveling light. But that's also when good lights can be the most important because if you're caught by darkness you can't just stop and camp on someone's lawn.

Most self-contained cyclists don't carry much in the way of a headlight. On the rare occasions when I've had to do more than bicycle to or from a restaurant after dark, I've been content to inch along by the weak glow of a handlebar strap-on, knowing that if conditions get really bad, I can give up and walk.

Coping with "Real" Rain

As a Pacific Northwesterner, I thought I knew all there was to know about riding in rain. Then I went to Iceland. It's a beautiful land with many things to recommend it—but climate isn't one of them. Studying weather data, I realized I was doing the equivalent of a time warp from August to November—without benefit of having September and October to acclimate. I wasn't sure my cycling gear was up to the challenge.

Several weeks later, I found myself standing in an Icelandic meadow, packing up for my last day on the road. "It's warm today," I thought as I pulled on a long-sleeved polypropylene jersey and midweight cycling tights. "I don't need my heavy clothes."

Then I got to wondering what I thought *warm* might mean after 1,000 miles just south of the Arctic Circle. I pulled out a thermometer and checked: 51°F. Obviously, my equipment choices had worked.

These choices would be equally appropriate for June touring in the northern Rockies or a fall century ride. At their core was a total absence of cotton. I had three polypropylene jerseys of different weights, sized so I could wear them all at once, if need be, two weights of tights, a vented Gore-Tex jacket, rain pants, Gore-Tex booties, long-fingered gloves, a rain hat, and a winter-weight fleece jacket and fleece pants, just in case. Unused clothes could be squashed into a compression stuff sack with my sleeping bag, and everything was made of fabrics that would keep me warm even if wet. In the preceding weeks I had occasionally been wind-blown, had frequently been damp, but had never been cold. And I rarely saw a temperature above 60°F. It may cost a bit of money, but you can indeed equip yourself to pedal comfortably in climates most people would shun.

The following summer I was back in Iceland, backpacking—and longing for a bicycle to ride between hikes.

GETTING THERE: PLANES, TRAINS, AUTOMOBILES, BUSES, AND FERRIES

11

MAKING A CHOICE

Unless a tour begins and ends at your front door, you'll need to get your bicycle to or from your destination.

By Car

Sometimes you'll want to avoid the hassles and expense of public transportation by driving. A sin-gle bike, sufficiently disassembled, fits the trunks of many sedans; two bikes, separated by a blanket to reduce scratching, fit in the back of a hatchback or station wagon. Pickup trucks and vans can carry even more. But most people will need bike racks, of which there are two traditional designs: roof racks and racks that mount to a trunk or the back of a hatchback.

Roof racks allow access to the trunk and let bicycles be taken on or off in a matter of seconds. Some can carry up to four bicycles on a passenger

car, more on a van. Roof racks, though, can be expensive and awkward to store when not in use. They also have to be left on the roof of the car when you're away cycling, although the best models have locks that greatly reduce the risk of theft. Some also have conversion kits that allow them to serve extra duty as ski or canoe/kayak carriers.

Rear-end racks are lighter and often fold compactly enough to fit in a closet—or a car trunk. The traditional design holds two bicycles, with the rack attached by hooks that fit into the crack formed by the trunk or hatchback door. Rubber feet help keep the rack from scratching your car but may leave black marks that are difficult to wash off.

Loading one of these racks, especially with two heavily customized touring bikes, is more time-consuming than loading a roof rack. Mount the bikes head to tail, and don't be surprised if pedals clash with spokes or derailleurs, handlebars with rear racks. Take heart; patience triumphs. To keep the rack from bouncing, fasten its lower end to the bumper or undercarriage with bungee cords or straps, being careful that hot exhaust can't damage the cords or your tires. Tie both bicycles securely to the rack, top and bottom, and use rags or old socks to prevent scratching.

When traveling with your bike on either kind of rack, remove anything that might fall off or be damaged by wind or rain. Pumps, cyclometers, and strap-on mirrors are obvious items. Also, make sure your handlebar bag is zipped shut; remove it if you don't want it bug spattered. Top-of-the-line roof racks have a cable to lock the bikes when they're unattended. A budget alternative is to pass a standard bike cable around both bicycles plus part of the rack.

Leaving a car. At your starting point, you need a safe and legal place to park. Many towns tow cars after a few days, so inquire at the city hall or police station. Probably you'll be given permission to park somewhere nearby. The smaller the town—as long as it's not too small for a police station—the more cooperative the officials are likely to be. Other good places to ask are state parks and national forest ranger stations.

By Plane

If you're flying, you can carry your bike with you as baggage. Many airlines supply boxes, obtainable at check-in. The boxes cost about $10, and there's also a sizable shipping fee (about $100 round-trip). Special rules apply to international flights (see page 145). Flights between the U.S. and Canada fall under domestic rules.

Boxing a bike takes only a few minutes, but allow enough time to avoid unnecessary panic. Loosen the handlebars, the same way you would alter their height (see pages 49–50) and turn them sideways, remove the pedals (see page 142), and then wheel the bike into the box. Put the pedals in your handlebar bag, if they fit, so you don't have to carry them as hand luggage. Don't leave the pump on the frame, or it'll fall off and rattle around. Similarly, remove your cyclometer head in case the bicycle winds up resting on its handlebars.

Tape the box liberally with nylon strapping tape or stout plastic tape supplied by the airline, running the tape completely around it in at least six places, three in each direction. This should hold the box together even if it gets badly sliced up. Write your name and address on the box in at least two places (also attach a name tag to the bicycle itself), and you're ready to go.

At your destination you'll need a pocketknife to cut the tape. These are legal to carry through airport security as long as the blade is no longer than a standard Swiss Army knife. The rest of your tools must be in your checked baggage. I usually put them in the handlebar bag so they can't get separated from my bicycle. When reassembling the bicycle, be careful not to strip the threads on your pedals.

If you're met by car you can carry the bike away, still boxed. If the box is damaged, open it immediately to check your bike; it's a lot easier to make a claim right away.

Not all that many years ago, airlines wouldn't insure a bicycle for anything but loss. But today, most accept responsibility for damage. When making reservations, inquire about this, and avoid carriers that aren't sure enough of their baggage-handling skills to take responsibility for them. Reduce handling by planning a minimum of connecting flights. Try not to mix carriers; not only does that increase handling, but you may have to pay fees to both airlines.

While making inquiries, check also on the availability of boxes. The airline almost certainly won't let you ship your bike without one, and lack of a box is a horrible way to get stuck an hour before a flight.

If you're planning on bicycling into or out of the airport, get a good map before you leave. In small-town airports, the way out by bicycle is often obvious, but in bigger cities, you'll need the map to locate a back door that isn't a freeway.

Bulletproofing your bike. Airline boxes are flimsy, protecting your bike only if it's reasonably well handled. As long as the airline takes responsibility, I accept the convenience of the box provided. If something goes wrong, I draw reassurance from the fact that any city large enough to have an airport will almost certainly have a bike shop. But if you want extra protection, there are sturdier ways to box your bike.

The simplest is by using some of your other baggage as padding. Camping gear, such as your sleeping bag, tent, and sleeping pad, is particularly useful. Putting this in your bike box is also a good way to consolidate baggage, although the extra weight increases the chance that the box will be torn during handling. Make sure your name is on everything in case the box bursts, and don't use small, loose items that can easily fall out of a small hole. Wadded-up newspaper is also good padding.

If you want a stronger box, ask a bike shop for a box that has been used to ship a new bike. If there's a charge, it won't be much. These shipping boxes are still cardboard, but they're sturdier, partly because they're smaller. Unlike the airline boxes, they come in a number of sizes, so get one that's big enough. For touring bikes, remember that the long wheelbase means you'll need a bigger box than was used to ship a similar-sized racing bike; if in doubt get the biggest box you can find.

Packing one of these boxes requires partially disassembling the bike. Doing this for the first time on the evening before a flight is a good way to wreck a night's sleep; if you've heavily customized your bike, everything from the water-bottle cages to the front and rear racks may get in the way, and much of it will have to be removed. Consider saving yourself a lot of grief by paying a shop to do the work.

For even greater protection, you can buy a hard-sided bicycle suitcase, but these aren't recommended for touring. They're expensive and are more likely to have been designed for racing bikes than for touring bikes, making fit a potential problem. It's also hard to figure out what to do with

them when you're on the road. On catered tours or organized event rides, you may be able to store such a case on the baggage truck or convert it to a suitcase, but ask in advance. Some rides have very limited baggage space.

Tandem riders will need special boxes, either by fabricating a tandem-sized box from two airline boxes or by acquiring a tandem box from a bike shop.

By Train

Trains are a good way to carry bicycles, especially because they stop in smaller towns than airplanes do, with the stations readily accessible by bicycle. And because reservation requirements aren't as restrictive as for airplanes, trains give you more schedule flexibility. A good way to plan a self-contained tour is by starting at one train station and ending up at another, which also gives you bailouts at intermediate stations along the way.

As with a plane, you need a box but can hope to get it at the station. You'll still have to pay for the box, but the shipping fee will probably be much smaller. Unfortunately, you can't ship your bicycle to or from every train station; some have no baggage facilities. Check this out in advance, along with the availability of boxes. Amtrak occasionally experiments with special bike-handling rules on some lines, allowing you to wheel your bike to the baggage car and collect it at your destination, even at stations with no baggage service. Hopefully, this European-style bike-friendly service will become the norm, but don't count on it.

By Bus

Buses have many of the advantages of trains, plus a much wider route network. It might take awhile, but you can get bus connections to or from almost anywhere. Like trains, buses carry bicycles at much more reasonable fees than airplanes. They too require boxes, though, and probably won't supply them, especially in small towns.

Finding a Box on a Tour

If you need a box at the end of a tour, start by looking for a bike shop. If none is around, fabricate a box from large pieces of cardboard scavenged else-

Avoiding Pedal Panic

The toughest aspect of shipping a bike is getting the pedals off in the airport, train station, or bus terminal. Many are threaded so they self-tighten under pedaling pressure—far better than having them come loose unexpectedly—-but this means they can be extremely tight. You may be able to remove them at home, at your leisure, but often you have to do so in a hurry, perhaps after having bicycled to the airport.

I've gotten pedals off many times with a midsized Crescent wrench, but there's always a moment of panic when they won't seem to budge. On a couple of occasions, only the adrenaline of "Oh, my gosh, I'm going to miss my flight" has finally allowed me to break them loose. For about $20 and a few ounces of extra weight, you can solve this by carrying a true pedal wrench. These are simply long, thin spanners, sized for the nuts on most pedals, designed to give you more leverage than you can get with adjustable wrenches. With these, anything but stripped threads will come off easily.

When removing your pedals, pay attention to the way they're threaded. If they're the self-tightening kind, one won't be a right-hand thread. If the pedal seems absurdly tight, ask yourself whether you might be turning it the wrong way. When putting them back on, lubricate the threads with bearing grease, chain lube, or oil to make them easier to remove next time.

Loosening a pedal. For the greatest torque, position the pedal wrench as close to parallel to the crank as possible, and brace the opposite pedal so the crank won't rotate. Block the rear wheel with your toe to keep the bike from rolling.

where—a furniture or appliance store, for example. The result will be nonstandard, but I've used such boxes by bus and even by plane. Check ahead to find out what's acceptable, and get to the station or airport far enough in advance that if the ticket agent has a different interpretation of the rules, you won't be stranded.

The carrier's interest in requiring a box is primarily to protect other people's luggage, so any contrivance that completely covers your machine will probably suffice. To increase the chances of its being accepted, remove the pedals and put extra padding at the ends of the axles. Don't expect an airline to insure a bike in such a jury-rigged box, but going uninsured is better than leaving your bike behind.

By Ferry

Ferries and bicycles go together. Not only do they take you to pleasant, low-traffic destinations, but carrying a bike by ferry is ridiculously easy: you simply walk up the ramp, pay a fee, and enjoy the ride. Reservations shouldn't be necessary; there's always room for a bike. Would that other forms of public transportation were so bike friendly.

By UPS

You can ship a bicycle by UPS, although that requires the "small" bike-shop style of box. The price depends on distance but is roughly comparable to airline oversized-baggage fees. The principal advantage of shipping by UPS is that it frees you of the need to handle the bicycle in transit. You'll need to ship your bike at least a week in advance, and you'll need someone at the other end who can be counted on to accept delivery. Organized tours often provide a volunteer at the town where the ride starts; ask the tour director. Other private shippers may also handle bicycles, but I've never known a cyclist to use a shipper other than UPS.

Special Concerns for Event Rides

Organized tours often begin or end with bus rides. Unless you ship your bike by UPS, you may have to pack it for shipment on a truckload of bikes that travels with the bus. Some tours want bikes boxed and expect you to bring them to the start already packed. If you've flown in from another city, this may mean you'll need a large cab or van to get your boxed bike from the airport to the starting point. Other tours supply boxes on-site, while still others would prefer not to have bikes in boxes due to space limitations on the truck. Read your registration packet carefully so you're not caught by surprise.

International Touring

There are few better ways to visit a foreign country than by bicycle. Just as it does at home, bicycling forces you to slow down and encounter a foreign land and its people on their own terms.

A multitude of destinations beckon. From the U.S. or Canada, probably the most popular is New Zealand—particularly because it's a good winter getaway. In the summer, Ireland is popular, as is much of mainland Europe. If you want to get off the beaten path, check out eastern Europe, particularly Hungary, Poland, and the Czech Republic.

If you're looking for something adventurous but not too culturally exotic, my favorite is Iceland. Few American cyclists visit, but to Europeans, this is the New Zealand of the North Atlantic; on a three-week trip, I met five to ten self-contained touring cyclists a day, mostly from Germany and Holland. That's more than you'll find anywhere in the U.S. or Canada.

Cycling-oriented information is scarce, but try starting with guidebooks designed more for the Europe-by-backpack crowd than for high-end luxury travelers. The *Lonely Planet* guidebooks, in particular, are outdoor oriented and often have information geared specifically for cyclists. They'll also give you the basics on subjects ranging from currency and ATM machines to shopping hours, holidays, tipping customs, and locations of hostels, inns, and campgrounds. More information can be obtained from your destination country's tourist bureau, listed in any good guidebook.

Another source of plentiful information is the Internet. Using your favorite search engine, type in your country's name and "bicycling," and see what comes up. Your best sources are likely to be local bike clubs. But there are also Web sites that compile bicycle travelogues from anyone who wants to post them. Take all these accounts with a grain of salt.

The best sources are people who've actually been there ahead of you. Seek referrals from your hometown bike club, or call up the tourist bureau for your destination and find a live person with whom to chat. Most people are delighted to share such information, and even if a U.S.-based tourist bureau employs only U.S. citizens, most of them will actually have visited the land they're representing.

Foreign Biking Basics

When traveling by bicycle, the information you most need involves public transportation, lodging, and road conditions.

In general, expect buses and trains to be much more bike friendly in the rest of the world than in the U.S. Often, you and your bike can just hop aboard if you get tired, behind schedule, or simply want to leapfrog ahead to an interesting destination. Lodging options are also different from what you may be used to. In much of the world

(continued next page)

International Touring
(continued from previous page)

campgrounds are often built on a European model. Instead of individual sites you'll find open fields where visitors are free to set up tents wherever they wish. Some campgrounds, particularly in cooler climates, have communal kitchen shelters with indoor tables, chairs, and cooking facilities. Camping fees are usually quite modest. And the communal atmosphere, coupled with late European dining hours, makes for great opportunities to meet fellow travelers. Language barriers are seldom a problem; English is often the lingua franca of these international tent cities.

Bed-and-breakfast accommodations are also common in much of the world. Guests may even have access to the home's kitchen, plus all of its cooking utensils. This means you may be able to lighten the load by leaving your own cooking equipment at home. Some B&Bs offer reduced-price "sleeping bag" accommodations, where guests bring their own bedding——a real bargain if you're mixing a camping and B&B trip and have a sleeping bag with you anyway.

Most important of all, of course, are maps. Luckily, Europe and the rest of the developed world generally has great road maps. You can find them at home in the best travel bookstores, or order them via the Internet. Another source of maps is the U.S. Central Intelligence Agency. Check the CIA's Web site (*www.odci.gov*) to see how to get copies.

Once you've gotten a map, you still have to figure out which roads offer the best bike routes. Many of the route-finding rules discussed on pages 112–15 still apply, but it's a good idea to understand the logic behind a nation's road-numbering system. In Britain, for example, there are four grades of rural roads: motorways, A highways, B highways, and lanes. Motorways are freeways, unsuitable for bicycling. The A roads are major thoroughfares, roughly comparable to U.S. highways. B roads are minor highways, and lanes are low-traffic farm roads. On first impression, one would expect the best bike routes to be the lanes, but that turns out to be true only if you don't mind steep hills and routes that meander aimlessly about the countryside. The B routes are often a better compromise.

In Iceland all roads are numbered and shown on the national highway map. This gives the misleading impression that they're all major routes. Actually, many are 4-wheel-drive tracks that can entail fording knee-deep rivers. The key to avoiding a rough adventure is to know that these routes are identified by numbers beginning with the letter *F*.

Traffic circles, weird road signs, and idiosyncratic bicycle laws are another aspect of international travel. The British are particularly fond of traffic circles, where a multitude of roads can come together in a tangle like a pair of mating octopuses.

Wherever you go, expect roads to be narrower than their U.S. counterparts. Road shoulders may also be rare—although some countries, such as the Netherlands, have extensive systems of rural, off-road bike paths. The narrow roads may not be quite as scary as they look. In many countries, bicycles are respected far more than they are in North America, and deliberately rude drivers are rare.

If you'd rather not trust these drivers' skills—and in some countries such trust can be a very bad idea—dodge the more heavily traveled routes or put fat tires on your bike so you can move out of the way onto grass or gravel shoulders.

Equipping a "World Bike"
North American cyclists need to remember that they're accustomed to one of the best road systems on the planet. The road bike that can easily carry you across the U.S. or Canada may work perfectly well in Denmark or Switzerland but be too spindly for Morocco. And U.S. road builders are averse to hills. Grades that we consider outrageously steep are taken for granted in other nations. Don't let a country's overall topography fool you. Mountainous lands often have gentler roads than

Icelandic traffic signs. International travel may present linguistic challenges.

countries that are merely hilly. England, for example, is a land that most people would rate as basically flat, but it has regions with hills as steep as 33 percent (the British call this a 1:3 grade). Mountainous Scotland, on the other hand, is devoid of such grades. But there are plenty of exceptions. Bicycling the mountainous coast of Norway, you'll hit at least one 6-mile, 10 percent grade—steep by anyone's definition.

Getting There

Most international tours begin at an airport. Page 140 discusses how to carry a bicycle on domestic flights. Internationally, it's a bit different, however.

You'll probably not have to pay an oversized baggage fee, but you'll have a very restrictive weight limit that includes the bicycle and (in theory, at least) your hand luggage. You can live with it, but you won't be able to carry everything. The precise limit varies with the destination; make sure you ask when making reservations.

Leaving the U.S., especially if you start with a connecting flight on a domestic carrier, you'll need a bike box, as with any domestic flight. When you're returning, boxes may not be available. Some foreign airlines use big plastic bags instead. They'll accept bike boxes—if you can find one and figure out how to get it to the airport—but they won't provide them.

The real problem is what to do with the rest of your baggage if you're on a self-contained tour. International rules typically give you a 2-bag limit, but on a self-contained tour you have 5 pieces: 2 front panniers, 2 rear panniers, and a tent/bedroll package. One solution is to carry an inexpensive duffel bag with you, large enough to hold several of these bags. The rest becomes hand luggage.

Another way to meet the rules is by offering to put all the pieces into a second plastic bike bag, checking this Santa's sack as a single "bag." But it may be better just to throw yourself on the mercy of the airline, particularly in a country that's used to seeing a lot of cyclists. Often the airline will let you check the pieces individually.

Bike Rental

You may decide it's easier simply to rent a bike. This is a bit risky because you're not likely to get a high-quality machine. Nor will it be custom adjusted for your body; you'll spend the first few days fine-tuning the saddle position. But the one time I tried this, on a combination cycling-and-auto vacation in Great Britain, I got a $1,000 bicycle, with panniers, for a very modest weekly fee.

Locating a shop that rents bicycles can be tricky. I found mine through a standard tourist guidebook. Also helpful are the Internet and international telephone operators. If all else fails, try calling at random to bike shops; the first one may not rent bicycles, but it may be able to make a recommendation. In searching for rentals in Europe or the British Commonwealth, remember that in British parlance, the word for *rent* is *hire*.

Border Crossings by Bike

Border crossings are exciting enough by car or bus. By bicycle they're even more exotic. In a car you're enclosed in a familiar environment; by bicycle there's nothing to separate you from the entire panoply of gates, customs agents, and multiple-language signs. Somehow, it all feels more real. The ceremony of border crossing also commemorates your progress across the map—or even the globe—far more thoroughly than simply crossing a state or provincial line.

That said, it's still an international crossing, with all of the attendant responsibilities. The same passport and visa rules apply to bicyclists as to anyone else, as does the need, in some countries, for up-to-date immunizations. Some countries can even turn you back if you don't have a credit card or enough money. Know the rules.

You also have to go through customs. Sometimes you'll just be waved through; other times you may have to face a thorough inspection.

Most people think of contraband as illegal drugs or large quantities of cigarettes or alcohol—things not commonly carried by health-conscious cyclists. But fresh fruit can also be contraband, and over-the-counter medications that are legal in one country may not be so in others. The most obvious example is codeine, which can be sold over the counter in Canada but is a controlled substance in the U.S. If in doubt about anything in your medical kit, find out in advance.

APPENDIX:
65 GREAT TOURS-AND MORE

Here's a list of 65 organized tours in 38 states, Canada, and Australia. From early June to mid-October there's usually at least one ride a week. There's something for everybody, ranging from the mammoth, rolling part of Iowa's RAGBRAI (8,500 riders) to tours limited to fewer than 100 people, from the laid-back 50-mile-a-day pace of Pedal Across Lower Michigan to mountain challenges in Arizona and Oregon. It's a great way to see the country—and where else can you get a weeklong vacation for as little as $300?

Most of these tours have run for several years, many for more than a decade. But the usual caveats apply: routes, dates, distances, group sizes, mailing addresses, and other contact information are all subject to change. Even well-established tours have been known to go out of business.

EAST

Maine

Coastal Tour—July or early August. Visits mountains and coastlands of surprisingly diverse state; 300 miles. Group size: 65. Established in 1998. Fee: $400 (includes some meals). Contact: Maine Wheels Bicycle Club, P.O. Box 229, Norway ME 04268; 207-743-5993; *info@CoastalTour.Com*; *www.coastaltour.com*.

MOOSA (Maine's Original Outstanding Super Adventure)—Late July. New route each year through Maine and (often) Québec. Distance: 300–400 miles with optional add-ons. Group size: 200. Established in 1993. Fee: $200 (meals extra). Contact: CAN-AM Wheelers, 140 Emerson Rd., Norway ME 04268; 207-743-9018; *Moosa@mega-link.net*; *www.megalink.net/~moosa*.

Moose Tour—Late July or early August. Maine isn't all rugged coastline. This tour goes through the inland mountains of western Maine; 300 miles. Group size: 150. Established in 1991. Fee: $285 (includes some meals). Contact: Maine Wheels Bicycle Club, P.O. Box 229, Norway ME 04268; 207-743-5993; *Info@MooseTour.com*; *www.MooseTour.com/*.

Maryland

Cycle Across Maryland—Late July. Stays more than one night at most locations, alternating between loop day rides and moves to a new camp; explores a different portion of the state each year. Distance: 300 miles plus options. Three-day, half-length option available. Group size: 1,500. Established in 1989. Fee: $210 (optional meal plan available). Contact: CAM Corp., 7 Church Ln., Suite 8, Baltimore MD 21208-3710; 888-CAM-RIDE (888-226-7433), 410-653-8288; *info@cyclexmd.org*; *www.cyclexmd.org*.

Massachusetts

MassBike Tour—July. Tour Massachusetts with a leading bike advocacy organization. Route varies annually; intends to visit all 351 of the state's towns and cities within 10 years. Some days have long and short distance options. Distance: 350–500 miles depending on choice of options. Group size: initially limited to 250 but expects to grow to at least 1,000. Established in 1998. Fee: $500–600 (includes all meals). Contact: 44 Bromfield St., #207, Boston MA 02108; 617-542-2453; *tour@massbike.org*; *www.massbike.org*.

New York

Bon Ton Roulet—Late July. Loop route through the glacial landscape of New York's Finger

Lakes region; 350 miles. Group size: 600. Established in 1997. Fee: $375 (includes meals, evening entertainment). Contact: Cortland YMCA, Attn. Bon Ton Roulet, 22 Tompkins St., Cortland NY 13045; 607-756-2893; *ahastin@aol.com*; *www.BonTonRoulet.com*.

Cycling the Erie Canal—Mid-August. Founded in 1999, this tour follows the Erie Canal between Buffalo and Albany. Much of the route is on off-road bike paths. Distance: 400 miles. Group size: 175. Fee: $325 (includes meals). Contact: New York Parks and Conservation Association, 29 Elk St., Albany NY, 12207; 518-434-1583; *canaltour@nypca.org*, *nypca@nypca.org*; *www.nypca.org*.

Pennsylvania

Pedal Pennsylvania—July. Route changes annually, with each event carrying a different name, such as Pedal Pennsylvania's Source of the Delaware to reflect each year's destination. May visit neighboring states. Some nights in college dorms. Group size: 200. Established in 1995. Partners with Rails-to-Trails Conservancy to show off state's 800 miles of rail-trail conversions. Fee: $800+ (includes dorm fees and all meals). Contact: Bob Ingersoll, Pedal Pennsylvania, 1914 Brandywine St., Philadelphia PA 19130; 215-561-9679; *bobi@pedal-pa.com*; *www.pedal-pa.com*.

Vermont

Cycle Vermont—Late August–early September. Mountainous tour of the East's premier biking state; don't be surprised to encounter 20,000 feet of cumulative elevation gain. Distance: 400 miles. Group size: 130. Established in 1998. Fee: $570 (includes catered meals). Contact: Adventure Cycling Association, P.O. Box 8308, Missoula MT 59807-8308; 800-755-2453, 406-721-1776; *tours@adv-cycling.org*; *www.adv-cycling.org*.

SOUTH

Alabama

BAMA (Bicycle Across Magnificent Alabama)—Early June, point-to-point, about 400 miles plus some options. Always connects with BRAG (Georgia) for a two-week southern tour. Organized in 1995. Group size: 300. Fee: about $125. Contact: Morton Archibald, Executive Director, 2117 Rothmore Dr. SW, Huntsville AL 35803-1431; 256-658-5189; *morton@bikebama.com*; *www.bikebama.com*.

Florida

Bike Florida—Early April, point-to-point or loop; about 400 miles. Sponsor hosts other events, summer and fall. Organized in 1994. Group size: 750. Fee: About $120; budget-priced meal package available (about $65). Contact: Bike Florida, P.O. Box 451514, Kissimmee FL 34745; 407-343-1992; *info@bikeflorida.org*; *www.bikeflorida.org*.

Florida Bicycle Safari—April. Based in northern Florida and sometimes venturing into Georgia, this is one of the oldest event rides in the South. Some days are spent exploring without changing base camp. Three-day option available. Distance: 275–500 miles. Group size: 200. Established in 1981. Fee: $250 for 6-day, $125 for 3-day (includes meals). Contact: Florida Freewheel, P.O. Box 916524, Longwood FL 32791-6524; 407-788-BIKE (407-788-2453); *ffwclub@aol.com*; *www.floridafreewheelers.com*.

Georgia

BRAG (Bicycle Ride Across Georgia)—June; 350–400 miles; always connects with BAMA. Organized in 1980. Group size: 2,500. Fee: about $125. Meals extra. Contact: P.O. Box 871111, Stone Mountain GA 30087-0028; 770-921-6166; *bragHQ@aol.com*; *www.brag.org*.

Louisiana

Cycle Louisiana—Early May. A 5-day tour across Cajun country; 300 miles. Group size: 300. Established in 2000. Fee: $150. Meals included. Contact: Louisiana State Games Foundation, New Orleans Centre, 1400 Poydras St., Suite 918, New Orleans LA 70112; 504-LA GAMES (504-524-2637); *avoge1@gnosf.org*; *www.louisianagames.com*.

Oklahoma

Oklahoma FreeWheel—Early June; 400–450 miles; route varies year to year. Group size: 1,500–2,500. Established in 1979. Fee: $40. Contact: Oklahoma FreeWheel, c/o Tulsa World, P.O. Box 21920, Tulsa OK 74121-1920; fax 918-581-8353; *okfreewheel@prodigy.net*; *www. okfreewheel. com*.

South Carolina

Cycle South Carolina—June. Route varies from year to year; about 450 miles. Organized in 1999. Group size: 500. Fee: $150. Meals extra. Contact: P.O. Box 3346, Spartanburg SC 29304; 800-636-6673 ext. 6664; *MR10speed@aol.com*; *members. aol.com/cyclesc*.

North Carolina

Cycle North Carolina—October. Route varies; usually point-to-point. Spectacular fall colors are likely; about 400 miles. Group size: 1,000. Established in 1999. Fee: $125 (meals not included). Contact: P.O. Box 12727, Research Triangle Park NC 27709; 800-277-8763; *ncas@interpath.com*; *www.cyclenorthcarolina.org*.

Tennessee

BRAT (Bicycle Ride Across Tennessee)—Late September. State-sponsored tour spends most nights in state parks; about 450 miles. Usually point-to-point. May take layover day. Group size: 500. Established in 1987. Fee: $100 (meals extra). Contact: 615-373-3467; *radnor@edge.net*; *www. state.tn.us/environment/parks*.

Texas

Texas Chainring Challenge—First full week of June. Scenic tour with varied terrain (rolling hills to flat river bottoms) on back roads of Texas. Loop route begins and ends in Longview; 450 miles. Group size: 175. Established in 1990. Fee: $200 (meal plan $100 extra). Contact: Longview Bicycle Club, 1609 Sweetbriar, Longview TX 75604; 800-374-2453; *leemccord@aol.com*; *www.texramp. net/~chainring*.

Virginia

Bike Virginia—Late June; about 350 miles. Group size: 2,000. Established in 1988. Fee: about $180 (meals extra). Contact Bicycling Education Association, P.O. Box 203, Williamsburg VA 23187-0203; *info@bikevirginia.org*; *www.bikevirginia.org*.

MIDWEST

Illinois

Around Illinois Bike Ride—Early August. Loop tour beginning and ending in Joliet; 450 miles. Group size: 300. Established in 1983, but only recently expanded to full week (was previously 4 days). Fee: $195 (includes some meals). Contact: Joliet Bicycle Club, P.O. Box 2758, Joliet IL 60436; *pukrat@netzero.net*; *www.jolietbicycleclub.org*.

Indiana

September Escapade TRIRI—Mid-September. A shorter-mileage, fall version of TRIRI (see below); 350 miles. Group size: 250. Established in 1998. Fee: approximately $235 (includes most meals). Inn option available for additional $160. Contact: TRIRI, P.O. Box 439, Clear Creek IN 47426; *jbanders @iquest.net*; *www.bloomington.in.us/~bbc/triri*.

TRIRI (Touring Ride in Rural Indiana)—Last full week in June; 450-mile tour of Hoosier country; spends each night in a state park. Sometimes takes layover days with optional loop rides. Group size: 500. Established in 1981. Fee: $250 (includes most meals). Contact: TRIRI (see above).

Iowa

RAGBRAI (*The Des Moines Register*'s Annual Great Bicycle Ride Across Iowa)—Late July. The ride that started it all, Missouri River to Mississippi River by new route each year; 450–500 miles. Group Size: 8,500 (largest in U.S.). Established 1973. Fee: $95. Entry by lottery from applications received by April 1. Contact: P.O. Box 622, Des Moines IA 50303-0622; 800-474-3342; *www.ragbrai.org*.

TOGIR (The Other Great Iowa Ride)—June; runs college-to-college with hot showers and dorm rooms every night; 400–450 miles. Group size: 100. Established in 1982 (with a multiyear hiatus in the 1990s). Fee: $400 (includes dorm accommodations, most meals). Contact: TOGIR, 1735 Piccadilly Pl., Davenport IA 52807-1121; 319-344-1379; *bike@togir.com*; *www.togir.com*.

Kansas

Biking Across Kansas—Early–mid-June. West to east across a state renowned for its hospitality to cyclists; about 450 miles. Indoor sleeping bag space provided nightly as an alternative to camping. Established in 1975. Fee: $140 (includes some meals). Contact: P.O. Box 8648, Wichita KS 67208-0648; 316-684-8184; *bakone@aol.com*; *www.bak.org*.

Michigan

DALMAC (Dick Allen Lansing to Mackinac Bicycle Tour)—Labor Day Weekend; 4- or 5-day event, with options to suit almost every level of ability. Each day, DALMAC offers route options from 60–100 miles—allowing the macho to do multiple, back-to-back centuries. Begins in East Lansing and culminates in a mass crossing of the Mackinac Bridge. Group size: 1,700. Established in 1971. Fee: $135–160 depending on options selected (includes meals). Contact: 517-882-3700; *dalmac@biketcba.org*; *www.biketcba.org*.

Michigander Ride—July. Sponsored by the Michigan chapter of the Rails-to-Trails Conservancy, this tour packs in as many railroad-to-bikeway conversions as possible—particularly appealing to mountain bikers, since some surfaces are gravel. About 50 miles a day (300 miles total). Group size: 2,000. Established in 1991. Fee: $225 (meals included). Contact: 913 W. Holmes Rd., Lansing MI 48910; *www.railtrails.org/MI*.

PALM (Pedal Across Lower Michigan)—Late June; west to east across southern Michigan at 50 miles a day, with longer options available. Because of its low mileage, this ride caters to beginners and families. Distance: about 270 miles, plus optional add-ons. Group size: 700. Established in 1982. Fee: $80 (meals extra). Contact: PO Box 7161, Ann Arbor MI 48107; *www.lmb.org/palm*.

Shoreline Bicycle Tours—Not a single event but a smorgasbord of weeklong outings in July and August, in a state that boasts the most paved roads (and the most miles of lakeshore) in the nation. Sometimes ferries across Lake Michigan visit Wisconsin's Door County. Mileage: 250–500. Group size: 125–500. Established in 1987. Fee: $235–300 (includes most meals). Contact: Shoreline Tours, League of Michigan Bicyclists, P.O. Box 16201, Lansing MI 48901; 517-334-9100; *LMBike@voyager.net*; *www.LMB.org*.

Minnesota

Habitat 500—July. Fundraiser for Twin Cities chapter of Habitat for Humanity, typically beginning in Minnesota and traveling to neighboring state or Canadian province. (One year's ride, however, went from Louisville KY to Atlanta GA.) About 500 miles. Group size: 115. Established in 1993. Fee: $100 plus $750 in pledges (includes meals). Contact: Twins Cities Habitat for Humanity, 3001 4th St. SE, Minneapolis MN 55414; 612-331-4090; *www.habitat500.org*.

TRAM (The Ride Across Minnesota)—Late July. A pledge ride for the Multiple Sclerosis Society, with a small minimum pledge compared to most such events. Traverses the state by a different route each year; 300 miles. Group size: 1,500. Established in 1990. Fee: $50 plus at least $200 in pledges (meals not included). Contact: MS Society, 200 12th Ave. S., Minneapolis MN 55415-1255; 800-582-5296, 612-335-7900; *msevents@mnms.org*; *www.mstram.com*.

Missouri

CAMP (Cycle Across Missouri Parks)—June; 400 miles. All nights in state parks or historic sites. Group Size: 300. Established in 1989. Fee: about $225 (includes shower truck and most meals). Contact: Hostelling International, 7187 Manchester Rd., St. Louis MO 63143; 800-334-6946; *nrkelld@mail.dnr.state.mo.us*; *www.mostateparks.com*.

Nebraska

BRAN (Bicycle Ride Across Nebraska)—Early June. Route varies each year, generally crossing state from west to east, ending near Omaha. Distance: 450–500 miles. Group size: 600. Established in 1981. Fee: $75 (meals extra). Contact: 10730 Pacific St., Suite 218, Omaha NE 68114-4780; 402-397-9785; *bran@radiks.net*; *www.bran-inc.org*.

North Dakota

CANDISC (Cycling Around North Dakota in Sakakawea Country)—First full week of August. Loop tour of western North Dakota, beginning and ending at Fort Stevenson State Park, Garrison; about 400 miles. May venture into Canada. Group size: 400. Established in 1993. Fee: $95/individual; $250/family (meals extra). Contact: P.O. Box 459, Garrison ND 58540; 701-337-5576; *www.state.nd.us/ndparks/*.

Ohio

GOBA (The Great Ohio Bicycle Adventure)—June; loop tour of a different part of Ohio each year; 300–350 miles. Nightly entertainment. Group size: 3,000. Established in 1989. Fee: $125 (meals extra). Contact: GOBA, P.O. Box 14384, Columbus OH 43214; 614-447-0971; *www.goba.com*.

Wisconsin

GRABAAWR (Great Annual Bicycle Adventure Along the Wisconsin River)—Early July. Explores a different route through the Wisconsin River country of central and southwestern Wisconsin each year; 450–500 miles. Gymnasium option every night. Group size: 1,100. Established in 1986. Fee: $175 with bus to start; $140 without (meals extra). Contact: Bike Wisconsin, P.O. Box 310, Spring Green WI 53588; 888-575-3640; *wisbike@mhtc.net*; *www.bikewisconsin.org*.

Northwoods to Capitol Tour—Late June–early July. Doesn't necessarily visit the state capitol; about 400 miles. Group size: 300. Established in 1999. Supports the Bicycle Federation of Wisconsin. Fee: about $300 (meals extra). Contact: P.O. Box 3142, Madison WI 53704; *bicycle@execpc.com*; *www.bikenorthwoods.com*.

POWWOW (Pedal Over Wisconsin—Week/ Weekend on Wheels)—College dorm or gymnasium accommodations on tours of rural Wisconsin. Several tours each summer. Fees vary with length: about $350 for week. Typically includes most meals. Group size: typically 150. Established in 1984. Contact: POWWOW Bicycle Tours, 3533 W. Lapham St., Milwaukee WI 53215; 414-671-4560; *dennard@ execpc.com*; *www.wisconsinbicycletour. com*.

SAGBRAW (Sprocket's Annual Great Bicycle Ride Across Wisconsin)—Late July–early August. The *S* in the sponsor's name of this venerable ride has changed over the years, but it's one of the Midwest's oldest, following a different route across the state each year. About 350 miles in a state renowned for its low-traffic, paved back roads. Group size: 750. Established in 1978. Fee: $170 with bus to start; $140 without (meals extra). Group size: 750. Contact: Bike Wisconsin, Box 310, Spring Green WI 53588; 888-575-3640; *wisbike @mhtc.net*; *www.bikewisconsin.org*.

WEST

Arizona

Great Arizona Bicycle Adventure—October. Explores the mountains and deserts of Arizona; 500 miles. Can be very hilly. Group size: 200. Established in 1981. Fee: $450 (includes most meals). Leadership rotates among Tucson bike club members, sometimes making the ride hard to contact for out-of-staters. Try: P.O. Box 40814, Tucson AZ 85717; 520-690-7900; *www.bikegaba.org*.

California

Sierra to the Sea—June. Tours the Gold Rush Country, Sacramento, Napa County wineries, and the Golden Gate Bridge; 400 miles. Weather can be very hot. Group size: 110. Established in 1987. Fee: about $400 (includes meals). Contact: Almaden Bicycle Touring Club, P.O. Box 7286, San Jose CA 95150; *s2s@actc.org*; *www.actc.org*.

Colorado

Bicycle Tour of Colorado—Mid-July. Route varies; typically a loop; 450-500 miles. Fundraiser for the Rocky Mountain Public Broadcasting Corporation, Inc. Group size: 2,000. Established in 1995. Fee: $400 (includes breakfasts and lunches; dinners extra). Contact: 3500 S. Wadsworth Blvd. #201, Lakewood CO 80235; 303-985-1180; *aj4BTC@juno.com*; *www.bicycletourcolo. com*.

The Denver Post Ride the Rockies—Mid-June (beginning the third Sunday); 380–450 miles through the Colorado mountains. Expect several passes with elevations well over 10,000 feet. Group size: 2,000. Fills by lottery in February (generally, 60–65% of applications make it in). Established in 1986. Fee: $215 (meals extra). Contact: Paul Balaguer, Ride the Rockies, The *Denver Post*, 1560 Broadway, Denver CO 80202; 303-820-1338; *rtr@denverpost.com*; *www.ridetherockies. com*.

Hawaii
Wheeling Hawaii—March. Circles the Big Island; 300 miles (held in most years, but not all). Group size: 100. Established in 1997. Fee: $600 for preregistration 18 or more months before the event, escalating stepwise to $1,000 in the days before departure (includes meals, shower truck). Contact: Tim Kneeland & Associates, Inc., 200 Lake Washington Blvd., Suite 101, Seattle WA 98122-6540; 800-433-0528; *timtka@aol.com*; *www.odyssey2000.com*.

Idaho
SPUDS—Cycling Around Idaho—First full week of August. Tours a little-known state that's one of the best biking venues in the nation. Distance: 450 miles. Group size: 150. Established in 1995. Fee: $400 (includes meals). Contact: Cyclevents, 888-733-9615; *spuds@cyclevents.com*; *www.cyclevents. com*.

Montana
Cycle Montana—Early August. Explores the mountains, rivers, valleys, battlefields, and hot springs of the Big Sky State; 300 miles and up; may take layover day with no scheduled riding. Group size: 375. Established in 1993. Fee: $600 (includes catered meals, shower truck). Contact: Adventure Cycling Association, P.O. Box 8308, Missoula MT 59807-8308; 800-755-2453, 406-721-1776; *tours@adv-cycling.org*; *www.adv-cycling.org*.

Nevada
OATBRAN (One Awesome Tour: Bike Ride Across Nevada)—Mid- to late September. California to Utah across U.S. 50, "The Loneliest Road in America"; 430 miles. Group size: 65. Fee: about $600 (includes all meals and bus back to start).

Contact: TGFT Productions, P.O. Box 5123, Lake Tahoe NV 89449; 800-565-2704; *tgft@sierra.net*; *www.bikethewest.com*.

Oregon
Cycle Oregon—Early to mid-September. Grand-daddy of Pacific Northwest rides often spends nights in tiny logging or ranching towns whose populations it outnumbers 10-to-1. Route varies; trend has been toward routes that feature layover days with optional century (or shorter) rides. High-caliber entertainment nightly. Distance: 450 miles. Group size: 2,000. Established in 1988. Fee: about $650 (includes shower trucks, catered meals). Contact: 8700 SW Nimbus, Ave., Ste. B, Beaverton OR 97008; 800-CYCLEOR (800-292-5367); *caryn@pjpco.com*; *www.cycleoregon.com*.

Oregon Bicycle Ride—Mid-August. Although this ride sometimes visits the coast, it specializes in the high desert and ponderosa pine forests of central and eastern Oregon. About 400 miles. Can be very mountainous. Group size: 350. Established in 1989. Fee: about $500 (includes shower truck and all meals). Contact: 1324 NW Vicksburg, Bend OR. 97701; *info@scenic-cycling.com*; *www.scenic-cycling.com*.

Utah
Cycle Utah—June. Loops through the national parks of southwest Utah; about 275 miles. Established in 1999. Group size: 150 (fills quickly). Fee: $550 (includes catered meals). Contact: Adventure Cycling Association, P.O. Box 8308, Missoula MT 59807-8308; 800-755-2453, 406-721-1776; *tours@adv-cycling.org*; *www.adv-cycling.org*.

Washington
Cascade Peaks—July. Route varies, but classic Washington sampler loop visits western Washington, the Cascade Mountains, and the east-side desert, with two crossings of the Cascades; 450–500 miles (expect 20,000 feet of cumulative elevation gain). Group size: 150. Established in 1995. Fee: $600; includes catered meals. Contact: Adventure Cycling Association, P.O. Box 8308, Missoula MT 59807-8308; 800-755-2453, 406-721-1776; *tours@adv-cycling.org*; *www.adv-cycling.org*.

Ride around Washington (RAW)—Late August. Point-to-point route tends to eschew common Seattle, Rainier, and North Cascades routings in favor of lesser-known portions of the state. Group size: 200. Established in 1999. Fee: $500 (includes most meals). Contact: Cascade Bicycle Club, P.O. Box 31299, Seattle WA 98103; 206-522-2453; *cbcevents@cascade.org*; *www.cascade.org*.

Wyoming

Tour de Wyoming—Mid-July. Point-to-point; 400 miles. Sponsored by the Wyoming Governor's Council for Physical Fitness and Sports. Group size: 130. Established in 1997. Fee: $125 (includes breakfasts). Contact: 1116 Albin St., Laramie WY 82072; 307-742-5840; *atravsky@wyoming.com*.

WYCYC (Wyoming Cycling Celebration)—Late August. Small but long-standing ride seeks out the best of Wyoming scenery. Usually does point-to-point crossing of the state, unlike other Wyoming rides, which are generally loops. Distance: 400–450 miles. Group size: 150. Established in 1990. Fee: $400 (includes all meals). Contact: Cyclevents; 888-733-9615, 307-733-9615; *wycyc@cyclevents.com*; *www.cyclevents.com*.

Wyoming Bicycle Adventure—July. Loop ride through Wyoming high country; may visit neighboring states; 400–500 miles. Group size: 75. Established in 1999. Fee: $250. Meals extra. Contact: Craig S. Carpenter, P.O. Box 37, Teton Village WY 83025; 307-733-9599; *info@BicycleWest.com*; *www.BicycleWest.com*.

CANADA

Tour du Canada—Late June–early September. The world's longest annual tour, crosses the continent in 66 days (with 10 rest days) or 74 days (with 14 rest days). Distance: 4,510 miles (82 miles/day average). Group size is limited to 28, but there may be multiple groups. Established in 1988. Fee: about $3,000 (Canadian) (includes meals, but cyclists help with food preparation). Contact: CycleCanada, 145 King St. W., Suite 1000, Toronto ON M5H 1J8, Canada; 800-214-7798; *sweep@CycleCanada.com*; *www.CycleCanada.com*.

British Columbia

TourBC—July. New route each year, usually in southern BC; 700 km (about 425 miles). Group size: 150. Established in 1996. Fee: $625 U.S. (includes all meals). Contact: 2025 Whyte Ave., Vancouver BC V6J 1B6, Canada; 800-330-9926; *tourbc@tour-bc.net*; *www.tour-bc.net*.

Maritime Provinces

Atlantic Canada Cycling Tours—Dates vary; a smorgasbord of small-group camping tours in the Maritime Provinces and Newfoundland, ranging from long weekends to full weeks. Destinations include Cape Breton Island, southern Nova Scotia, and Prince Edward Island. Average daily mileage about 40 miles. Group size: 20–50. Established in 1987. Fees: $300–550 U.S. (includes meals). Contact: P.O. Box 1555, Station Central, Halifax NS B3J 2Y3, Canada; 902-423-2453; *cycling@atl-canadacycling.com*; *www.atl-canadacycling.com*.

Lighthouse Tour—Late July or August. New route each year along the Maine coast and/or Nova Scotia, New Brunswick, and Prince Edward Island; 300–400 miles. Group size: 200. Established in 1995. Fee: $300 U.S. Contact: CAN-AM Wheelers, 140 Emerson Rd., Norway ME 04268; *Moosa@megalink.net*; *www.megalink.net/~moosa*.

Ontario

Braunstorm (formerly CYCLONE)—Late June. Canada's largest event ride rotates among five Ontario destinations: Manitoulin Island, Huron–Bruce County, Niagara, Ottawa area, and Point Pelee; 350 miles. Group size: 650. Established in 1996. Fee: $175 U.S. (meals extra). Rent-to-own bicycles available. Contact: Blair Keller, Manager, Tours & Charity Events, Touring with Brauns, 27 Scott St., Kitchener ON N2H 2P8, Canada; 519-586-TOUR; *touring@brauns.com*; *www.touring.brauns.com*.

Québec

See MOOSA (Maine) on page 146.

AUSTRALIA

The Great Tasmanian Bike Ride—Mid-January (expect weather equivalent to Northern Hemisphere July). Explores Australia's southern island, home of some of the country's most unusual flora, fauna, and scenery. Distance: about 250 miles. Group size: 700. Established in 1994. Fee: about $500 (Australian, includes most meals). Contact: Bicycle Victoria (Bicycle Institute of Victoria), 19 O'Connel St., N. Melbourne, Victoria 3051, or GPO Box 1961R, Melbourne, Victoria 3001, Australia; (+61) 3-9328-3000; *bicyclevic@bv.com.au*; *www. bv.com.au*.

The RTA Big Ride—Late March–early April (that's early autumn in the Land Down Under). Two-week tour explores New South Wales at 50 miles a day (700 miles total, with a few rest days). Group size: 1,500. Established in 1990. Fee: $920 (Australian) in 2000 (meals included). Contact: Bicycle New South Wales, GPO Box 272, Sydney NSW 2001, Australia; (+61) 2-9283-5200; *info@bicyclensw. org.au*; *www.ozemail.com.au/~bikensw*.

MULTISTATE

Cycle America—June–August. This Minnesota-based touring company, in business since 1987, specializes in tours that can be combined into longer vacations. Offerings vary from year to year; the most ambitious is a series of 9–12 back-to-back cross-state rides that collectively span the continent at about 440 miles a week (with lay-off days between segments), from Washington State to New England. Riders may take as many segments as they desire or come back summer after summer to complete the entire trek in installments (although the route may change in the interim).

Cycle America also sponsors a series of National Park Rides (about 400–500 miles a week) which visit the greatest scenic attractions of the U.S. and Canada, mostly in the West. Destinations vary from year to year but popular routes are repeated—although not necessarily each year. Again, what distinguishes Cycle America is that it's easy to do more than one tour. A tour of Yellowstone and the Grand Tetons, for example, might be followed by a week in Glacier–Waterton, and another week in Banff and Jasper. Shuttles carry riders between tours.

Group size: 100. Fees: $425–700 (includes meals). Airport shuttles and intertour shuttles extra

(typically $25–70). Hotel/inn lodging package available for extra fee on some national park routes. Contact: P.O. Box 485, Cannon Falls MN 55009; 800-245-3263, 507-263-2665; *info@ CycleAmerica.com*; *www.CycleAmerica.com*.

New England Adventure—Mid-August. Three-state tour of Massachusetts, New Hampshire, and Vermont. All accommodations are in inns; 225–320 miles, plus optional add-ons. Group size: 80. Established in 1995. Fee: $600+ (includes most meals, train ride back to start). Contact: P.O. Box 809, Saratoga Springs NY 12866-0809; 800-727-9711, 518-885-3102; *tmcbike@aol.com*; *www.NewEnglandAdventure.com*.

Pedal the Peaks—June–July. A pass-bagging challenge in Colorado, Wyoming, New Mexico, or other Rocky Mountain state. At 500 miles, and with cumulative elevation gains that can be truly Himalayan, this is for experienced riders seeking a challenge. Has had upward of 34,000 feet of climbing in a week (nearly 5,000 feet per day). Group size: 450. Fee: $545 (includes meals). Established in 1987. Contact: Pedal the Peaks, Cycle America, P.O. Box 485, Cannon Falls MN 55009, 800-795-0898; *mail@pedalthepeaks.com*; *www. pedalthepeaks.com*.

Santa Fe Trail Bicycle Trek—September. Semiannual, 3-week, 1,100-mile pilgrimage along the route of the historic Santa Fe Trail (Santa Fe NM to New Franklin MO). Group size: 50. Established in 1989. Riders can sign up by the day, week, or for the whole event. Fee: $30 a day (4-day minimum; includes meals). Contact: 885 Camino Del Este, Santa Fe NM 87501; 505-982-1282; *chilcott1@ aol.com*.

ADVENTURE CYCLING ASSOCIATION

Formerly called Bikecentennial (because it was organized for the 1976 U. S. Bicentennial), this 30,000-member nonprofit organization is the Sierra Club of bicycle touring: part outing organizer and part guardian of bicycle tourists' interests.

The organization has mapped thousands of miles of cross-country routes, including a mountain biking route along the Continental Divide. For self-contained touring, its superb maps make for easy

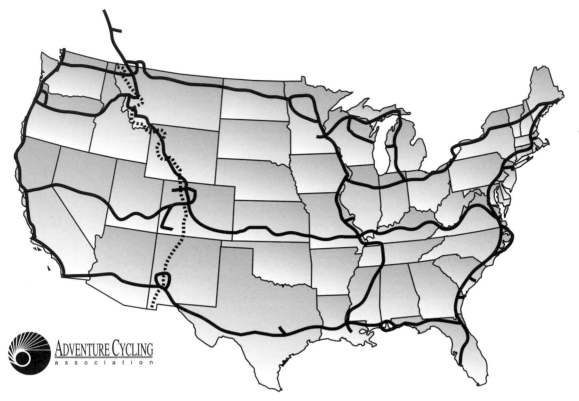

Adventure Cycling Association's National Bicycle Route Network, with the Great Mountain Bike Route shown as a dashed line.

route finding. The popularity of these routes also increases the chances of meeting other cyclists along the way. Adventure Cycling's annual *Cyclists' Yellow Pages* is also a handy compendium of information.

Adventure Cycling also organizes tours, ranging from event rides (Cycle Vermont, Cycle Montana, Cycle Utah, and Cascade Peaks, listed above) to inexpensive, carry-your-own-baggage camping trips. Specialties include summer-long coast-to-coast outings and trips up the Alaskan Highway. All are camping trips, with meals prepared by the group. Average daily mileage: about 50. Contact: P.O. Box 8308, Missoula MT 59807-8308; 406-721-1776; *www.adv-cycling.org*.

INDEX

Numbers in **bold** refer to pages with illustrations

toe touching cautions, 72
tool kits, 103, 104–**5**
topographic maps, 113
towing gear with trailers, 102
towns and cycling, 110, 111, 115–16
traffic riding: bike lanes and paths, 57; changing lanes, 55; children hazards, 56–57; common sense and, 58; corners, 57; dangers, 126; defensive cycling, 56–57; driveway hazards, 57; highways, 56; intersections, 54–**55**, 57; lane use, 53–**54**, 57; laws, 57–58; looking behind you, **53**, 55, 56; oncoming traffic, 56; one-way streets, 57; parked-cars hazards, 55–56; passing-cars hazards, 53; pedaling cadence, 51–52; right-hand side of road riding, 52, 53, **54**, 57; sensors at low-traffic intersections, 55; shoulder use, 56; side-street hazards, 57; sidewalks, 57–58; signaling, **54**, 60; stoplights, 55; stopped-car hazards, 57; stopping, **54**, 57; swerving avoidance, **53**; taking the lane, 53, 55, 56, 129–**30**; truck hazards, 56; turning, **54**, 55, 56; two-abreast riding, 57; unguarded intersections, 57
trailers: for children, **31**; for towing gear, 102
training: base training, 65–68, **67**; body, listening to, 65; century rides, 64, **74–75**; changing training cautions, 67; commuting, 74; cross training, 70; cue sheets for century rides, 75; Dan Henrys, **75**; diary for,

67; exercise bicycles, 52, 70–72; flexibility for, 67; focused training schedule, **69**; fun and, **73**; goals, 65; hard-easy pattern for, 66; heart rate, 68; indoor trainers, 70, **71**; injuries, 66, 67, 68, 75; interval work, **67**; layoffs and, 65; overtraining, 70; pace work, **67**; panniers (full) and, 69; recovery, 66–67; recumbent riding, **17**, 71–72; sickness and, 67; speed training, 67; spring training, 65; stretching, 66, **72**–73; tour training, 68–**69**; upper-body strengthening, 73–74; warm-ups, 67; weekly mileage, 65–**67**, **69**; weight lifting, 73–74; winter training, 70–72, **71**
trains for traveling to tours, 141
TravelChair, 80
traveling to tours: bike racks, **139**–40; border crossings, 145; boxing bikes for travel, 140–43; buses for, 141; cars for, **139**–40; event rides, 78, 82, 143; ferries for, 142; international touring, 143–45, **144**; packing tips, 80, 97–101, **99**, 107, 141; pedal removal, **142**; planes for, 140–41; rear-end bike racks, 140; renting bikes for foreign tours, 145; roof bike racks, 139–40; trains for, 141
truck hazards, 56
T-shape lashing, **99**
tubes, **21**
tuck position for descents, 124
tunnels danger, 130–31
turning, **54**–56
Twain, Mark, 10, 53
two-abreast riding, 57

underwear, 39, 43
unguarded intersections, 57
upper-body strengthening, 73–74
upshifting, 123
U.S. Geological Survey (USGS), 113
used bikes, 24, 32

van-supported tours, 8, **85**, 88
VBT Bicycling Vacations, 87
vehicle laws and bikes, 57–58
visibility problems, 127

warm-ups, 67
warning pennants, 127
water, 103–**4**, 120, 128–**29**
water-bottle cage, 16
water bottles, **25**, 26, 103–**4**
waterproof-breathable fabrics, 40, 41, 42, 90
weekly mileage, 65–**67**, **69**
weight distribution tips, 97–101, **99**
weight lifting, 73–74
western tours, 150–53
wheel-retention devices, 22
wheels, 20–**22**
wicking fabrics, 38–39, 42, 43
widths of tires, 15–16
wind, riding and, 58–**60**, 109
wind chill, 125
wind shells, 40
winter training, 70–72, **71**
women's: cycling shorts, 39; heart rates, 68; saddles, 22, 49; special concerns, **121**
wrist problems, 66

zipper serenade, 78

ACKNOWLEDGMENTS

My thanks to the many people who contributed to this book: to Elizabeth for her excellent drawings and willingness to sweat the details, to Vera not only for photographs but also for input into many sections of the book, and to Robert Grott for being our guinea pig and model on the road. I also thank Dick and Pat Lovett, Kelly Scott, Sherry Lais,and Brett Flemming for reading and commenting on drafts, and the Eastside Bike Gallery in Portland, Oregon, (especially Brett, Sarah Perrault, and David Feldman) for fielding innumerable technical questions. Thanks also to the following equipment manufacturers whose products appear in photos: Bridgestone, Madden, Blackburn, Avocet, Pearl Izumi, REI, Ortlieb, Yakima, Outdoor Research, MSR, Camelbak and Giro. Thanks also to Greg Siple of the Adventure Cycling Association. And finally, thanks to Jim Babb, Tom McCarthy, Dan Kirchoff, and the other folks at Ragged Mountain Press.